TONY OPPÉ
BASS ACADEMY

This book is dedicated to
the love & spirit of Harriet Gedge

WISE PUBLICATIONS
PART OF THE MUSIC SALES GROUP
LONDON / NEW YORK / PARIS / SYDNEY / COPENHAGEN / BERLIN / MADRID / HONG KONG / TOKYO

Published by
Wise Publications
14-15 Berners Street,
London W1T 3LJ, UK.

Exclusive Distributors:
Music Sales Limited
Distribution Centre, Newmarket Road,
Bury St Edmunds, Suffolk IP33 3YB, UK.
Music Sales Corporation
180 Madison Avenue, 24th Floor,
New York NY 10016, USA.
Music Sales Pty Limited
Units 3-4, 17 Willfox Street, Condell Park
NSW 2200, Australia.

Order No. AM1004531
ISBN 978-1-78038-483-2

Edited by Sam Lung.
Music processing and layout by Camden Music Services.
Essential Bass Library compiled by Tom Farncombe, Tom Perchard and Paul Reynolds.
Photographs courtesy of Ingrid Hertfelder, Jonas Persson and Fodera.
Design by Ruth Keating.
DVD production by Wild Apple Design.

Printed in the EU.

Your Guarantee of Quality
As publishers, we strive to produce every book to the
highest commercial standards.
This book has been carefully designed to minimise awkward
page turns and to make playing from it a real pleasure.
Particular care has been given to specifying acid-free, neutral-sized paper
made from pulps which have not been elemental chlorine bleached.
This pulp is from farmed sustainable forests and was
produced with special regard for the environment.
Throughout, the printing and binding have been planned to
ensure a sturdy, attractive publication which should give years of enjoyment.
If your copy fails to meet our high standards,
please inform us and we will gladly replace it.

www.musicsales.com

Contents

Enrol in the Tony Grey Bass Academy online!

Visit the Tony Grey Bass Academy website for more tutorials and expert advice on mastering the bass guitar. Frequently updated with the latest video lessons, master classes and tips from Tony himself, the site is the ultimate online companion to the Tony Grey Bass Academy book.

Registration is simple! Unlock a library of playalong tracks and learning materials, vital for players of any level or background—you don't even need to be able to read music to benefit.

- Learn to play bass from beginner to advanced—and beyond!
- Bass guitar lessons like you've never seen or experienced before from world-class musician, Tony Grey
- Free playalong tracks and supporting documents included
- Contact Tony via the online forum for tips and advice
- Join a vibrant community of aspiring and inspiring musicians

Access your lessons online at **tonygreybassacademy.com** and start the next chapter in your bass playing journey today!

Also visit the Tony Grey website at **tonygrey.com** for even more videos, links, news and tour info.

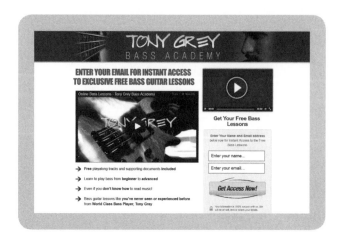

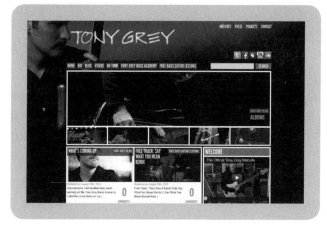

The DVD

Music can be incredibly complex to understand, and sometimes reading a book just isn't enough to get a feeling for the concepts of theory, playing technique or many other aspects.

The enclosed DVD contains over 100 minutes of guidance, explanation and demonstration, where I go through some of the chapters in this book. I believe it's extremely important to 'hear' music, and so you'll be able to find demonstrations of any part of the book where a DVD logo is indicated:

This DVD is, however, just a starting point—once you can grasp the beginning concepts of each musical principle or exercise I will leave you to digest the remainder of the Bass Academy.

For more video lessons and tutorials, including further advanced concepts and techniques, you can visit the Bass Academy website, as highlighted at the beginning of this book.

The Essential Bass Library

On almost every page of this book I've suggested an album featuring a great jazz bass player for you to check out. This list runs from the early days of swing through to contemporary fusion, and includes both acoustic (double) bass players and electric bass guitarists.

The albums listed aren't directly connected to the musical content on the page where they appear—this is an alphabetical list running throughout the book that will hopefully inspire you to listen to and learn from the masters as you develop as a musician.

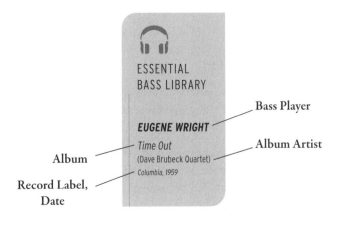

WORDS OF ADVICE FROM TONY

CREATIVITY AND PRACTICE SCHEDULES

Throughout this book we will cover many different topics for study, however my overall aim is to give you the tools and ideas to organise your practice time and to help you learn in a more creative way. With these skills you can begin to play music with the freedom required to master your instrument.

This book can be used as a comprehensive study for beginners, a guide for intermediate musicians to inspire new ideas and skills, as well as a resource for advanced musicians to vary their practice technique.

There are many aspects to playing music, and a number of these are important in jazz. By maintaining good practising habits you'll be able to tackle all of these elements, but first there are a few topics we should discuss.

Understanding Harmony

Having a good knowledge of harmony is fundamental to understanding how to write, improvise, and analyse music. Throughout this book we will look at many different aspects of harmony:

- Creating scales and intervals, and playing them across the whole fretboard
- Soloing through different keys using the 'linear line' concept
- Constructing chords (triads and 4-note chords)
- Creating walking bass lines

Listening To Music

Sometimes continual practice can be far too intensive, and it can be far more constructive to spend some time away from your instrument.

Although I am passionate about jazz music I can sometimes forget about the beauty found in other styles. In my experience, I practised far too much and tended to only listen to jazz—I thought this was the only way to learn how to be a great musician.

You should never be ashamed of loving any music that moves you. For sure, it is important for every musician to learn and understand all types of music, but I feel that true self-expression is only really possible when you are being honest to yourself. You cannot force what you do not feel. The listener will feel what you feel, and it will not sound right.

Nevertheless, this book primarily focuses on jazz technique, and throughout the book I have suggested some essential tracks for you to listen to. These are recordings by some great jazz bassists, as well as some from albums you may not necessarily know. Remember to keep expanding your listening playlists!

They're singing your praises while stealing your phrases.

— **Charles Mingus**

Improvising Solos

Improvising a solo is one of the ultimate ways of fulfilling self-expression. Every great improviser has their own voice, and so I feel it is important to listen to many soloists, in many different styles.

The great soloists tell stories within their improvisations, and it is important to listen to different instrumentalists—not only bassists—such as John Coltrane (saxophone) or Oscar Peterson (piano).

There are many elements to a good improvisation. You should listen out for:

- Dynamic range
- Technique during both faster and slower passages
- Melodic development
- Harmonic tension and chromaticism
- Variety of rhythm
- Phrasing, using space to allow the line to 'breathe'

Transcribing is the key to understanding how to solo and I feel it is important to do this first. Try analysing or even copying some of your favourite lines. Ultimately, your goal should be to create your own unique voice in music.

Playing and Interacting

You can practise and work on music by yourself all day long, but no amount of practice can compare to interacting with another musician. As you're only really able to control what you do, you will have to think differently to be able to react to both another instrument and another person.

> *You not only have to know your own instrument... You must know the others and how to back them up at all times. That's jazz.*
>
> — Oscar Peterson

I believe it is crucial for your own growth to spend time doing this, and although you may feel you are not yet ready, you should regularly be playing with others. You might think that you need more time to work on things on your own, but you need to push past this.

Organise your practice schedule, and stick to it. Once you are finished for the day, leave it until tomorrow and get out of the practice room. Go and play and have fun! Apply what you have been working on. Enjoy playing, don't get too serious, and try to remember why you started in the first place.

Creating

In my opinion, being creative is one of the most important factors in music. Don't be scared to try new things!

Push yourself to deal with difficult musical situations. Many times during my career I have been in a position that I thought was far too much for me to cope with. At first these challenges seemed impossible however, once I put my mind to it, I ended up surprising myself.

Whenever I ask my students if they write music, many times the answer is "No, because I can't". I think anyone can—you just have to go for it. Every piece of music does not have to be a masterpiece. You can learn a lot about yourself musically from what you write.

Composing melodies and chord progressions can really shape your own personal voice as a musician. Try not to judge yourself too much. Let it go and, like anything else, the more you do it the better you will become. Also try to finish what you start. It can be bad to develop a habit of thinking something is no good and starting over again. Always remember that a bad idea can lead to a great one so just be patient and don't give up. If you have the courage and perseverance, your imagination can take you anywhere.

"The best advice I ever had..."

It is great to be hungry and enthusiastic about improving your playing, but it can turn into an obsession. You might burn out and stop developing, which could make you become more mechanical and less musical. You may also become a little self-obsessed, or even injure yourself from the excessive strain.

My mother once said to me:

> *Why are you always practising by yourself? You have become anti-social. How can you speak to people through music if you have no life?*

This is the best advice I ever had. Music is about expressing life and emotions through your art. If you are boring and self-obsessed, what do you have to talk about?

I decided to restrict the time I spent practising, and began organising my schedule to make the most of this time. Since organising my practice...

- I have become more focused
- I have more energy and enthusiasm
- I retain more information
- I have become more creative
- I have a life outside of music which in fact benefits my music
- I spend more time listening to other music and enjoy it much more
- I achieve more because I am organised.

Anyone can do it. Organisation is just a habit, like anything else.

Organising Practice Schedules

In my opinion, it is most important for your practice sessions to be organised. This will also aid your development. I used to practise up to and over 12 hours a day and found my lack of growth frustrating. I ended up not enjoying practising or indeed enjoying my life. Music is about expressing emotions and life. Of course, the more knowledge and vocabulary you have the better qualified you are to express exactly what you mean. However, the golden word here is 'life' and that is what it is all about.

I quickly found that organising and documenting my practising schedule allowed me to stay fresh and focused on what I was working on. I could always see the light at the end of the tunnel and see and feel my progress.

Sometimes, the more you try to do something the harder it becomes—it can be better to leave it alone and come back to it fresh. You will find that problems become much more manageable once you return from a break, whether you give it five minutes, a day, or even a week.

To be a good musician takes a lot of patience and realism. Every step of your musical growth has much to offer and can be fun too. It is important to understand you cannot become the musician you want to be overnight. Just be clear in your mind what you want and how to achieve it. Enjoy the stage of development that you're at and stay positive. I try to make my practising a combination of hard work, fun and creativity.

"

We had to do a lot of rehearsals to get it so that it was playable. What it did was make you practise. That's good for any musician to have that kind of pressure. It brings things out of you that might not come out if you don't have to reach for something all the time.

— **Ray Brown**

Everyone has their own schedule and time they are able to commit to practising. I think it is important to be aware of what you can commit to, whether it be 1 hour a day or 4 hours a day. You should use some kind of note book or diary specifically for marking down your practice schedule.

At the end of this book you will find a one-week practice diary for you to use. Make copies of this and be sure to make note of the progress you make during your practice sessions.

I recommend you re-write the things you are working from (onto manuscript paper); for example, the fingering patterns in this book, as they may not fit your style of playing. My fingering patterns work for me—treat them as starting points, or just as examples to help you find your own. Also, my written examples are only in the key of C. As you move through the keys you will need to write them out.

I also recommend you have different manuscript books for the different topics you are working on. That way, you don't have a book that is all mixed up.

Next, you should identify what you want to work on. You need some level of consistency when practising, without burning yourself out.

The way I practise is that I first write out the topics I want to study, for example:

- Neck Study
- Technique
- Ear Training (and 'Listening')
- Bebop Exercises

I have four topics listed, and will spend no more than 30 minutes on each one of them. Therefore, in total there are two hours of practice material here. If I do this over two days, it is basically one-hour-per-day practice.

This can give me the opportunity to stay fresh with each topic I am working on.

This is an example of how I record my practice:

I write the exercises I want to practise at the top, and underneath I signify the key, perhaps a different one for each day. I also show the time I practised for and the bpm I've reached. If I complete what I wanted to practise then I put a tick next to it.

The next day I will start the exercises from previous tempos and aim to increase the bpm for each exercise.

If, for whatever reason, you cannot commit to your daily schedule, you simply continue when you can from the topic next in line. This way of working allows you to give each topic you are working on equal priority.

Next, I will go through the sort of aspects and topics that you can work through, beginning with some overall technique exercises.

TECHNIQUE

These exercises are designed to develop dexterity, stamina, strength and tone. They are patterns and should not be analysed as anything else.

In total there are 7 daily exercises, each using different co-ordination skills. Spend no longer than 30 minutes on each of these exercises per day.

Start at a tempo that allows you to play these exercises accurately. Patience is always important, so give it time. It is important to be able to play these exercises clearly and comfortably before increasing the tempo. I never practise these exercises above 60bpm, with the metronome on beats

2 and 4. Definition and accuracy are the goals here. Speed and agility will come from playing these exercises.

I have developed a system to help the student learn how to read and stay in position. For these exercises you will notice a number followed by a letter written underneath the note.

The number represents the finger used (0 = open string). The letter indicates the string the note is played on.

Technique Day 1

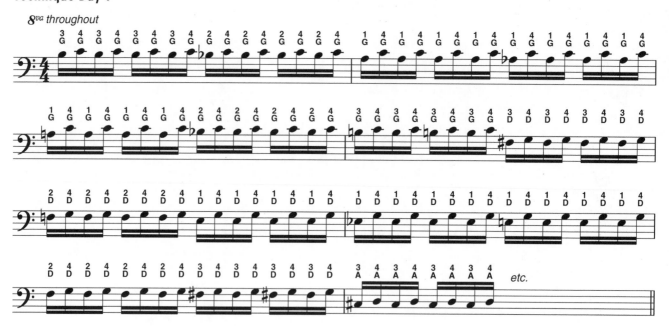

This exercise is played one octave up with the note B played on the 16th fret of the G string. This pattern is played over 5 frets using all fingers and a 5-fret stretch. Play this exercise as written continuing across all the strings. Once you arrive at the lowest string (in this case E) play the pattern and without stopping move to the next note up on the G string. The next note up will be a B♭ on the 15th fret.

Keep playing the exercise without stopping until your 1st finger stretch is between the 1st and 5th fret. Once you have worked your way down, without stopping, work your way back up to where you started. This exercise will build up stamina in your fingers. Try to relax during this exercise and use the metronome on beats 2 and 4.

Technique Day 2

Play this exercise across all strings E, A, D and G and without stopping move chromatically up to the next note and repeat. Once you reach the 12th fret descend back down to the 1st fret and repeat 3 times. Play pattern with metronome on beats 2 and 4.

This pattern is played over 3 strings then repeated on the next string up. Continue the pattern up in half-steps until you reach the 12th fret then descend. Repeat the exercise 3 times without stopping. This exercise uses the 1st, 2nd and 3rd fingers only.

This exercise is the same as the previous one. This time, use the 2nd, 3rd and 4th fingers only.

This exercise is played over 2 strings using all 4 fingers. It helps your hand and finger positioning on the neck with the left hand and develops alternate string skipping with the right hand.

Play the pattern across the strings then, without stopping, move up the neck chromatically to the 12th fret and back down. Repeat this exercise 3 times with the metronome on beats 2 and 4.

This exercise is similar to the previous one above. The only difference is the 4th note skips 2 strings instead of one. Again, the pattern is played over 4 frets developing the positioning of the left hand and string skipping with the right. This pattern is played down the strings then moving up across the neck chromatically until you reach the 12th fret with your 1st finger. Once you are there, without stopping, return to the 1st fret.

Again, without stopping repeat this exercise 3 times with the metronome on beats 2 and 4.

ESSENTIAL
BASS LIBRARY

JEFF ANDREWS
Where We Come From
(Vital Information)
Intuition, 1998

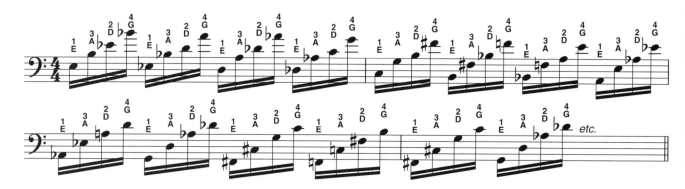

This exercise is played across 4 strings and 4 frets. It strengthens finger positioning with the left hand and works the right hand technique because every note is played on the next string up. Start this pattern on the 12th fret and chromatically work your way down the neck to the 1st fret and back up. Repeat this exercise 5 times without stopping with the metronome on beats 2 and 4.

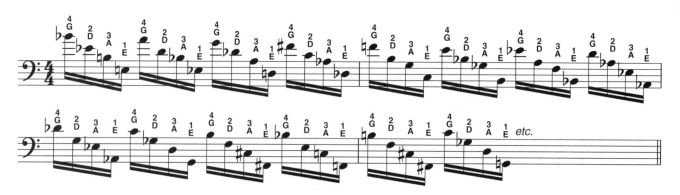

This exercise is the same as the previous one. The only difference is that you play from the highest string working your way down to the lowest.

Technique Day 3

This exercise is a variation of the Day 1 Technique work out. The exercise is played an octave up with the note F♯ played on the 16th fret of the D string. As in Day 1 this pattern is played over 5 frets using all fingers with a 5 fret stretch. The 3rd finger in the exercise is played on the string above (G string).

Play this exercise as written continuing across all the strings. Once you arrive at the lowest string continue playing the exercise and without stopping move to the next note up on the G string. The note in this case will be an F on the D string. Continue until the 5 finger stretch brings your 1st finger to the 1st fret. Again, without stopping, continue chromatically back down the fretboard to the original position on which the exercise started.

Technique Day 4: Part 1

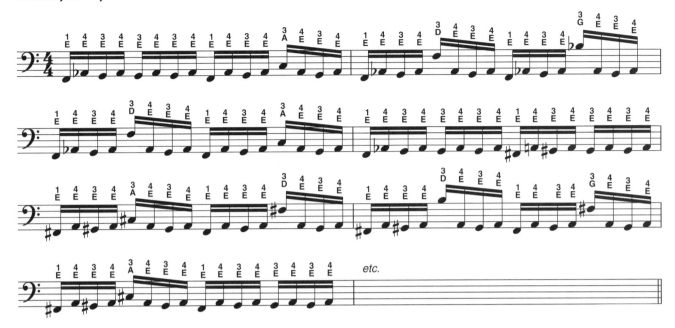

This exercise is designed to build strength and stamina in the right and left hands. The pattern is played over 4 frets and across 4 strings.

Part 1 concentrates on strengthening the 3rd finger by string skipping from the E to the A, E to D and E to G strings. The fingering pattern is the same throughout the exercise: 1, 4, 3, 4, 3, 4, 3, 4.

Play the pattern once then move up chromatically repeating the pattern until you reach the 12th fret with the 1st finger. Once you have reached the 12th fret, without stopping, work your way back down to the 1st fret. Again, without stopping, repeat the exercise 3 times.

Technique Day 4: Part 2

Part 2 of the technique Day 4 exercise is a variation of part 1. Again, it concentrates on strengthening and stamina using the 3rd finger. The pattern is also played over 4 frets and across all 4 strings. The fingering pattern is 1, 4, 3, 4 and every time the 3rd finger is used the next string up is played. Repeat the pattern moving up chromatically all the way to the 12th fret on the 1st finger. Once you have reached the 12th fret without stopping work your way back down to the 1st fret. Again, without stopping, repeat this exercise 3 times.

ESSENTIAL
BASS LIBRARY

VICTOR BAILEY

Low Blow
(Victor Bailey)
EFA Medien, 1999

Technique Day 5

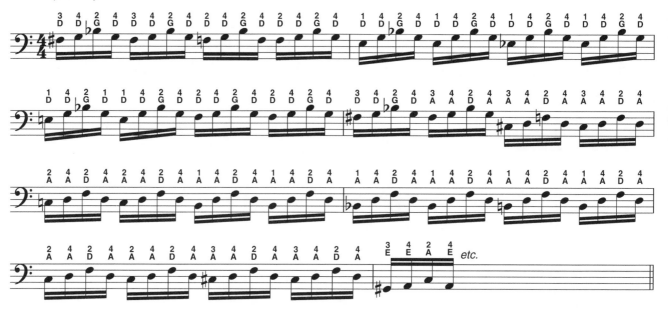

This is a variation of the Day 1 and Day 3 technique work out exercises. The exercise is played an octave up with the F♯ played on the 16th fret of the D string. In this case the 2nd finger is played on the string above. Play this exercise as written continuing across all strings. Once you arrive at the lowest string (E) continue playing the exercise and, without stopping, move to the next note up on the D string. The note in this case will be an F on the 15th fret of the D string. Continue in this matter until the 5 fret stretch brings your 1st finger to the 1st fret. Without stopping, continue chromatically back down the fretboard to the original position on which the exercise started.

Technique Day 6: Part 1

This is a variation of the Day 4 technique workout exercise. Again, the exercise is designed to strengthen the left and right hands. The pattern is played over 4 frets and across 4 strings.

Part 1 concentrates on strengthening the 2nd finger by string skipping from the E to A, E to D and E to G strings. The fingering pattern is the same throughout the exercise and is: 1, 4, 2, 4, 2, 4, 2, 4. Play the pattern once then move up the neck chromatically repeating the pattern until you reach the 12th fret with the 1st finger. Once you have reached the 12th fret without stopping work your way back down to the 1st fret. Again, without stopping, repeat the exercise 3 times.

Technique Day 6: Part 2

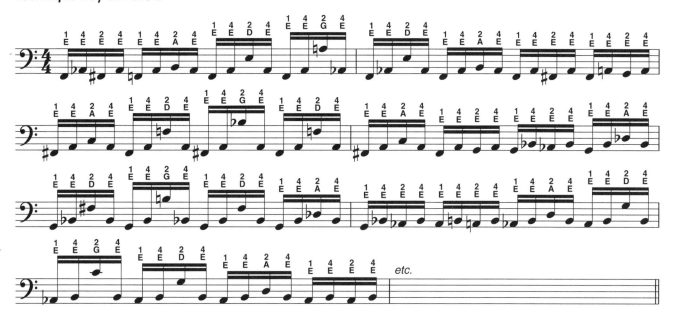

Part 2 of the technique Day 6 exercise is a variation of Part 1. Again, it concentrates on strengthening and stamina using the 2nd finger. The pattern is also played over 4 frets and across 4 strings. The fingering pattern is the same throughout the exercise: 1, 4, 2, 4 and every time the 2nd finger is used the next string up is played. Repeat the pattern moving up chromatically all the way to the 12th fret on the 1st finger. Once you have reached the 12th fret without stopping work your way back down to the 1st fret. Again, without stopping, repeat the exercise 3 times.

Technique Day 7

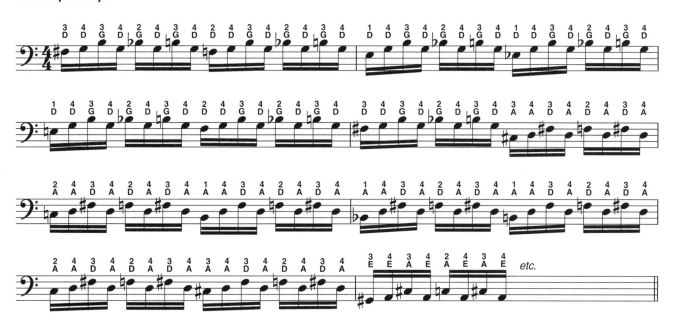

This exercise is a variation of the Day 1, Day 3 and Day 5 technique work outs. The exercise is played an octave up than written with the note F♯ played on the 16th fret of the D string. As in Days 1, 3 and 5 the pattern is played over 5 frets using all fingers with a 5-fret stretch. The 3rd and 2nd fingers in this pattern are played on the string above. Play this exercise as written continuing across all the strings. Once you arrive at the lowest string (E) continue playing the exercise, without stopping, move to the next note up on the D string. The note in this case will be an F on the D string. Continue in this manner until the 5-finger stretch brings your 1st finger to the 1st fret. Again, without stopping, continue chromatically back down the fretboard to the original position on which the exercise started.

Apply any number of these daily technique exercises to your practice schedule and you will find that, in time, your familiary with your instrument will vastly improve.

ESSENTIAL BASS LIBRARY

JIM BARR

All Is Yes
(Get The Blessing)
Candid Productions, 2008

MORE PRACTICE SCHEDULE TOPICS

1. Neck Study (fingering patterns)

Start with the C major modes fingering patterns. Learn the whole range fingering pattern starting at a slow tempo, e.g. 40 bpm on beats 2 and 4. Play through the pattern ascending and descending without stopping 3 times then raise the metronome increments by 2–5 bpm and repeat.

Work your way up to a challenging tempo, e.g. 120 bpm on beats 2 and 4. Once you are comfortable with the exercise move on to the C Ionian fingering pattern. Work on this scale in the same way. This time once you have worked your way up to a challenging tempo write a simple melody using scale fragments.

Go back to your slow tempo, set up a drone or a sustained C^{maj7} chord and play through the fingering pattern once, then play your melody. Use the melody as a starting point for your own improvisations. Don't stick to the fingering patterns when improvising, just have the concept of the position shifts and let go.

Use a timer for 3–5 minutes at each tempo you work on. Once you have reached your challenging tempo move on to the D Dorian scale and repeat the process. This time set your drone to a D or a sustained Dm^7 chord.

All these scales contain the same notes so it is important to get the sound and characteristics of the scale into your improvising.

Repeat this process for each mode in the key of C and over each interval. Next, learn the Linear fingering patterns and try to imply them into your improvisations.

Once you have finished with the C major modes move on to the C melodic minor modes, C harmonic minor modes, C diminished, etc. nRepeat this whole process then start again in the key of F.

Your musicality will improve all the time whilst working on these exercises. Your instinctive nature of playing economically around the fretboard will improve immensely. Be patient and stay with it. Remember 30 minutes each time you practise is enough.

2. Linear Solo Concepts

Start with exercise one at a slow tempo, e.g. 60 bpm. If you can record a sequence to play along with the result will be better. You can play along with the included recorded track at a fixed tempo. However, if it is not possible to play along with a track just have the sound of the chords in your head.

Set a timer for 5 minutes, play a quarter or half-note line for 2½ minutes, and if you are comfortable, improvise a solo for the remaining time. Use as much of the fretboard as possible and if you have trouble in one area focus on that. Once comfortable at one tempo raise the increments 2–5 bpm and repeat.

Work your way through the exercises then move on to the melodic minor linear solo exercises and repeat. Try experimenting with your own progressions and play to challenging tempos.

This exercise is a great way to improve your ears, melodic development, fingering shapes and the ability to play musically through chord changes.

3. Chord Study (triads, 4-note chords, linear solo concepts)

Start this topic by learning or reviewing all the available triads and their inversions.

Next, learn the one octave diatonic triad patterns then practise them over the whole range of the fretboard.

Start these whole range patterns at a slow tempo along with a drone or related sustained chord. Play through the pattern 3 times before raising the tempo. Play up to a challenging tempo then return to your slow starting tempo and improvise and try to imply the pattern into your phrasing.

When you are at the improvisation section set a timer for each tempo you are working from for 3–5 minutes. Once comfortable with the exercise move on to the next pattern and repeat the process. Once you are happy with the triad patterns in the key of C major, move on to different keys and repeat.

After the triad patterns in major keys study or review the construction of 4-note chords and their inversions. Learn the one octave patterns then practise them with the triads over the whole range of the fretboard. Again start these whole range patterns at a slow tempo along with a drone or sustained related chord. Play through the pattern 3 times before raising the tempo.

As before, go back to your starting tempo and improvise implying the pattern as much as necessary and move on to the next pattern and repeat. Don't forget to use a timer raising the metronome increments 2–5 bpm each time.

Once comfortable with the diatonic 4-note chords in the key of C move transpose patterns through all 12 keys and repeat the concept.

Next, move on to the moving 4-note chords through non-related chord changes patterns. This chapter is a variation of the linear solo concept chapter only this time you are ascending and descending with 4-note chords.

Work your way through each exercise slowly before moving on to the triads found within the melodic minor modes and repeat.

ESSENTIAL
BASS LIBRARY

JEFF BERLIN

High Standards
(Jeff Berlin)
M.A.J. Records, 2010

4. Walking Bass Lines

Work your way through these exercises, slowly and methodically. After each exercise try implying the concept over your choice of 10 standard jazz tunes. Pick ones that are different from one another, e.g. A Blues, Rhythm Changes, Be Bop, Minor Blues, etc.

After you have completed playing the exercise over the standards at various tempos pick up a recording of a standard or bass player you like and transcribe their walking bass line.

One or two choruses to start with are fine. Try to analyse and play along with the recording. The dynamics and time feel of a walking bass line is essential to the authenticity of the genre.

Next, move on to the following exercise and repeat.

Remember, the bass player's main function is to support and not step on the soloist. Be mindful and focus. Try to memorize the songs and form. These exercises are a great way to learn tunes.

5. Be Bop (upper structure, target note approaches)

Start with the tensions and upper structure exercises for the chords found within the major modes. Remember these are exercises developed to familiarize you will the upper structures of the chords.

It is important for you to recognize these exercises as ear training exercises and not technical ones. Play these upper structure tension patterns over the cycle of 5ths progressions starting at a slow tempo.

Next work through the 4-part approach to target note exercises. These exercises are a great way to learn how to move around chords in an interesting way. These techniques are very commonly used by the jazz greats and are well worth all the work.

Try to emply these concepts over your 10 standards you are working on in the Walking Bass Line topic.

After you are finished with the chords found within the major modes move on to the melodic and harmonic minor modes.

6. Blues Scale Soloing

The Blues scale is a very simple and very effective way of soloing through a Blues progression. I have written out 3 steps to practise. Work your way through the steps in each key. Force yourself to write out patterns. This is a great way to practise developing your melodic statements.

Practise these exercise in all keys.

7. Technique

These technique exercises can be practised daily or every other day. They have been designed to develop different areas of your technique from speed and dexterity to stamina.

It is important to stretch and loosen up before your start working on these exercises. I personally go no faster than 60 bpm on beats 2 and 4. Speed comes from accuracy, comfort and execution. It is important to keep focused on your right and left hand. If you feel pain, stop. Try to stay relaxed if you can't play these exercises comfortably just slow the tempo down. Start at 40 bpm on beats 2 and 4.

Each time you complete the cycle of daily exercises raise the increments 2 bpm and continue. A good technique is vital to be able to play what you desire. Be patient and consistent and your technique will develop with no bad habits.

Certainly one of the more common experiences in the jazz field is discovering someone new. Improvising musicians are capable of being musical travelers, voyagers. We want to join in on whatever we hear. There is a freedom to wander the musical landscape.

— **Gary Burton**

Some Final Thoughts

- Use this book as a guide to help you through your own journey.

- It is important to realize there is no right or wrong way to practise.

- Enjoy your growth—never force it. If you work hard with diligence and patience you will reach your goals. There are no shortcuts, so accept and enjoy where you are musically.

- Each step of your journey is valuable. A solid foundation of knowledge will aid your growth.

- Don't forget it is important to take breaks as you need time to reflect and absorb all the information you have gathered.

- You learn best when you are focused and have a desire to practise...
  If you are hungry—EAT
  If you are tired—SLEEP
  If you want to practise—PRACTISE

- When you need inspiration, it is good to refresh yourself. Listen to music, watch a show, watch a movie, read a book or go for a walk.

Inspiration can be found everywhere. Enjoy your journey.

TONY GREY

2013

Part 1

The Basics:
Major Modes
Fingering Patterns
Linear Solo Concepts
Inversions and Triads

CHAPTER 1.1

Key Signatures and Major Modes

In this chapter I will explain about key signatures and their construction using the cycle of fifths. I will also discuss the major modes and their relationships with one another.

THE CHROMATIC SCALE

A half-step is also known as a *semitone*. Likewise, a whole step is also known as a *whole tone*, or often simply a tone.

A chromatic scale is a 12-note scale built in half-steps. The scale contains all the notes available in conventional Western harmony, and accordingly, all Western harmony is derived from notes in the chromatic scale.

Ascending chromatic scale

Descending chromatic scale

There are many further scales which use some of the notes of the chromatic scale. In this book we will concentrate and discuss the structure of the more common scales and their modes, as they are used in Western popular and Jazz music.

Here are the six common scales we will be analysing, all shown in the key of C major:

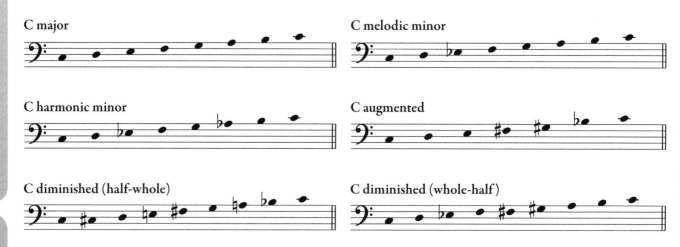

C major

C melodic minor

C harmonic minor

C augmented

C diminished (half-whole)

C diminished (whole-half)

ESSENTIAL
BASS LIBRARY

JIMMY BLANTON

*The Blanton-Webster
Years*
(Duke Ellington)
Bluebird, 1939-1942

KEY SIGNATURES

A key signature shows all the accidentals within the key on the right side of the clef before the time signature.

Example 1

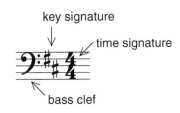

The key signature indicates what key a piece of music is in. It is a way of organising scales with accidentals.

Example 2

| D natural | D sharp | D natural | D flat |

Example 2 shows the note D being played 4 times. After the first D the following D's have accidentals placed in front of them.

♯   a sharp raises the note a half-step

♮   a natural returns the note to its original standing

♭   a flat lowers the note a half-step

In Example 1 there are two accidentals in the key signature: F♯ and C♯. These two pitches will remain altered throughout the piece of music unless otherwise indicated.

There is a pattern which structures the relationship between the different key signatures you'll use. This pattern is called the cycle of 5ths. Let's start from C major, which has no key signature, because all its notes are natural.

If you look at a piano all the white keys belong to the C major scale. The notes from one C to the next C create the C major scale. The pattern of notes in this scale is the same pattern from which all major scales are formed. Later in this chapter we will analyse the construction of scales.

Continuing with the cycle of 5ths from C up a 5th gives us G. The key signature for G is one sharp (F♯). Moving up another 5th gives us the key signature for D major—two sharps (C♯ and F♯). Continuing in this way uncovers patterns which govern the construction of each subsequent key signature in the cycle.

Every time you raise the key a 5th one sharp is added to the key signature. There are two key patterns to this cycle:

1. The added sharp is always the seventh degree of the new key, e.g. in the key of G major, F♯ is the seventh degree of the G major scale, and so the added sharp is F♯.

2. The added sharp is always a 5th above the last one in the cycle, e.g. in the key of D major—two sharps—the added sharp is C♯, which is a 5th above F♯ in the key of G major.

Continuing up the cycle of 5ths, once you reach F♯, it is more common to continue the cycle using flats. Although it is not incorrect to see a C♯ key signature (seven sharps) D♭ is the same note and is often more convenient to use, as there are fewer accidentals in the key signature. D♭ is called an enharmonic of C♯.

ESSENTIAL BASS LIBRARY

JIMMY BLANTON

1939-1941 The Jimmy Blanton Era (Duke Ellington, Jimmy Blanton) *Saar, 1939*

Every time you lower the key by a 5th or raise the key by a 4th one flat is added to the new key signature. There are two key patterns to this cycle:

1. The accidental (flat) is the previous key is always the name of the new key, e.g. the key of F has the key signature with one flat. The flattened note is the key
   of F is B♭. The next scale in the cycle of 5ths is the key of B♭.

2. The added flat to the new key signature is always a perfect 4th above the last one, e.g. the key of F has one flat in its key signature, which is a B♭. A perfect 4th above B♭, E♭, is the added flat to the next key signature.

It is not so common to use the key signatures for G♭ and C♭; it is more common to use F♯ in place of the G♭ and a B in place of C♭. Again, it is not actually incorrect to use either key signatures because they are simply enharmonics, but it is generally easier to use the key signature that has fewer sharps or flats. The placement of flats, as with sharps, always remains the same.

The pattern of the cycle of fifths can be seen clearly here.

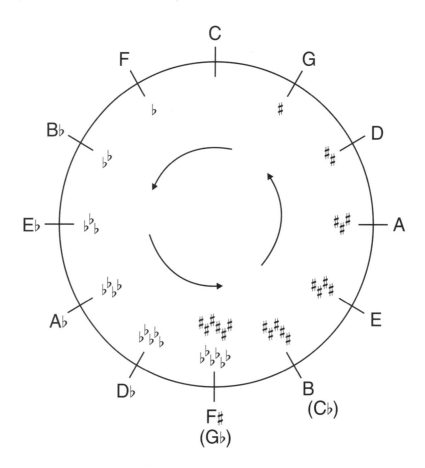

Following the cycle anti-clockwise from C major, the keys go down in perfect 5ths, adding a flat to each subsequent key signature.

When the cycle reaches G♭ we can change the key signature from flats to sharps—in fact, from 6 flats to 6 sharps. The cycle continues from F♯ (G♭) down a perfect 5th, subtracting a sharp from each subsequent key signature. When it reaches C the cycle starts again.

Major Modes

The major scale is made up of a series of steps. They are: W, W, H, W, W, W, H.

W= whole step H= half-step

You can build a different scale off each note (or *degree*) of the major scale. These new scales form a group of scales called the major modes. As before, a good way to see this is to start by looking at the white notes on a piano, i.e. all the notes of C major.

A new mode can be formed by starting on a particular degree of the scale, and then only using notes in the pre-existing major key to establish a new 7-note scale. Each scale built off the major scale has its own unique series of intervals, and this is what gives each mode its particular qualities and characteristics.

Here are the seven modes from the major scale:

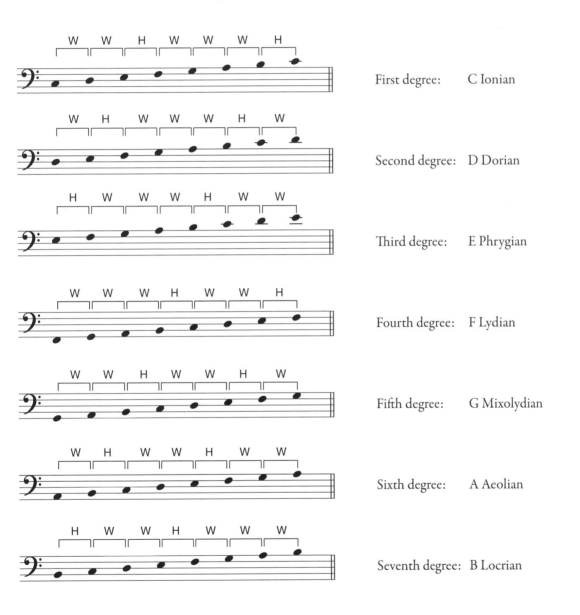

First degree: C Ionian

Second degree: D Dorian

Third degree: E Phrygian

Fourth degree: F Lydian

Fifth degree: G Mixolydian

Sixth degree: A Aeolian

Seventh degree: B Locrian

You might notice that the C major scale and the C Ionian mode are identical. When we talk about the notes of a particular key, we refer to those notes as belonging to the major scale. However, when talking specifically about the scale built on the first degree of the key, we give that scale its modal name—Ionian. Another way to put this is that all of these scales are modes of the C major scale; the Ionian is the mode derived from the first note.

ESSENTIAL BASS LIBRARY

WELLMAN BRAUD

Duke Ellington & His Orchestra: Early Ellington, 1927-1934 (Duke Ellington)
Decca, 1927-1934

C Ionian

The major 3rd and major 7th degrees make the C Ionian a major scale. The most common chord to play this scale over is a C^{maj7}.

The intervals between the notes of each mode give that mode its particular characteristics. A good way to hear the qualities of each mode is to compare each mode of the C major scale with the major scales of the keys of each root. For instance, comparing D Dorian—the mode built off the second degree of the C major scale, with no sharps—with the D major (Ionian) scale, which has two sharps.

D Dorian

The D Dorian scale is the scale built off the second degree of the C major scale (the Ionian mode).

When you compare the D Dorian scale against the D Ionian you will notice that the third and seventh degrees are flattened.

The minor 3rd and minor 7th degrees make the D Dorian a minor scale. The most common chord to play this scale over is Dm^7.

D Dorian

E Phrygian

The E Phrygian scale is the scale built off the third degree of the C major scale (the Ionian mode).

When you compare the E Phrygian scale against the E Ionian you will notice the second, third, sixth, and seventh degrees are flattened.

The minor 3rd, perfect 5th and minor 7th degrees make the E Phrygian a minor scale. The b2 and b6 give this scale a Spanish sound. The most common chord to play this scale over is Em^7.

E Phrygian

F Lydian

The F Lydian scale is the scale built off the fourth degree of the C major scale (the Ionian mode).

When you compare the F Lydian scale against the F Ionian scale you will notice the fourth degree is raised a half-step.

The major 3rd, perfect 5th and major 7th degrees make the F Lydian a major scale. The most common chord to play this scale over is F^maj7.

F Lydian

F Ionian

G Mixolydian

The G Mixolydian scale is the scale built off the fifth degree of the C major scale (the Ionian mode).

When you compare the G Mixolydian scale against the G Ionian scale you will notice the seventh degree is flattened.

The major 3rd, perfect 5th and minor 7th degrees make the G Mixolydian a dominant scale—identifying scale functions, such as tonic and dominant, will be discussed later in the book. The most common chord to play this scale over is G^7.

G Mixolydian

G Ionian

A Aeolian

The A Aeolian scale is the scale built off the sixth degree of the C major scale (the Ionian mode).

When you compare the A Aeolian scale against the A Ionian scale you will notice the third, sixth, and seventh degrees are flattened.

The minor 3rd, perfect 5th and minor 7th degrees make the A Aeolian a minor scale. The Aeolian scale is also known as a natural minor scale. The most common chord to play this scale over is A^m7.

A Aeolian

A Ionian

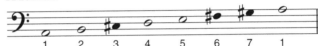

B Locrian

The B Locrian scale is the scale built off the seventh degree of the C major scale (the Ionian mode).

When you compare the B Locrian scale against the B Ionian scale you will notice the second, third, fifth, sixth, and seventh degrees are flattened.

The minor 3rd, diminished 5th and minor 7th degrees make this uncommon scale B Locrian a half-diminished scale. The most common chord to play this scale over is a B^m7♭5.

B Locrian

B Ionian

Much European folk music uses the Lydian mode, with a distinctive sharpened fourth. The opening theme from *The Simpsons* is a well-known example of this.

The flattened seventh of the Mixolydian mode gives it both a folky and slightly unresolved quality. As the Blues almost entirely uses flattened seventh (dominant) chords, the harmony could be conisidered to be somewhat Mixolydian.

The Aeolian mode sounds like a minor scale with the 'leading note' (seventh degree) flattened. Compared to the Dorian mode, the sixth degree is also flattened. This mode was frequently used in Ancient music.

The more unusual nature of the Locrian mode means that it is used less frequently than the other modes, however this unusual sound has been exploited by many, including Debussy (in the orchestral piece 'Jeux') and Björk (in 'Army Of Me').

ESSENTIAL
BASS LIBRARY

RAY BROWN

Dizzy Gillespie: The Complete RCA Victor Recordings 1937 - 1949 (Dizzy Gillespie) *Bluebird, 1937-1949*

1.2

CHAPTER 1.2

Intervals and Diatonic Fingering Patterns for the Major Modes

This chapter focuses on fingering patterns for the C major modes and their intervals.

I wrote out the whole range of the modes from the lowest note to the highest note on the instrument (NB these fingering patterns are written for a 4 string Bass, E to G, with 24 frets). The idea of this exercise is to find the perfect fingering pattern to play across the whole instrument with ease.

Firstly, I wrote out the C major scale, starting with the lowest note available (an E on the E string) up to the highest note available (G on the 24th fret of the G string).

Next, I wrote out C Ionian, from the lowest C on the lowest string E to the highest available C on the highest string, G. Again, I worked out the perfect fingering pattern, and continued this exercise throughout all the C major modes: D Dorian, E Phrygian, F Lydian, G Mixolydian, A Aeolian and B Locrian. There is a different fingering pattern, position and range for each exercise.

Next, I applied the same concept to the major modes of C major by writing out fingering patterns for all the intervals: 3rds, 4ths, 5ths, 6ths, and 7ths.

Let's start by analysing exactly what an interval is.

INTERVALS

An interval describes the relationship between two notes. They measure the distance of the lower note to the higher note.

There are five types of intervals:

1. Major (maj)
2. Minor (min)
3. Perfect (P)
4. Augmented (aug)
5. Diminished (dim)

There are 7 notes in a common major scale and there are 7 different sizes of interval.

They are: Unisons, 2nds, 3rds, 4ths, 5ths, 6ths, and 7ths.

Octaves (8ths), complete the scale with the same note as the starting note, and are essentially the same as unisons.

Diatonic Intervals in the key of C major

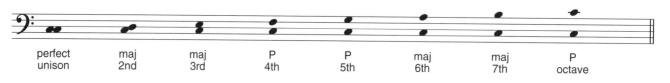

| perfect unison | maj 2nd | maj 3rd | P 4th | P 5th | maj 6th | maj 7th | P octave |

In the key of C major, all the ascending intervals are major or perfect. The 2nd, 3rd, 6th and 7th intervals are major. The unison, 4th, 5th and octave are all known as perfect intervals. Using these intervals I can define the other intervals (minor, augmented, and diminished).

ESSENTIAL BASS LIBRARY

RAY BROWN

This One's For Blanton
(Duke Ellington)
Original Jazz Classics, 1972

Minor Intervals

A minor interval is a major 2nd, 3rd, 6th, or 7th lowered by a half-step.

A major 3rd in the key of C major:

The upper note is E making the interval a maj 3rd

A minor 3rd in the key of C major:

The E is now lowered a half step to E♭ making this interval a minor 3rd.

Augmented Interval

An augmented interval is a major or perfect interval raised a half-step.

An augmented 5th in the key of C major:

The upper note is G (perfect 5th) raised a half-step to a G♯ making this interval on augmented 5th.

Diminished Interval

A diminished interval is a minor or perfect interval lowered a half-step.

A diminished 5th in the key of C major:

The upper note is a G (perfect 5th) lowered a half-step to a G♭ making this interval a diminished 5th.

You can adjust intervals to make new intervals:

- A major interval raised a half-step becomes augmented
- A major interval lowered a half-step becomes minor
- A major interval lowered a whole step becomes diminished
- A minor interval raised a half-step becomes major
- A minor interval lowered a half-step becomes diminished
- A minor interval raised a whole step becomes augmented
- A perfect interval raised a half-step becomes augmented
- A perfect interval lowered half-step becomes diminished

INVERSIONS OF INTERVALS

An inversion of an interval is created by raising the lower note by an octave.

maj 6th

This is an interval of a major 6th

maj 6th   min 3rd

Raising the lowest note (C) up are octave changes the interval from a major 6th into a minor 3rd.

ESSENTIAL
BASS LIBRARY

RAY BROWN

Magical Trio 2
(James Williams)
EmArcy, 1987

Here is a list of possible intervallic inversions from the C chromatic scale.

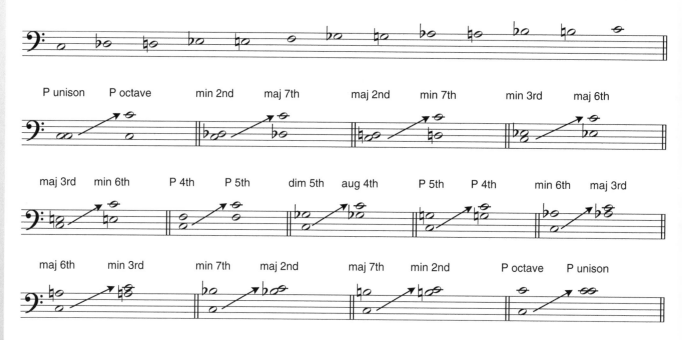

As you analyse the previous chart of intervals built off the chromatic scale you will notice some patterns:

- When a perfect interval is inverted it remains a perfect interval.
- When a major interval is inverted it becomes a minor interval.
- When a minor interval is inverted it becomes a major interval.
- When an augmented interval is inverted it becomes a diminished interval.
- When a diminished interval is inverted it becomes an augmented interval.

DIATONIC FINGERING PATTERNS

These following fingering patterns are designed for you, the student, to understand your instrument. The goal of this is to develop a strong knowledge of the fingerboard and an instinctive feel for your instrument, enabling you to play with more freedom and allowing you to play more from your heart and ears. These exercises only cover the key of C major (and the modes that are derived from it), but I strongly advise you to repeat these exercises in all keys. For these exercises I am using this following system:

Above the note head you will find a number followed by a letter.

In this case, the number '3' represents the fret-hand finger to use and the letter 'A' represents the string this applies to.

The number 0 indicates an open string. So in this case the note is D open string.

All of these following exercises are played on all 4 strings. These fingering patterns are my own way of moving around the fingerboard. There are endless possibilities; if these fingering patterns feel unnatural to your way of playing then find your own way. My method, as you'll see if you analyse these patterns, is: when ascending I tend to lead with my index finger (1), and when descending I tend to lead with my little finger (4).

Practice and patience will help you play with more fluidity and help you develop a strong melodic sense. I feel it is important to practise these patterns as written but it is more important to practise things in a creative way, and later I will discuss other ways to practise these exercises using melodies and melodic development.

I recommend practising these exercises with the metronome on beats 2 and 4 (instead of on beats 1 and 3, to add a bit of a rhythmic drive), starting at 40bpm. Repeat five times up and down the fretboard without stopping, and then increase the metronome speed in increments of 2bpm, and repeat. I perform these exercises until the metronome is at 120bpm (on beats 2 and 4). However, play at the tempo which is most comfortable for you. **Speed is not the point of this exercise.**

I recommended practising this for no more than 30 minutes a day. Once your time is up, make a note of the tempo you reached and continue from that point the next time you practise.

C MAJOR MODES

Whole Range

This exercise covers the whole range of the C major scale that is available, starting on the lowest note available, the open E string (E), to the highest note available, a top G on the G string (G).

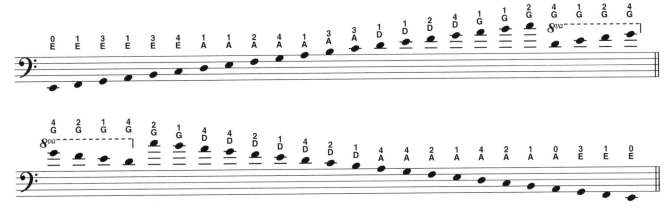

C Ionian

This exercise covers the C Ionian scale from the lowest root (C) on the E string to the highest root (C) on the G string.

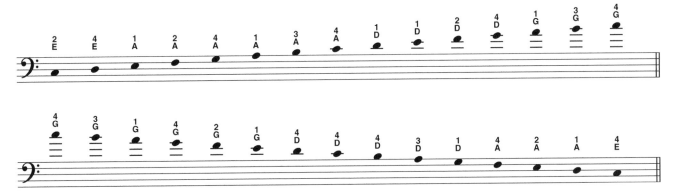

D Dorian

This exercise covers the D Dorian scale from the lowest root (D) on the E string to the highest root (D) on the G string.

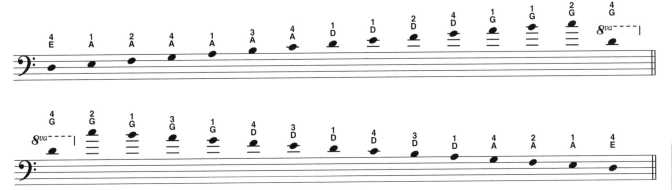

ESSENTIAL
BASS LIBRARY

RAY BROWN

We Get Requests
(Oscar Peterson Trio)
Verve, 1964

E Phrygian

This exercise covers the E Phrygian scale from the lowest root (E) on the E string to the highest root (E) on the G string.

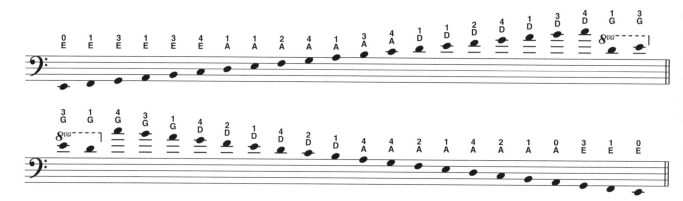

F Lydian

This exercise covers the F Lydian scale from the lowest root (F) on the E string to the highest root (F) on the G string.

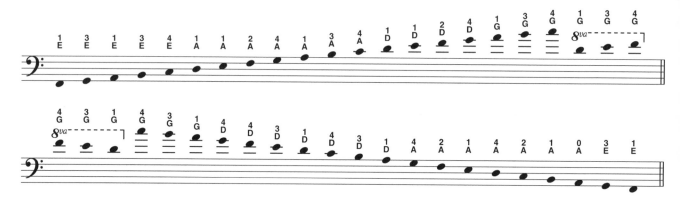

G Mixolydian

This exercise covers the G Mixolydian scale from the lowest root (G) on the E string to the highest root (G) on the G string.

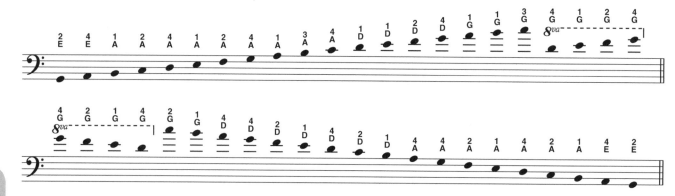

ESSENTIAL
BASS LIBRARY

RAY BROWN

Some Of My Best Friends Are...The Sax Players
(Ray Brown)
Telarc, 1996

A Aeolian

This exercise covers the A Aeolian scale from the lowest root (A) on the E string to the highest root (A) on the G string.

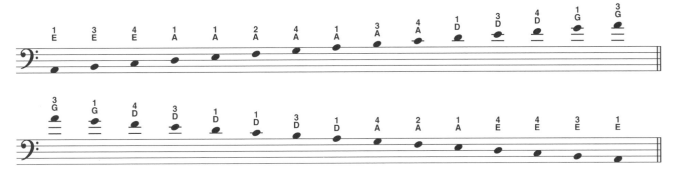

B Locrian

This exercise covers the B Locrian scale from the lowest root (B) on the E string to the highest root (B) on the G string.

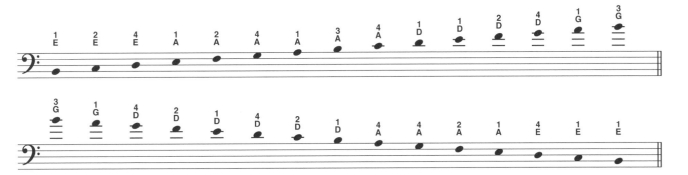

SCALES IN 3RDS

Whole Range in 3rds

This exercise covers the whole range of the C major scale in intervals of 3rds, moving from the lowest note on the E string (E) to the highest note on the G string (G).

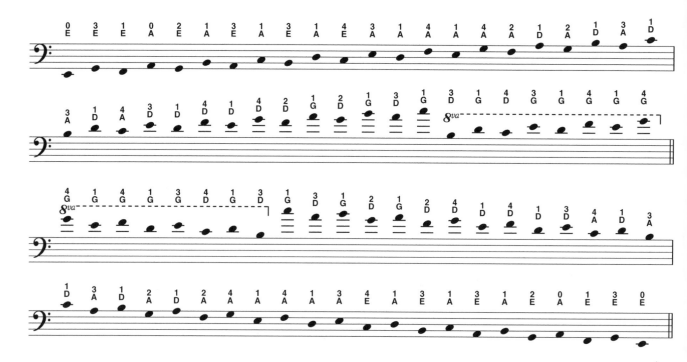

C Ionian in 3rds

This exercise covers the C Ionian scale in 3rds from the lowest root (C) on the E string to the highest available interval from the root (E) on the G string.

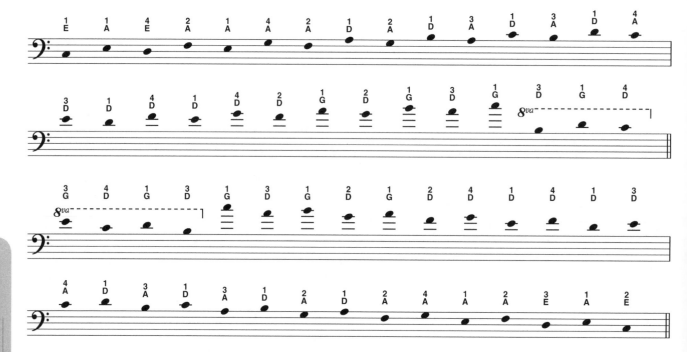

D Dorian in 3rds

This exercise covers the D Dorian scale in 3rds from the lowest root (D) on the E string to the highest available interval from the root (F) on the G string.

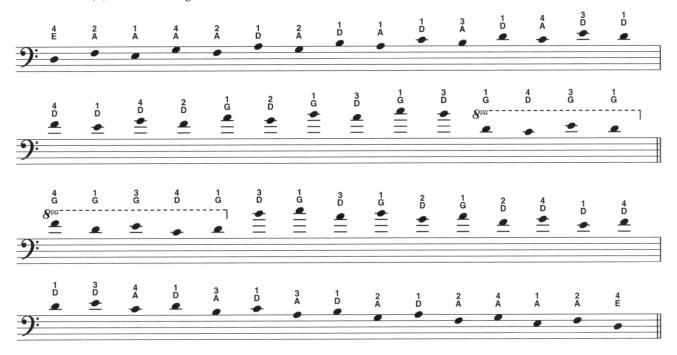

E Phrygian in 3rds

This exercise covers the E Phrygian scale in 3rds from the lowest root (E) on the E string to the highest available interval from the root (G) on the G string.

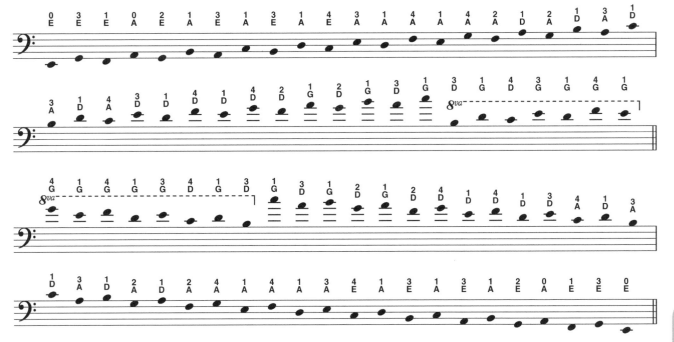

F Lydian in 3rds

This exercise covers the F Lydian scale in 3rds from the lowest root (F) on the E string to the highest available interval from the root (A) on the G string.

G Mixolydian in 3rds

This exercise covers the G Mixolydian scale in 3rds from the lowest root (G) on the E string to the highest available interval from the root (B) on the G string.

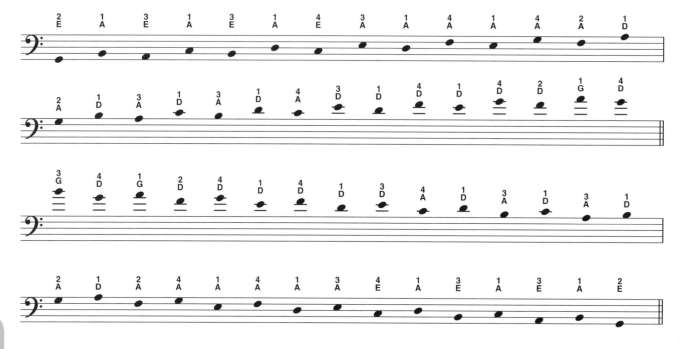

A Aeolian in 3rds

This exercise covers the A Aeolian scale in 3rds from the lowest root (A) on the E string to the highest available interval from the root (C) on the G string.

B Locrian in 3rds

This exercise covers the B Locrian scale in 3rds from the lowest root (B) on the E string to the highest available interval from the root (D) on the G string.

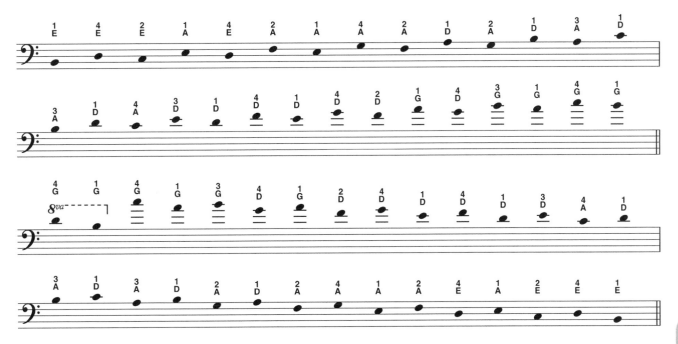

SCALES IN 4THS

Whole Range in 4ths

This exercise covers the whole range of the C major scale in intervals of 4ths moving from the lowest note on the E string (E) to the highest note on the G string (G).

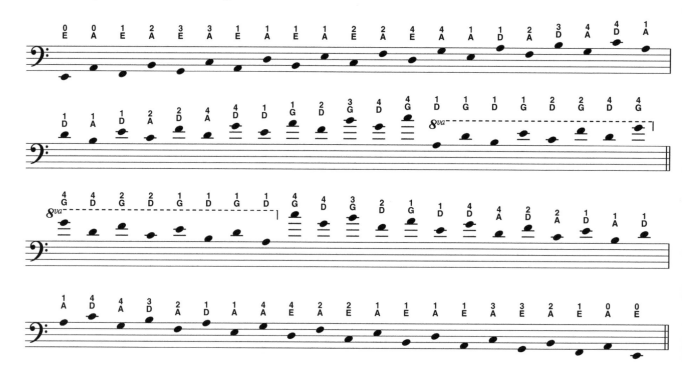

C Ionian in 4ths

This exercise covers the C Ionian scale in 4ths from the lowest root (C) on the E string to the highest available interval from the root (F) on the G string.

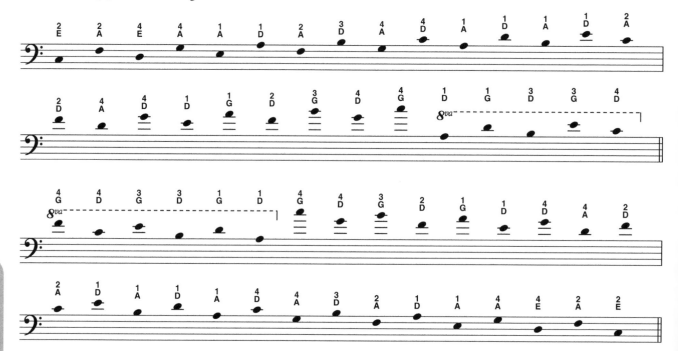

D Dorian in 4ths

This exercise covers the D Dorian scale in 4ths from the lowest root (D) on the E string to the highest available interval from the root (G) on the G string.

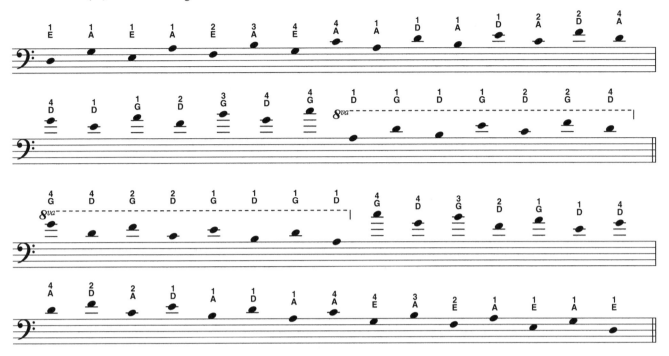

E Phrygian in 4ths

This exercise covers the E Phrygian scale in 4ths from the lowest root (E) on the E string to the highest available interval from the root (A) on the G string.

ESSENTIAL
BASS LIBRARY

**RED CALLENDAR,
TOMMY POTTER,
NELSON BOYD**

*Complete Savoy And
Dial Master Takes*
(Charlie Parker)
Savoy, Dial, 1944-1948

F Lydian in 4ths

This exercise covers the F Lydian scale in 4ths from the lowest root (F) on the E string to the highest available interval from the root (B) on the G string.

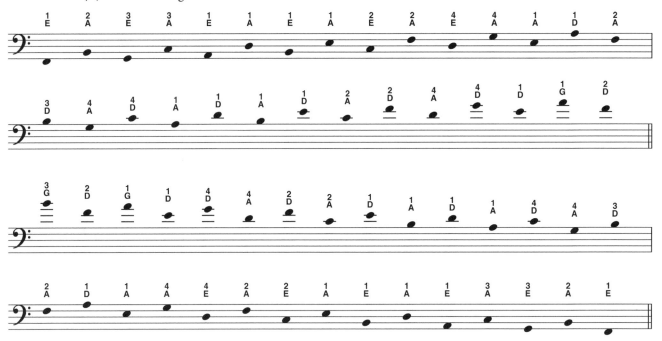

G Mixolydian in 4ths

This exercise covers the G Mixolydian scale in 4ths from the lowest root (G) on the E string to the highest available interval from the root (C) on the G string.

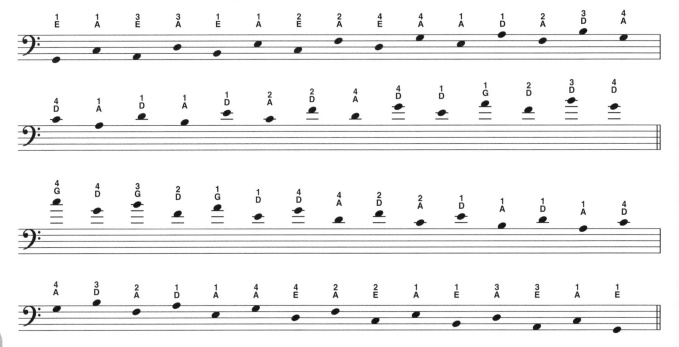

A Aeolian in 4ths

This exercise covers the A Aeolian scale in 4ths from the lowest root (A) on the E string to the highest available interval from the root (D) on the G string.

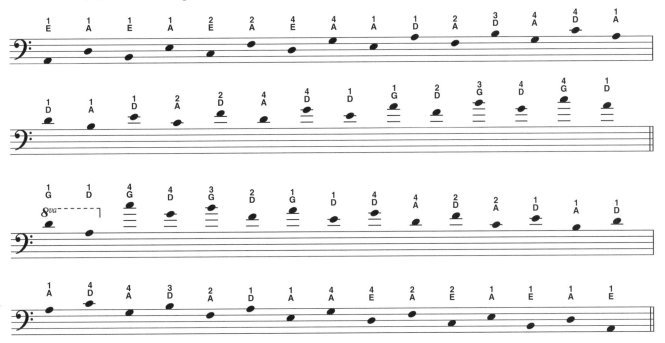

B Locrian in 4ths

This exercise covers the B Locrian scale in 4ths from the lowest root (B) on the E string to the highest available interval from the root (E) on the G string.

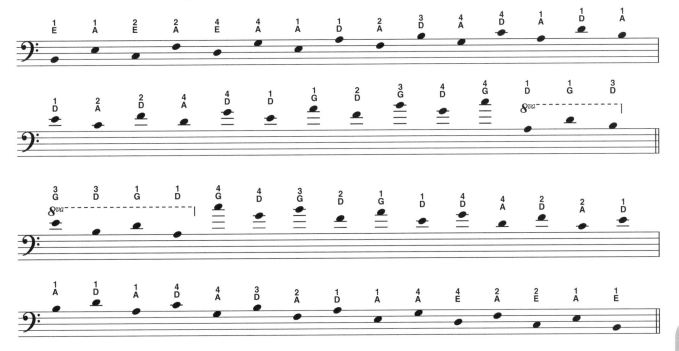

ESSENTIAL
BASS LIBRARY

RON CARTER

*Bill Frisell, Ron Carter,
Paul Motian*
(Bill Frisell, Ron Carter,
Paul Motian)
Nonesuch, 2006

SCALES IN 5THS

Whole Range in 5ths

This exercise covers the whole range of the C major scale in intervals of 5ths, moving from the lowest note on the E string (E) to the highest note on the G string (G).

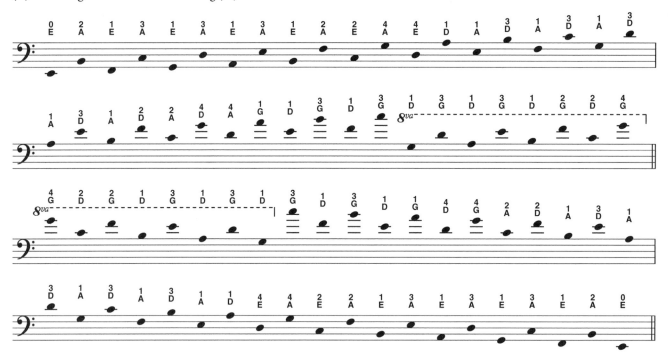

C Ionian in 5ths

This exercise covers the C Ionian scale in 5ths from the lowest root (C) on the E string to the highest available interval from the root (G) on the G string.

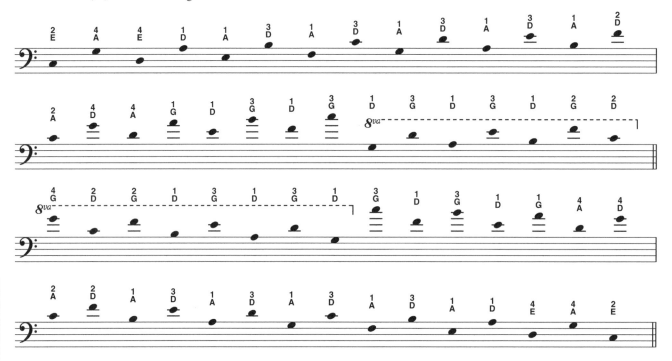

ESSENTIAL
BASS LIBRARY

RON CARTER

Maiden Voyage
(Herbie Hancock)
Blue Note, 1964

D Dorian in 5ths

This exercise covers the D Dorian scale in 5ths from the lowest root (D) on the E string to the highest available interval from the root (A) on the G string.

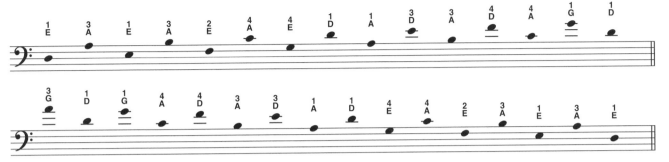

E Phrygian in 5ths

This exercise covers the E Phrygian scale in 5ths from the lowest root (E) on the E string to the highest available interval from the root (B) on the G string.

ESSENTIAL
BASS LIBRARY

RON CARTER

The Real McCoy
(McCoy Tyner)
Blue Note, 1967

F Lydian in 5ths

This exercise covers the F Lydian scale in 5ths from the lowest root (F) on the E string to the highest available interval from the root (C) on the G string.

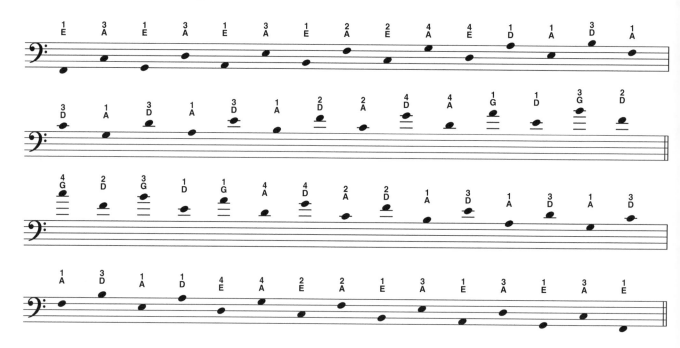

G Mixolydian in 5ths

This exercise covers the G Mixolydian scale in 5ths from the lowest root (G) on the E string to the highest available interval from the root (D) on the G string.

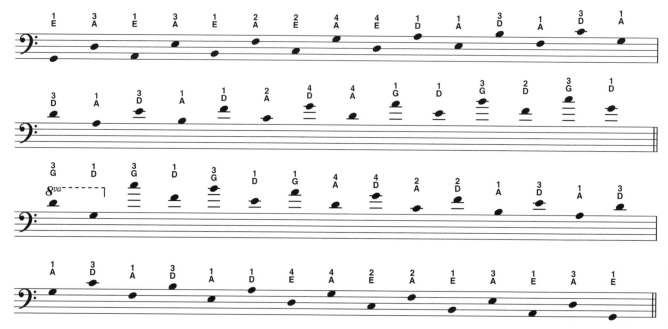

A Aeolian in 5ths

This exercise covers the A Aeolian scale in 5ths from the lowest root (A) on the E string to the highest available interval from the root (E) on the G string.

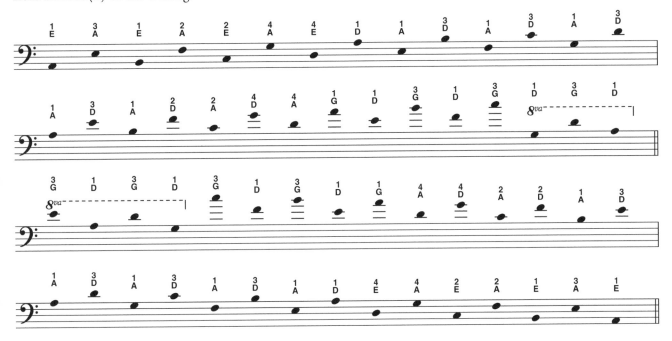

B Locrian in 5ths

This exercise covers the B Locrian scale in 5ths from the lowest root (B) on the E string to the highest available interval from the root (F) on the G string.

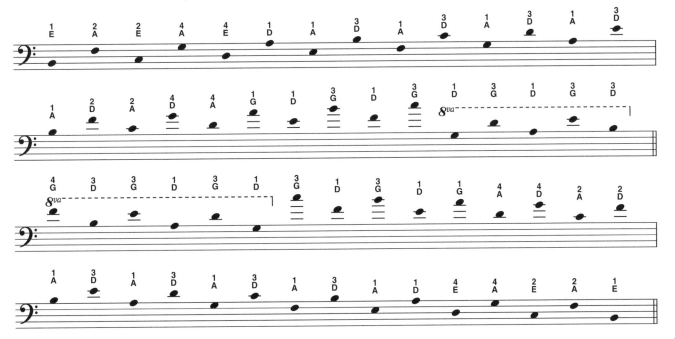

Practising Fingering Patterns for the Major Modes

PRACTISING THE DIATONIC FINGERING PATTERNS

I feel it is important to practise in a creative way. If all you practise is scales and modes your melodic phrasing can become stagnant, unmusical and boring. However, it is important to get the basics and foundation of harmony, ear training and fingerboard knowledge together. It will free you up to react in a more creative way.

> "
> *Concentrate when practising...*
> *... Relax and practise slowly.*
>
> — **Wynton Marsalis**

Firstly, I will show you some linear fingering patterns which you can include in your improvisations. They are a combination of fluency, ear training and technical exercises.

Next, I will write out some simple melodies for each of the modes, outlining the important characteristics of each scale. This will be a basis for your own improvisations, helping you to instinctively hear and create melodies and colours within harmonic boundaries.

LINEAR FINGERING PATTERNS

These patterns are to be played and studied across the entire fingerboard. They have been written in the key of C, but learn them in all keys. Practise these exercises starting at a slow tempo, e.g, 40bpm. Repeat without stopping, five times, and then increase the tempo by 5bpm and repeat.

It is important to play these exercises steadily and accurately. They will help improve your sound, touch, technique, and melodic development. Examples like these can be heard quite frequently during a solo.

Exercise 1

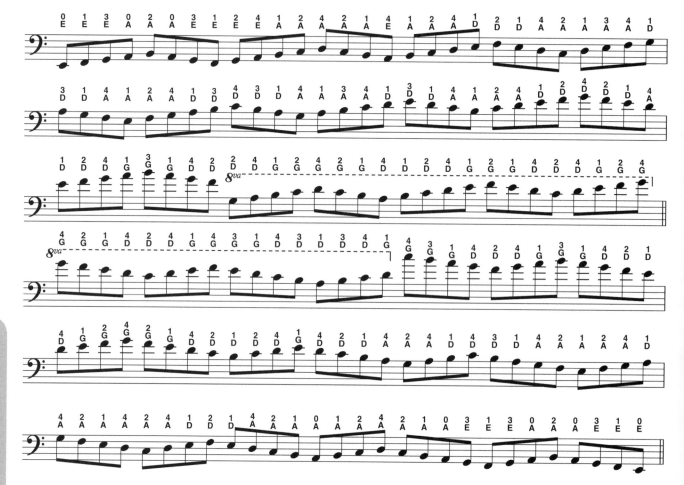

Exercise 2

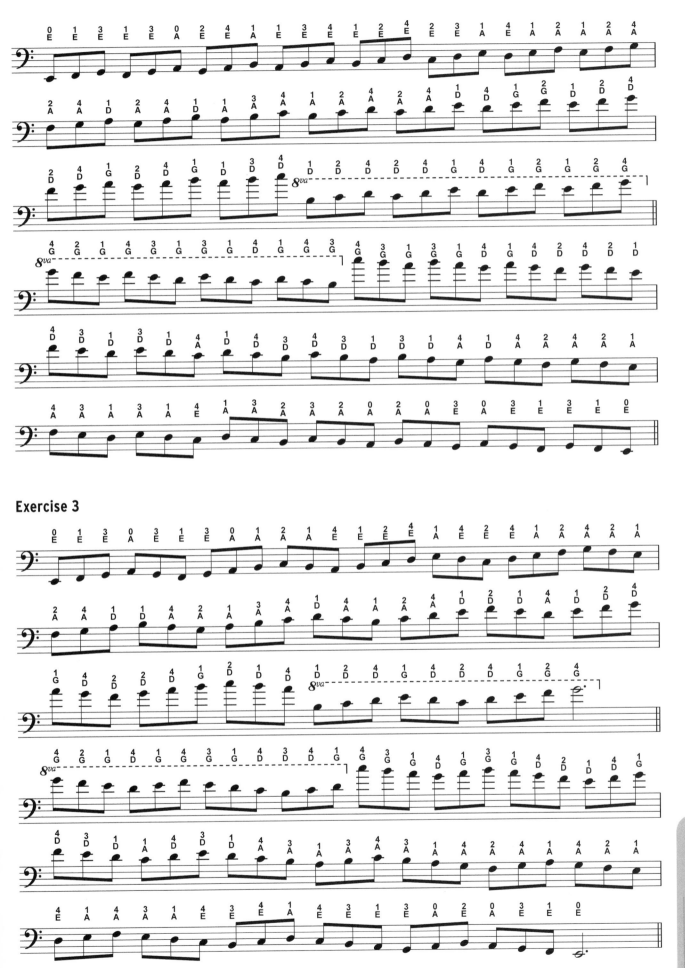

Exercise 3

IMPROVISING WITH THE DIATONIC FINGERING PATTERNS

The following are some melodies that I wrote using the different modes within the key of C major. I took each of the modes and wrote a simple melody. Using the characteristics of the scale along with the use of different interval shapes, I tried to keep the sound of the scale in my playing.

HOW TO PRACTISE THIS CONCEPT

1. A good way to help keep the characteristics is to play along with a drone (low root and 5th of a chosen scale).

A drone for the key of:

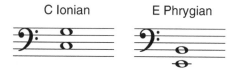

2. Set up a groove on a drum machine or simply use a metronome clicking on beats 2 and 4.

3. Set up a timer so you can record how long you practise each tempo. I recommend practising 3–5 minutes for each tempo. There is a lot to do, and it is good to practise at many tempos, slow to fast. Giving yourself a time limit can help you keep moving forward.

4. After setting up your drone, tempo, groove and timer, start by recapping the whole range of the scale in question. Next, play your melody and use it as a basis for your own improvisations. When you improvise try to use as much of the whole range as possible.

The point of the diatonic fingering patterns is not to tell you or restrict you how to play. The point is to create a sense of freedom and natural instinct in the way you move around the fret board. Combined with the ear training and linear fingering patterns, you can develop a melodic approach to playing. Again practise these melodies/improvisations at different tempos. Start at 40bpm, and after your selected time is up, increase the tempo increments by 5 degrees and repeat, working your way up to 240 bpm (which is 120 bpm with the metronome on beats 2 and 4). Try to practise this for 30 minutes each time you work on it. Make a note of where you are after 30 minutes, then the next day or time you revisit this exercise, continue where you left off. There are a lot of scales and modes to work with so it is important to keep moving forward. Perfecting things is not the point; it is all about expanding your ideas and ears.

Melodies with the use of intervals and linear fingering patterns

C Ionian

D Dorian

E Phrygian

F Lydian

G Mixolydian

A Aeolian

B Locrian

RECAP

The point of this exercise is to keep your ideas simple, so that you make a strong melodic statement within the given scale. Use different intervals and rhythms to make your lines interesting. You should practise these improvisations in all keys and different tempos. Remember the character of the scale sound should always be heard for these exercises.

ESSENTIAL BASS LIBRARY

RON CARTER

Stardust
(Ron Carter)
Toshiba EMI, 2003

1.3

CHAPTER 1.3

Linear Solo Concepts Through The Changes Using Diatonic Major Harmony

In this chapter you will learn how to tackle playing through a series of non-related chords within a progression. These exercises are designed to help you play through chord and key changes while keeping a linear shape. This chapter focuses on the use of major harmony.

LINEAR SOLOING

The concept of these exercises is to learn how to change keys without losing the direction of your line or position of the fingerboard. The aim of working through these exercises is to play through chord changes in a smooth and melodic fashion.

These 4 exercises are only a starting point. Continue each exercise after the written demonstrations to create your own lines.

Exercise 1

The first exercise is to take any two chords from different keys and write out a never-ending scale through the progression. As the chord changes, adjust the chord scale chromatically or in a stepwise order depending on the flow of the line.

While playing through the changes mix up the direction of the scale in order to keep the line spontaneous and to refrain from being repetitive. You can start the scale on any note within the related chord scale. This will develop your ears to hear the relationship of tensions, chord tones and colours against the chord.

The first two chords I am using are **Fm⁷** and **Am⁷**

These two chords are completely unrelated: they are from different chord scales.

Fm7 (F Dorian)

F Dorian is the 2nd mode of E♭ major

Am7 (A Dorian)

A Dorian is the 2nd mode of G major

Musicians and composers often try to exploit the lack of relation between a number of chords to make the music more interesting. One great example of this is John Coltrane's 'Giant Steps', which continuously shifts between unrelated chords, making it both interesting to listen to and notoriously difficult to play!

ESSENTIAL BASS LIBRARY

RON CARTER

Speak No Evil
(Wayne Shorter)
Blue Note, 1964

Exercise 2

In exercise 1 the rate of the chord change was every 4 bars. In this exercise the rate changes to every 2 bars.

This is good practice to help you in dealing with more rapid chord and key changes.

Exercise 3

As in the previous exercise the rate of chord change has been doubled again. This time the chord will change every bar.

ESSENTIAL
BASS LIBRARY

PAUL CHAMBERS

Soul Station
(Hank Mobley)
Blue Note, 1960

Exercise 4

In exercise 4 the idea continues with chords from three keys instead of two. The chords and chord scales being used in this exercise are as follows:

Fm⁷ (F Dorian)

F Dorian is the 2nd mode of E♭ major

E maj7 (E Lydian)

E Lydian is the 4th mode of B major

Am⁷ (A Dorian)

A Dorian is the 2nd mode of G major

G sus2/B (G Ionian)

This chord works with the G Ionian scale and the G major modes

G sus2/B

This is the voicing used for G sus2/B

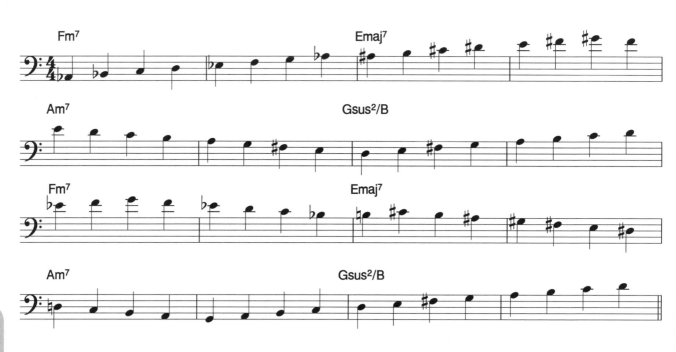

Here are some things to keep in mind when improvising a solo using these concepts and techniques.

- Keep your position on the fretboard
- Use the next note available during the chord change
- Identify some common tones (notes that work over more than one chord)
- Take your time—use space, and do not overplay
- Really listen to the tensions and colours you are creating over the progression
- Be musical

CHAPTER 1.4

1.4

The Construction of Triads and their Inversions

In this chapter I discuss how to build a triad and its inversions. I will also explain about diatonic chords within the major modes. There are a few variations used to describe the different types of triad. Here are a few that are commonly used. In this book I use only the first example for each triad type:

Major	=	no chord suffix, or **maj**
Minor	=	**m, min,** or **-**
Augmented	=	**aug** or **+**
Diminished	=	**dim** or **°**
Suspended 4th	=	**SUS4**

Also in this chapter I use double flats (♭♭) and double sharps (✕).

A double flat is used to flatten a note twice.

Here is a C double flat.

C double flat is the same pitch as B♭

A double sharp is used to sharpen a note twice.

Here is a C double sharp.

C double sharp is the same pitch as D

There are many ways of expressing a particular chord type, and each method is often derived from different notational or performing circumstances. For example, some musicians will refer to a suspended 4th chord simply as a "sus" chord, especially during practical rehearsals. Some will prefer to use shorthand symbols, whereas others may prefer to abbreviate the name of the chord. It is good to be aware of these differences in chord symbol notation, even though the chords will often be interpreted in exactly the same way.

As with enharmonics (i.e. using a B#, even though it is the same as a C), it is often necessary to maintain the sequence of note letters (A, B, C, D, E, F, G) within a scale. This sometimes requires the need for double sharps or double flats to augment the note letter until it is the correct pitch.

TRIADS

A triad is a group of three notes played together to form a chord. There are 5 different types of triad chord quality. They are: major, minor, diminished, augmented and suspended 4th.

Triads are chords built in intervals of thirds, with the exception of sus4 chords for example:

C major

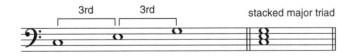

The exception to this pattern of triads built in 3rds is the sus4 chord. The fourth degree replaces the third in the sus4 chord.

C sus4

Now let's analyse all of the commonly used triads.

ESSENTIAL BASS LIBRARY

PAUL CHAMBERS

Giant Steps
(John Coltrane)
Atlantic, 1959

Major Triad

The construction of the major triad is:

The root followed by a major 3rd, followed by a further minor 3rd or an interval of a perfect 5th from the root.

C major triad

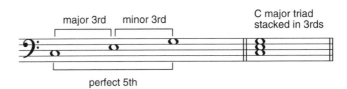

Minor Triad

The construction of the minor triad is:

The root followed by a minor 3rd, followed by a further major 3rd or an interval of a perfect 5th from the root.

C minor triad

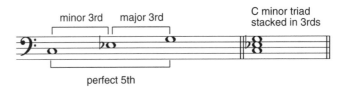

Diminished Triad

The construction of a diminished triad is:

The root followed by a minor 3rd, followed by a further minor 3rd or an interval of a diminished 5th from the root.

C diminished triad

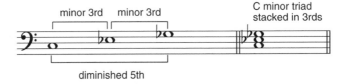

Augmented Triad

The construction of an augmented triad is:

The root followed by a major 3rd, followed by a further major 3rd or an interval of a augmented 5th from the root.

C augmented triad

Sus4 Triad

The sus4 triad is unique because it is not built in intervals of a third. The 4th degree replaces the 3rd degree.

The construction of a sus4 triad is:

The root followed by a perfect 4th, followed by a further major 2nd or an interval of a perfect 5th from the root.

C suspended 4th triad

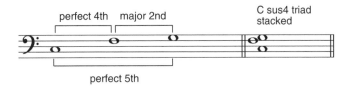

A Summary of Triads in the Key of C

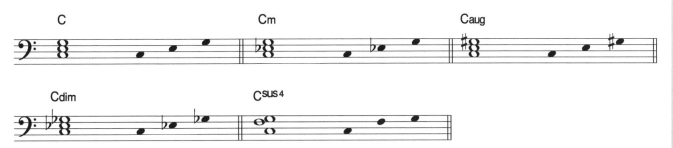

The suspended chord has been used since early Western harmony. It was the intention to hold back the 3rd by using a 4th instead, to create some feeling of unresolution, and so these particular chords are known as 'suspended' chords. In conventional harmony, they are often followed by a chord which resolves this suspended 3rd.

ESSENTIAL
BASS LIBRARY

PAUL CHAMBERS

At Newport
(Miles Davis)
Columbia, 1958-1961

INVERSION OF TRIADS

An inversion of a triad is similar to an inversion of an interval in the sense that you raise the bottom note up one octave.

Example:

The A raised up one octave creates the inversion, although with simple interval inversion the result can be expressed as an alternative interval. In this example, inverting a perfect 5th produces a perfect 4th. However with triads it is usually the case that the inversion cannot be expressed as a different triad, but rather the same triad 'in an inversion'.

In an interval there is just one possible inversion when raising the bottom note up one octave, however there are 3 notes in a triad so there are 3 possible inversions—or rather, 2 inversions and the original root position triad.

Following the root position, there are 2 notes to be raised an octave. Raising the root note and middle note gives us 1st inversion and 2nd inversion respectively.

Example:

Root position:
The root positioned on the bottom followed by the third and fifth degrees.

1st inversion:
The third degree on the bottom followed by the fifth degree, and root raised an octave.

2nd inversion:
The fifth degree on the bottom, followed by the root and the third both raised an octave.

A Summary of all the triad inversions in the key of C

DIATONIC TRIADS

A diatonic triad is a particular chord that is related to a specific scale. Although there are many types of triads in this chapter I will mainly focus on the major modes.

C major Scale

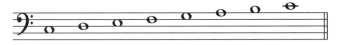

If you stack two diatonic 3rds in the key of C on top of each of the 7 scale degrees you will get the 7 diatonic triads related to the major modes.

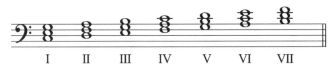

In jazz and popular music (and often in the analysis of tonal classical music), roman numerals are commonly used to classify and label chords, referring to their position within the home scale or key. This helps when expressing chord progressions, crucially describing the function of a chord rather than simply its specific name.

When you analyse these triads you will notice there are 3 different chord quality types: major, minor, and diminished.

The I, IV, and V chords are all major:

The II, III, and VI chords are all minor:

The VII chord is diminished:

Review of diatonic triads in various keys

Example 1

In G:

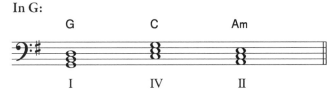

Example 2

In B♭:

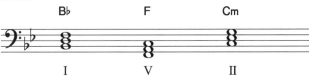

Example 3

In D:

Example 4

In A:

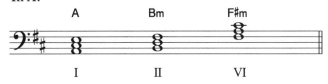

A broken triad or broken chord is when you play the notes of one chord in sequence, either from the bottom note through to the top, or vice-versa.

Reviewing and practising triads

After you have studied and learned all the diatonic triads in all keys, try putting together sequences to help you become more fluent and melodic with these patterns. Here are two one-octave diatonic patterns in the key of C major.

1. Ascending diatonic broken triads across the whole range of the instrument followed by descending diatonic broken triads back down to the starting note. Begin this exercise moving from the lowest note available within the key up to the highest note then returning back down the fingerboard.

I have written out a suggested fingering pattern which will help you move around your instrument in a comfortable and economical fashion.

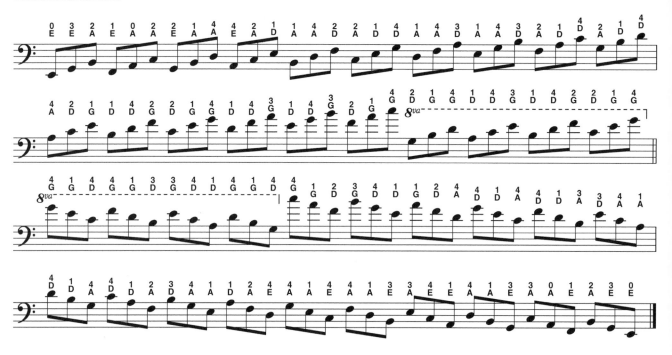

Learn this pattern in all keys.

ESSENTIAL BASS LIBRARY

PAUL CHAMBERS
Workin'
(Miles Davis)
Original Jazz Classics, 1956

2. Ascending a diatonic broken triad followed by descending a diatonic broken triad across the whole range of the instrument. Reverse the pattern on the way back down to the starting note.

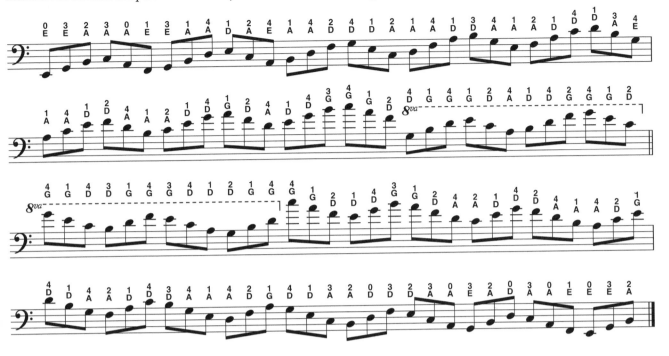

Again, learn this pattern in all keys.

Recap of complete range triad patterns

Practise theses full-range triad patterns at a slow tempo, concentrating on the neck position.

The idea of these patterns is to create an instinctive fluidity to your playing whilst improvising.

For example, play through the sequence ascending and descending three times without stopping with your metronome at 40 bpm (beats 2 and 4). Once you're comfortable with that, raise the tempo in increments of 2–5bpm and repeat.

Play up to a challenging tempo, e.g. 120 bpm (beats 2 and 4) then move on to the next exercise.

Once all exercises are completed you can recap each exercise by playing along with a sustained drone or a related diatonic chord progression. Play once through the sequence along with a drum machine or metronome and improvise using the idea of the pattern along with scale fragments. Again, start this at a slow tempo and after five minutes of improvising increase the tempo increment by 5bpm and repeat.

It is so important to study in a focused way and then apply the concepts in a musical way. Practise this no more than 30mins per day, mark down your progress and continue from that point next time.

Do this for all keys.

ESSENTIAL
BASS LIBRARY

PAUL CHAMBERS

Whims Of Chambers
(Paul Chambers)
Blue Note, 1956

Part 2

Major Modes:
4-Note Chords
Chord Changes
Tensions & Approaches To Chord Tones

2.1

CHAPTER 2.1

The Construction of 4-Note Chords and Their Inversions

In this chapter I discuss how to build a 4-note chord and its inversions. I will also explain about the diatonic 4-note chords within the major modes.

A 4-note chord is a triad with an added note. There are 11 different 4-note chords that we will look at, some of which are more common than others. As with the triads, there is more than one way to express them:

Major 7	=	maj7	or	△						
Minor 7	=	m7	or	min7	or	-7				
Half diminished	=	m7♭5	or	min7♭5	or	-7♭5	or	ø		
Dominant 7	=	7	or	dom7						
Minor (maj7)	=	mmaj7	or	minmaj7	or	-maj7	or	min△	or	m△
Major 7 aug	=	maj7♯5	or	maj7aug5	or	△aug				
Dominant 7 aug	=	7♯5	or	7aug						
Diminished 7	=	dim7	or	o7						
Dominant 7 (sus4)	=	7SUS4								
Major 6	=	6	or	maj6						
Minor 6	=	m6	or	min6	or	-6				

Later in this chapter I will go deeper into 4-note chords found within the major modes.

These 4-note chords are mainly built in stacked intervals of thirds. The suspended 7, minor 6 and major 6 are the exceptions.

Major 7

A major 7 is a 4-note chord built from intervals of 3rds. It is constructed from a major triad by adding a maj 3rd to the fifth degree (or a maj 7th to the root).

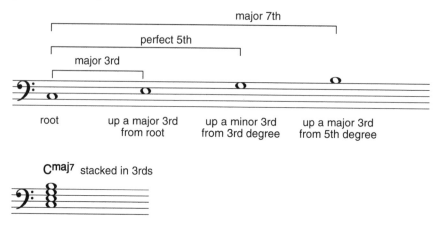

So that there is no ambiguity with the expression of chord symbols for half-diminished or augmented chords, they will occasionally be expressed as ♭5 or ♯5 chords.

ESSENTIAL
BASS LIBRARY

PAUL CHAMBERS

The Complete Vee Jay Paul Chambers-Wynton Kelly Sessions
(Paul Chambers, Wynton Kelly)
Vee Jay, 1954-1961

Minor 7

A minor 7 is a 4-note chord built from intervals of 3rds. It is constructed from a minor triad by adding a min 3rd to the fifth degree (or a min 7th to the root).

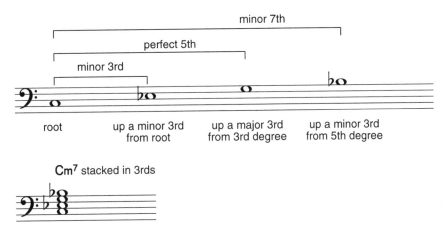

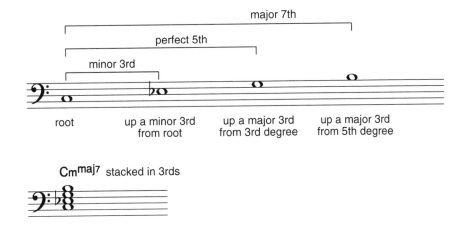

Dominant 7

A dominant 7 is a 4-note chord built from intervals of 3rds. It is constructed from a major triad by adding a min 3rd to the fifth degree (or a min 7th to the root).

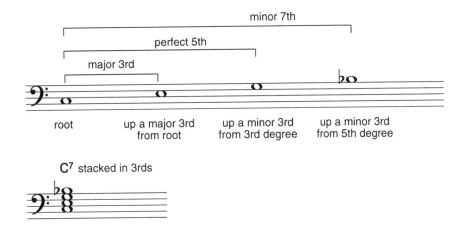

Minor (maj7)

A minor (maj7) is a 4-note chord built from intervals of 3rds. It is constructed from a minor triad by adding a maj 3rd to the fifth degree (or a maj 7th to the root).

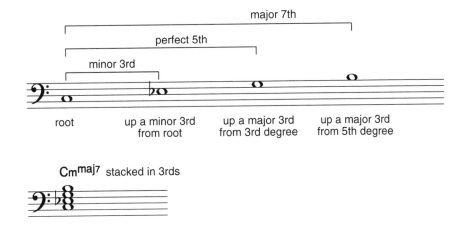

ESSENTIAL
BASS LIBRARY

**JEAN-FRANÇOIS
JENNY CLARK**

*Symphony for
Improvisers*
(Don Cherry)
Blue Note, 1966

Half Diminished

A half diminished (or minor 7♭5) is a 4-note chord built from intervals of 3rds. It is constructed from a diminished triad by adding a maj 3rd to the fifth degree (or a min 7th to the root).

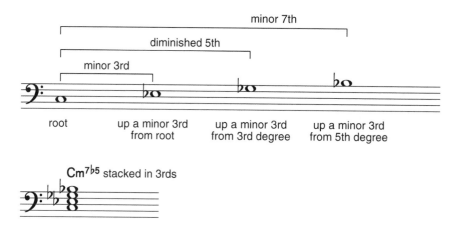

Major 7 Aug

A major 7 aug (or major 7♯5) is a 4-note chord built from intervals of 3rds. It is constructed from an augmented triad by adding a min 3rd to the fifth degree (or a maj 7th to the root).

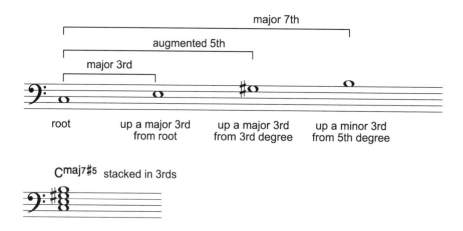

Dominant 7 Aug

A dominant 7 aug (or 7♯5) a 4-note chord built from intervals of 3rds. It is constructed from an augmented triad by adding a diminished 3rd to the fifth degree (or a min 7th to the root).

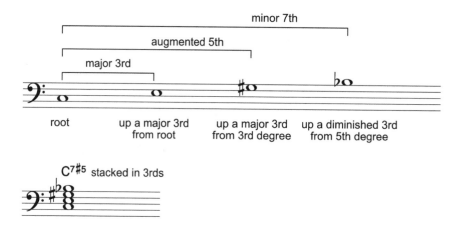

Diminished 7

A diminished 7 is a unique 4-note chord built from intervals of 3rds. It is constructed from a diminished triad by adding a min 3rd to the fifth degree (or a diminished 7th to the root).

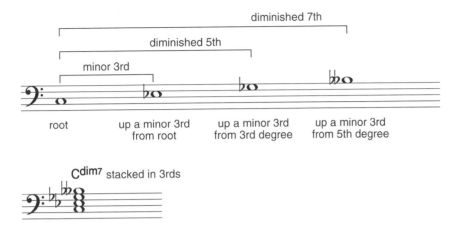

Dominant 7 (sus4)

A dominant 7 (sus4) is a 4-note chord. It is constructed from a sus4 triad by adding a min 3rd to the fifth degree (or a min 7th to the root).

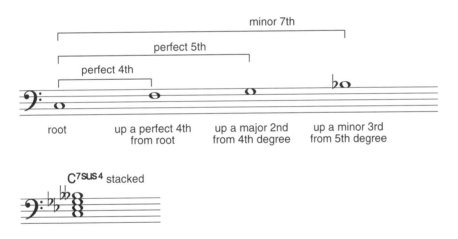

Major 6

A major 6 is a 4-note chord. It is constructed from a major triad by adding a maj 2nd to the fifth degree (or a maj 6th to the root).

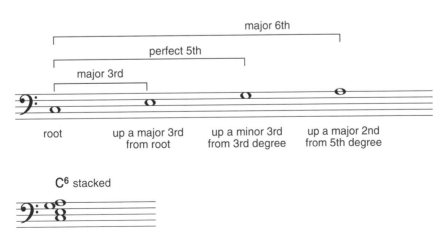

The diminished 7 chord is a very unique chord with many harmonic implications. In early Western music, it was often referred to as the 'Devil's chord', due to its inclusion of tritones (aug 4ths, or dim 5ths)—considered to be a very unnatural interval

An easy way to build a 7sus4 chord is to start with the 5th and stack intervals of perfect 4ths on top of each other. For example, C7sus4 can be played as (from the bottom note): G, C, F, Bb. Another example is an inverted chord of A7sus4, which is: E, A, D, G - the same as the open strings on the bass guitar.

A major 6 chord and its relative minor 7 chord consist of the same notes, and are effectively inversions of one another.

ESSENTIAL
BASS LIBRARY

STANLEY CLARKE

Light As A Feather
(Return To Forever)
Polydor, 1972

Minor 6

A minor 6 is a 4-note chord. It is constructed from a minor triad by adding a maj 2nd to the fifth degree (or a maj 6th to the root).

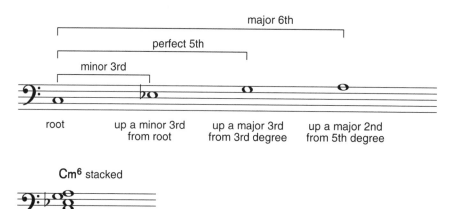

Examples of 4-Note Chords

Tony's Phrygian Chord:

INVERSION OF 4-NOTE CHORDS

An inversion of a 4-note chord is similar to an inversion of an interval or triad.

The additional note results in an additional inversion, and so there are 3 possible inversions in a 4-note chord (not including the root position).

The inversions of these chords are created by raising the bottom notes up one octave, giving us the following positions:

Root position:  The F^maj7 chord with the root positioned on the bottom, followed by the third, fifth and seventh degrees.

1st inversion:  The F^maj7 chord with the third degree on the bottom, followed by the fifth and seventh degree, followed by the root raised one octave.

2nd inversion:  The F^maj7 chord with the fifth degree on the bottom, followed by the seventh degree, followed by the root and the third degree both raised one octave.

3rd inversion:  The F^maj7 chord with the seventh degree on the bottom, followed by the root, third degree and fifth degree all raised one octave.

DIATONIC 4-NOTE CHORDS

As with the diatonic triads there are seven diatonic 4-note chords with the major modes.

These chords are constructed in the same way as the diatonic triads.

For this example I will use the key of F major:

If you stack three diatonic 3rds on top of each scale degree of a major scale you will get the seven diatonic 4-note chords related to the major modes.

Here are the diatonic 4-note chords in the key of F:

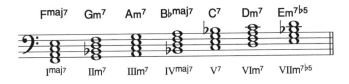

When you analyse these 4-note chords you will notice that there are four different chord quality types. They are: major 7, minor 7, dominant 7 and half diminished.

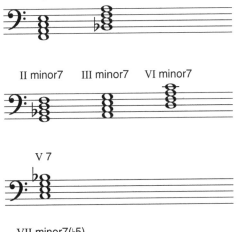

The I and IV are both major 7 chords
The II, III, and VI are all minor 7 chords
The V is a dominant chord
The VII is half diminished

Review of Diatonic 4-Note Chords in Various Keys

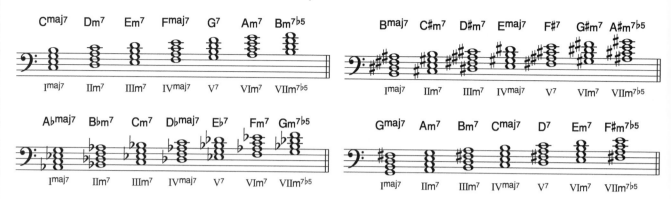

Reviewing and Practising 4-Note Chords

After you have studied and learned all the diatonic 4-note chords in all keys try putting together sequences to help you be more fluent and melodic with these chords and scales.

1. As with the triad exercises; ascending diatonic 4-note broken chords across the whole range of the instrument followed by descending diatonic 4-note broken chords back down to the starting note in the key of C major Begin this exercise moving from the lowest note available within the key up to the highest note then returning back down the fretboard. Again, I have suggested a fingering pattern to help you move around the fretboard more comfortably.

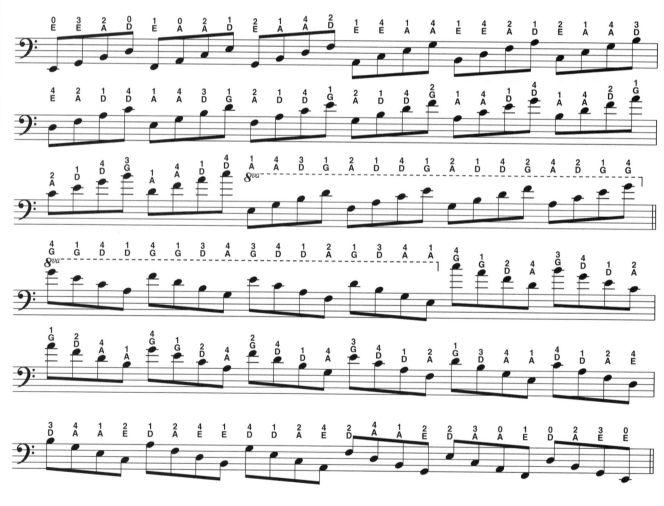

Learn this pattern in all keys.

ESSENTIAL
BASS LIBRARY

LAURENCE COTTLE

Five Seasons
(Laurence Cottle)
JMS Records, 1992

2. Ascending a diatonic 4-note broken chord followed by descending a diatonic 4-note broken chord, across the whole range of the instrument. Reverse the pattern on the way back down to the starting note.

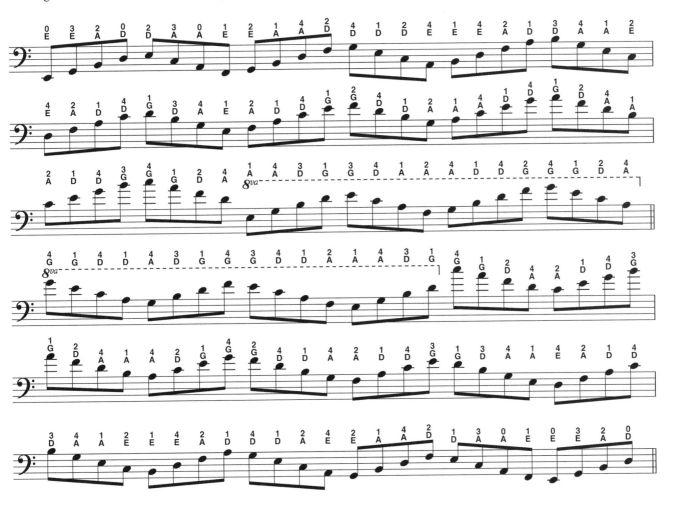

Learn this pattern in all keys.

How To Practise These Exercises

Practise these fingering patterns starting at a slow tempo. Repeat without stopping, ascending and descending five times at one tempo before increasing the metronome increments.

Please note these are my fingering patterns suited to the way I play. If they feel unnatural or uncomfortable for you then try making your own.

Practising in this way conditions the mind and fingers to play in a more logical and economical way. By starting these exercises at a slow tempo you will develop your memory of the shape, touch and technique. Practising things slowly can become boring, making it easier to lose focus. If you do find yourself losing focus then you should concentrate on other things such as your time feel, touch (etc.). Also building up the tempo slowly helps to build a solid technique. Try to avoid developing bad habits in your practice and playing.

Here is an example of how I practise each exercise. Start with the metronome at 40 bpm on beats 2 and 4 (see below). Repeat the whole exercise five times without stopping and then increase the tempo 2bpm—from 40 bpm to 42 bpm— and start again.
Keep going until the tempo is 100–200bpm and then move on to the next exercise.

ESSENTIAL
BASS LIBRARY

LAURENCE COTTLE

Laurence Cottle Quintet-Live!
(The Laurence Cottle Quintet)
Jazzi, 1995

2.2

CHAPTER 2.2

Moving 4-Note Chords Through Non-Related Chord Changes (Major Harmony)

In this chapter you will learn how to tackle playing through a series of non-related chords within a progression. In a previous chapter we looked at how to play through chord changes in a linear fashion. Now in this chapter we will look at how to play through chord changes using ascending and descending 4-note (broken) chords. This is a great mental exercise and will really develop your knowledge of the fretboard.

Exercise 1

The idea of this exercise is to take two non-related chords and play a continuous progression of ascending and descending 4-note broken diatonic chords. With each bar, a different 4-note broken chord is played in rising or falling 3rds, and each broken chord is connected to the broken chord of the next bar by moving in a stepwise motion to the nearest note of that key.

The two chords used for Exercise 1 are **Fm⁷** and **Am⁷**. These two chords are completely unrelated and are from different chord scales and different keys. As a result of being from different keys, each mode has a different set of diatonic chords.

For the **Fm⁷** we'll use the F Dorian scale (the second of the E♭ major modes).

For the **Am⁷** we'll use the A Dorian scale (the second of the G major modes). By stacking 3rds on top of each degree of the two scales we can see which chords are available to use.

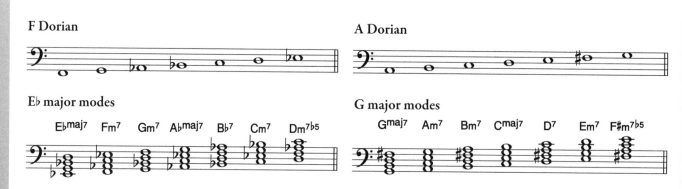

F Dorian

E♭ major modes

A Dorian

G major modes

Continue this exercise for as long as you want, and try to use as much of the fretboard as possible. Change direction of the line randomly to avoid repeating chords that have already been used.

Exercise 2

In Exercise 1 the rate of harmonic change is every 2 bars. In this Exercise 2 the harmonic change rate has doubled—every bar. The chords remain Fm⁷ and Am⁷.

For these exercises we are using the same progressions as in the linear soloing chapter. However I advise you to experiment with other progressions that can help you improve your skill in this concept.

For this chapter we will concentrate on the major modes and harmony.

Later we will look at the chords and harmony of the melodic minor modes, and combining the major and minor modes.

ESSENTIAL
BASS LIBRARY

BOB CRANSHAW

The Sidewinder
(Lee Morgan)
Blue Note, 1964

Exercise 3

This exercise introduces a third key centre.

The chords we're using for this exercise are Fm⁷, Emaj⁷, Am⁷ and Gsus²/B.

In Exercise 1 we looked at and analysed two chords—Fm⁷ and Am⁷.

In Exercise 3 we have added Emaj⁷ and Gsus²/B. I have not analysed the Gsus²/B in any of the previous chapters, but it is essentially a Gsus² triad with a B as the lowest note in the voicing. There is no particular significance to this chord—I have just experimented with voicings to find a chord scale that fits. I recommend that you find your own unconventional chords to play with.

For the Gsus²/B chord we'll use the G Ionian scale (the first degree of the G major modes).

For the Emaj⁷ chord we'll use the E Lydian scale (the fourth degree of the B major modes). When you play or listen to the natural fourth/eleventh degree against a major 7 chord it sounds very harsh. The fourth being a half-step above the third degree creates the dissonance. A #4 or #11 is more commonly used. This is borrowed from the Lydian scale. Therefore, major 7 chords tend to use sharpened fourths/elevenths.

The Am⁷ chord in this progression uses the A Dorian scale (the second degree of the G major modes). And as before, the Fm⁷ uses the F Dorian (the second degree of the E♭ major modes).

Recap: the Gsus²/B (G Ionian) and Am⁷ (A Dorian) are both from the G major modes. The Emaj⁷ uses the

E Lydian from the B major modes. The Fm⁷ uses the F Dorian scale from the E♭ major modes.

G Ionian

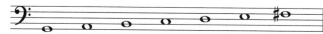

G major modes

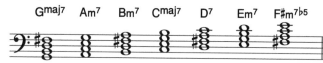

E Lydian

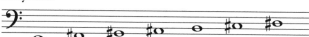

B major modes

F Dorian

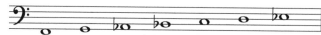

E♭ major modes

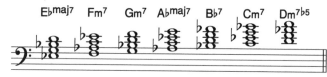

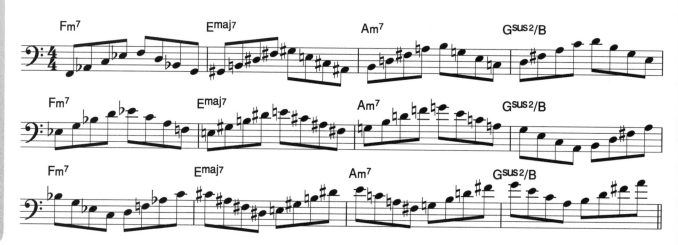

As in the linear solo concept chapter, these exercises are only a starting point. Work your way through the exercises starting at a slow tempo, increasing the speed by small increments each time you perform them.

Take your time to master each exercise before you move on to the next one. Create your own chord progressions in different keys.

Later we will be discussing the melodic minor modes and diatonic chords and how to incorporate them into your progressions.

Try incorporating all the techniques that you have learned so far into your improvisations. These exercises are a great way to move between chord changes and will really help you learn your instrument. They are also a great exercise for your mind, helping you think quickly so that you can adjust your lines during solos with ease and agility.

ESSENTIAL BASS LIBRARY

BOB CRANSHAW

The Bridge
(Sonny Rollins)
Bluebird, 1962

CHAPTER 2.3

Tensions And Upper Structures For Chords Found Within The Major Modes

Tensions and Upper Structures Commonly Used in Major Diatonic Harmony

When soloing/improvising it is more colourful to use notes that are not part of the given chord you are playing over. Tensions Tensions are the notes in between chord tones with in a scale. There are two kinds of tensions.

The natural tension is a note diatonic to the scale in question, and the altered tension is a non-diatonic note related to the chord or scale. Here is a 2-octave C major scale highlighting the available natural tensions.

As tensions are commonly used on top of a triad or 4-note chord, the numbers above the octave (beyond '8') are used. The natural tensions available are the second, fourth, sixth, ninth, eleventh, and thirteenth degrees. You will notice that the second degree is the same as the eleventh degree, and likewise with the fourth and eleventh degrees, and the sixth and thirteenth degrees.

Another way to build natural tensions is to keep building a scale in diatonic 3rds. Here is C Ionian built in 3rds:

Once you arrive back at C the cycle begins again.

To 'alter' a tension (i.e. change it from a natural tension to an altered tension) you simply raise or lower the tension by a half-step. A second or ninth degree lowered a half-step becomes a ♭2 or ♭9. A second or ninth degree raised a half-step becomes a ♯2 or ♯9. Lowering a fourth or eleventh degree by a half-step would make it the same pitch as a third (or tenth) degree, so this is avoided. Instead, raising by a half-step produces a ♯11. A sixth or thirteenth degree lowered a half-step becomes a ♭6 or ♭13. A sixth or thirteenth degree raised a half-step becomes a ♯6 or ♯13. A ♯13 tension is uncommon over a 'major chord' as it is the same as a flattened-seventh chord tone.

Some tensions sound good with chords and sometimes do not. It is important to judge for yourself which of the tensions sound good or functional to the ear. A harmonic tension is a note a whole step above a chord tone. For example:

In general, notes a half-step above a chord tone sound dissonant and sound as if they need to resolve.

ESSENTIAL
BASS LIBRARY

ISRAEL CROSBY

Ahmad Jamal Trio
(Ahmad Jamal)
Epic, 1955

C major 7 Harmonic Tensions

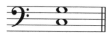

| | 1 | 3 | 5 | 7 | **9** | **♯11** | **13** |

Remember that for major 7 chords we use the Lydian option to avoid the fourth degree in the Ionian (an avoid note). The Lydian scale played against the major 7 chord has no avoid notes.

If you look at the pattern of notes you can see there are several arpeggios/chords that include the harmonic tensions.

- Em⁷ gives us the tension 9 (the 7th of Em⁷ being a D)
- Gᵐᵃʲ⁷ gives us the tensions 9 and ♯11 (the 5th being a D and the 7th being an F♯)
- Bm⁷ gives us the tensions 9, ♯11 and 13 (the 3rd being a D, the 5th being an F♯ and the 7th being an A)
- D⁷ gives us the tensions 9, ♯11 and 13 (the root being a D, the 3rd being an F♯ and the 5th being an A)
- F♯m⁷♭⁵ gives us the tensions ♯11 and 13 (the root being an F♯ and the 3rd being an A)
- Am⁷ gives us the tension 13 (the only tension being the root—the A)

You can superimpose these chords over a Cᵐᵃʲ⁷ to add colour to the harmony.

A bassist, pianist or guitarist accompanying a soloist would generally cover the root and chord tones. So as a soloist the understanding and usage of tensions is vital for creating interesting solos.

A good way to practise the tensions is to play a drone related to the chord or the chord in question sustained.

For example, for Cᵐᵃʲ⁷ play along with:

Playing along with a drone as a reference helps you hear the colours created.

Next, play the chord tones and tensions on a single string in order. For example, on the E string you would play

| | 3 | 5 | 7 | **9** | **♯11** | **13** | **RT** |

Ascend all the way up the string to the highest tension or chord tone available, and from there descend back to where you started.

Next, repeat the exercise starting from the second lowest tension or chord tone available. F♯ is the next note available. So the pattern is as follows:

| | **♯11** | **13** | **RT** | 3 | 5 | 7 | **9** |

Again, ascend up to the highest chord tone or tension then descend back down to the starting point.

Do not treat this exercise as a technique exercise but as an ear training exercise. I want you to become familiar with the colours you are creating. Playing on a single string forces you to hear the tensions as it is not part of a pattern. It also makes you play and learn less common areas on the fretboard.

After studying the major chord tensions we will look at the minor 7 chord. For Dm⁷ we will continue building the chord in diatonic 3rds related to the key of C.

ESSENTIAL
BASS LIBRARY

ISRAEL CROSBY

Ahmad Jamal at the Pershing Vols. 1 & 2
(Ahmad Jamal)
Argo, 1958

1	3	5	7	**9**	**11**	**13**

The natural tensions in D minor are 9, 11, and 13. The tensions here are also harmonic tensions as they are all a whole step above the chord tones, and when played on top of a Dm⁷ chord they sound rested and pleasant to the ear.

The other minor chords within the C major modes, Em⁷ and Am⁷, contain the tensions ♭9 and ♭13 for the Phrygian and ♭13 for the Aeolian.

When these tensions are played against the chord they sound dissonant and unsettled. As with the tension 11 of the Cᵐᵃʲ⁷, we raise the ♭9 and ♭13 a half-step, giving the harmonic tensions you can see in Dm⁷. Please note that all the notes within a scale are very important and usable.

For example, the ♭9 and ♭13 in the Phrygian scale give the scale its unique and beautiful sound and using these tensions can bring a special sound to your melodies and solos.

Here in this chapter we are looking at the different available chords within the major modes, which are major 7, minor 7, dominant 7 and minor 7♭5. The chords found in the minor 7 chord with harmonic tensions are:

1	3	5	7	**9**	**11**	**13**

Fᵐᵃʲ⁷, Am⁷, Cᵐᵃʲ⁷, Em⁷, G⁷, Bm⁷♭⁵

Am⁷ gives you the tensions 9 and 11 (the 5th being an E and the 7th being a G)

Cᵐᵃʲ⁷ gives you the tensions 9, 11 and 13 (the 3rd being an E, the 5th being a G and the 7th being a B)

Em⁷ gives you the tensions 9, 11 and 13 (the root being an E, the 3rd being a G and the 5th being a B)

G⁷ gives you the tensions 11 and 13 (the root being a G and the 3rd being a B)

Bm⁷♭⁵ gives you the tensions 13 (the only tension being the root—the B)

You can superimpose these chords over a Dm⁷ to add colour.

Again, another great way to practise these tensions is to play them across each of the strings on your instrument. Playing the sequence in order from the lowest available chord tone or tension up to the highest available chord tone or tension then back down to where you started.

On the E string the lowest available note is the E, which is tension 9. In sequence the notes are (E string):

9	**11**	**13**	RT	3	5	7

Again repeat the exercise starting from the next lowest available chord tone or tension which is F (the third)

The new sequence will be (E string):

3	5	7	**9**	**11**	**13**	RT

Again I recommend you play these exercises along with a drone or chord representing the tonality. In this case use a D drone or a sustained Dm⁷ chord.

The exercise should be played across each string. Again this is not a technical exercise but an ear training exercise that takes away the pattern and shape to force you to hear the colours.

ESSENTIAL
BASS LIBRARY

PALLE DANIELSSON

Witichi-Tai-To
(Jan Garbarek)
ECM, 1973

So far within the major modes we have looked at the harmonic tensions available for the diatonic major and minor chords. The chord we will now look at is the dominant 7 chord. The dominant chord, when analysed harmonically and within progressions, has a very special function. Due to its unstable sound when used, it implies motion or movement so that there is a sense of resolution. It is a kind of pivotal chord.

The G⁷ contains the notes B and F, which are unstable sounding notes in the C major scale. The B and F are 3 whole steps apart, or a diminished 5th (augmented 4th), also known as a tritone. The B sounds as if it wants to resolve up a half-step to a C (the root of a C chord) and the F sounds like it wants to resolve down a half-step to an E (the 3rd of a C chord).

The most common movement for a dominant chord is up a perfect 4th. So in the key of C major the G⁷ will usually be followed by the C^maj7.

Now let us look at the G⁷ chord built in 3rds.

As you analyse the tensions available you will notice that, as with the C^maj7, there is the tension 11, which clashes with the third degree. Written as the fourth degree (i.e. down an octave), it is a half-step from the third, making it dissonant and unstable.

For the C^maj7 we borrowed a note (F♯) from the relative Lydian scale, which gave us a more stable whole step above the chord tone. In the case of a dominant chord we can also raise the fourth/eleventh degree a half-step, giving us an interesting colour known as the Lydian ♭7. This chord scale comes from the fourth mode of the melodic minor.

The altered tensions ♭9, ♯9, ♯11, ♭13 are commonly employed over the dominant chord and come from a variety of chord scales, i.e. diminished, melodic minor, harmonic minor, extended and secondary dominants, which will all be discussed later.

To determine which tensions are available on the dominant 7 chord in question depends on the function of the V⁷ chord and where it is going. In diatonic harmony, the V⁷ chord usually resolves to the I^maj7 chord, so the available tensions are 9 and 13.

Within the dominant 7 chord, the chords with harmonic diatonic tensions are:

Bm⁷♭⁵, Dm, Em⁷

Bm⁷♭⁵ gives us the tension 9 (the 7th of Bm⁷♭⁵ being an A)

Dm gives us the tension 9 (the 5th being an A)

Em⁷ gives us the tension 13 (the root being an E)

As with the major and minor chords we can practise the dominant 7 chord with its diatonic harmonic tensions across the fretboard using single strings.

Again start with the lowest available chord tone or tension and play the sequence in order all the way to the highest chord tone or tension available back down to the lowest.

The order will be (E string):

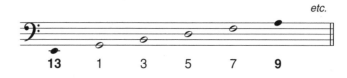

Now repeat the exercise starting with the second lowest available tension or chord tone. The next sequence is as follows (E string):

| 7 | 9 | 13 | RT | 3 | 5 |

Again, I recommend that these tensions are played along with a drone or chord built from the root. Play these exercises ascending and descending across all strings. Note these exercises focus on ear training and harmonic understanding, not technique. Make sure you can hear the relationship between the tensions and the chord tones. The last chord within the major modes that we have not yet looked at is the minor 7♭5. In the key of C major that is the Bm⁷♭⁵.

Like the dominant 7 chord, the minor 7♭5 chord is very unstable and also contains a tri tone (3 whole steps apart). For the Bm⁷♭⁵, the tri tone is the B to the F.

As with the dominant chord the available tensions and function of the chord depends on the harmonic movement of the chord.

Probably, the most common usage of this chord is part of a minII–V–I movement, which comes from the harmonic minor modes. In the key of C harmonic minor the chords that make up the II–V–I movement would be:

$$Dm^{7♭5}—G^{7♭9}—Cm^{maj7}.$$

We will look further at the minor modes and the corresponding chords later.

In major diatonic harmony, the minor 7♭5 chord forms the seventh mode, using the Locrian scale. Now let us look at the Bm⁷♭⁵ chord built in 3rds to find the upper extensions.

| 1 | 3 | ♭5 | 7 | ♭9 | 11 | ♭13 |

As with all the other chords, to hear which tensions sound good we simply play them against the chord. Tension ♭9 sounds quite harsh and unstable. Tension 11 and ♭13 sound colourful and stable due to them both being a whole step above a chord tone. Instead of tension ♭9, tension 9 is commonly used as it sounds nice against the chord.

Tension 9 when played on top or against a VIIm⁷♭⁵ (Bm⁷♭⁵) in the key of C major is a C♯, which is not a diatonic pitch. The natural 9 on a m7♭5 chord comes from the sixth mode of the melodic minor and the second mode of the harmonic minor modes. Again, we will discuss these other minor modes later. For now, the available harmonic diatonic tensions over a Bm⁷♭⁵ (VIIm⁷♭⁵) are 11 and ♭13.

ESSENTIAL
BASS LIBRARY

PALLE DANIELSSON

My Song
(Keith Jarrett)
ECM, 1977

The chords we find within the Bm7♭5 with harmonic diatonic tensions are:

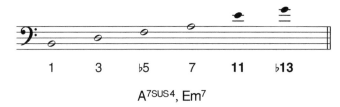

| 1 | 3 | ♭5 | 7 | **11** | ♭**13** |

A⁷ˢᵘˢ⁴, Em⁷

A⁷ˢᵘˢ⁴ gives us the tensions 11 and ♭13 (the 5th being an E and the 7th being a G)

Em⁷ gives us the tensions 11 and ♭13 (the root being an E and the 3rd being a G)

Practise the Bm7♭5 chord with harmonic diatonic tensions across all the strings in order, starting from the lowest available chord tone or tension up to the highest available chord tone or tension available and back down.

The order will be (E string):

| **11** | ♭**13** | RT | 3 | ♭5 | 7 |

Now repeat the exercise starting with the next lowest available tension or chord tone.

The next sequence is as follows (E string):

| ♭5 | 7 | **11** | ♭**13** | RT | 3 |

Here is a list of all the harmonic diatonic tensions in major harmony:

Major 7:	9, ♯11, 13
Minor 7:	9, 11, 13
Dominant 7:	9, 13
Minor 7♭5:	11, ♭13

Here is a list of the commonly used non-diatonic tensions over chords found within the major modes:

| Dominant 7: | ♭9, ♯9, ♯11, ♭13 |
| Minor 7♭5: | 9, 13 |

Here is a list of all the non-harmonic diatonic tensions over chords found within the major modes:

Major 7:	11
Minor 7:	♭9, ♭13
Dominant 7:	11
Minor 7♭5:	♭9

Practise playing the upper structure harmonic diatonic tensions over these following progressions.

Cycle of 5ths, major 7 chords in all keys, from root:

Cycle of 5ths, minor 7 chords in all keys, from root:

Cycle of 5ths, dominant 7 chords in all keys, from root:

ESSENTIAL
BASS LIBRARY

ART DAVIS

Ready for Freddie
(Freddie Hubbard)
Blue Note, 1961

Cycle of 5ths, minor 7♭5 chords in all keys, from root:

Major 7 arpeggios plus harmonic diatonic tensions from third degree:

Minor 7 arpeggios plus harmonic diatonic tensions from third degree:

Dominant 7 arpeggios plus harmonic tensions from third degree:

Minor 7♭5 arpeggios plus harmonic diatonic tensions from third degree:

ESSENTIAL
BASS LIBRARY

RICHARD DAVIS

The Blues Book
(Booker Ervin)
Original Jazz Classics, 1964

Only harmonic diatonic tensions over this cycle of 5ths progression:

Available harmonic diatonic tensions over this cycle of 5ths diatonic chord progression:

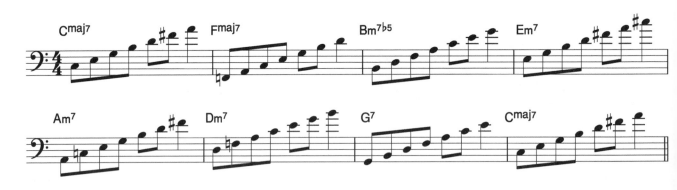

Play this exercise in all keys.

ESSENTIAL
BASS LIBRARY

RICHARD DAVIS
Out to Lunch
(Eric Dolphy)
Blue Note, 1964

Available harmonic diatonic tensions from the third degree over this cycle of 5ths diatonic chord progression:

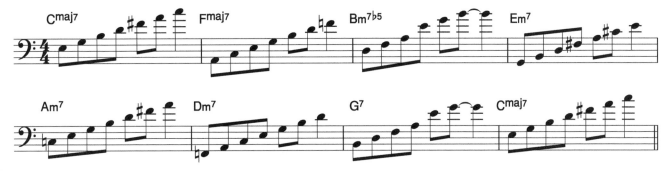

Play this exercise in all keys.

Only the available diatonic harmonic tensions over this diatonic chord progression:

Play this exercise in all keys.

TENSIONS (SUMMARY)

Making music is about making choices. Ultimately, you play what sounds good to you, and what you enjoying hearing. There are no rules for what you think sounds good—you just have to trust your ears and enjoy it.

Learning these tensions and how they sound, good or bad, will give you an insight of how they work and how they can be used.

Although the non-harmonic diatonic tensions sound harsh when played against their relative chords, this does not mean that they are not usable or unimportant to that particular scale.

For example, tension ♭9 and ♭13 is what makes the Phrygian scale so unique and beautiful.

By analysing tensions we are simply looking at what sounds dissonant (needing resolution) and what sounds rested (resolved).

Harmonic tensions sound best on strong beats of the measure or phrase.

Non-harmonic diatonic tensions are very important and sound best when used as a passing tone or a weak beat during a measure or phrase.

STRONG BEAT, WEAK BEAT

The placement of notes within a phrase or measure is vital to how they sound. We have seen and heard at this point that tension (11) played against a major 7th chord does not sound so good. However, saying you can never play it against that chord would be wrong.

Every one of the 12 notes (chromatic scale) is available on any chord. It is just how you use them and the strength of the direction your line is going in.

A $\frac{4}{4}$ measure has 4 beats and naturally within the beats there are strong ones and weak ones.

The downbeat or 1st beat is the strongest of the 4 in question. The 3rd beat being another strong beat as it is the half way point in the measure.

The 1st beat establishes the harmonic movement so therefore it would require a stable sound or part of a strong phrase.

Beats 2 and 4 are less strong and require less attention regarding strength of a scale tone.

In between all 4 beats there are the upbeats again which are weaker than the downbeats.

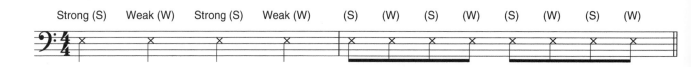

You will learn how to play your phrases naturally; this is not really a concept you think of whilst improvising.

> "
> *A chimpanzee could learn to do what I do physically. But it goes way beyond that. When you play, you play life.*
>
> — **Jaco Pastorius**

Learning your tensions and how to use them is a great step in how to improvise solos and write melodies. Understanding the strong/weak beat concept is also important to how your solos and melodies will sound.

Here is a simple melody to demonstrate how certain avoid notes work within a phrase.

As you can see and hear in the 1st of the two examples all the chord tones are on the upbeats and the tension (11) is on the strong downbeats.

In example 2 we have chord tones on the downbeats using the F (tension 11) as a passing tone making the phrase work and sound strong.

Both examples are using almost the same notes.

You should experiment writing out different passages and melodies to hear and see for yourself how it works and sounds.

1. Weak sounding phrase

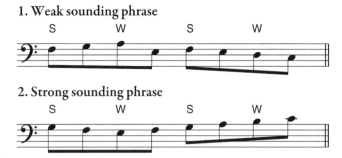

2. Strong sounding phrase

Try playing these two melodies over a **Cmaj⁷** drone.

CHAPTER 2.4

Approach to Target Note Exercises
For chords found within the Major Modes

Understanding chord tones is vital to understanding how to improvise over a series of chord progressions. If we only used chord tones and extensions our melodic content would be limited and become predictable.

These next exercises are based on using chord tones as target notes and finding different ways to approach them. A strong line or phrase is really important to writing a melody or improvising a solo.

The use of chromatic notes and non-related scale tones are very much usable and important to create tension within the music. A chord tone is the most important and significant note you can use to outline a chord.

These exercises will help you understand and appreciate the value of chord tones.

It also will give you a better knowledge of harmony and your instrument, along with some usable melodic content.

ESSENTIAL
BASS LIBRARY

GEORGE DUVIVIER

Out There
(Eric Dolphy)
Original Jazz Classics, 1960

APPROACHING CHORD TONES FROM A SCALE DEGREE ABOVE—THE UPPER APPROACH (DIATONIC)

The upper approach always uses a diatonic scale degree above the target note (the chord tone).

Major 7 chords have two choices depending on the function of the chords in question. The available scales are Ionian for I^{maj7} chords and Lydian for IV^{maj7} chords.

Minor 7 chords have three choices depending on the function of the chords in question. The available scales are Dorian for IIm⁷ chord, Phrygian for IIIm⁷ chords and Aeolian for VIm⁷ chords.

Here are all the scale degrees using the upper approach concept for all the diatonic chords found within the major modes:

Chord extensions are frequently altered with sharps or flats, which are expressed in the chord symbol. However, the third and seventh degrees may be altered depending on whether the chord is major or minor. Although the third or seventh of a minor chord wouldn't typically be referred to as a ♭3 or ♭7, when discussing tensions it is easier to use this approach to distinguish the differences between the many different chord types.

ESSENTIAL BASS LIBRARY

GEORGE DUVIVIER

Screamin' The Blues
(Oliver Nelson)
Original Jazz Classics, 1960

4 WAYS TO PRACTISE THE APPROACH NOTE EXERCISES

It is important to study and learn all these concepts but it is also important to be creative and musical with them too. Here are the 4 study concepts we will be using for these Approach To Target Note exercises.

Part 1: Single String

As with the upper extension tension exercise I believe it is a great idea to practise these different approaches to target note exercises over the whole range of a single string.

The reason for the single concept is that it really helps you get away from playing these exercises as patterns and helps you hear the approach. This makes the exercise more of an ear training exercise rather than a technical one. It also teaches you parts of the fretboard you may not be so familiar with.

Playing with some kind of drone or sustained chord based on the root is a good idea as it helps to give you a reference to the approaches you are using.

The upper approach exercise across the whole range of the E string using C^{maj7} (I^{maj7}) (Ionian). Move from the lowest available chord tone (with the upper approach note) in sequence, up to the highest available upper approach note, and back down.

The order is:

etc.

| 4 | 3 | 6 | 5 | RT | 7 | 2 | RT | 4 | 3 |

Practise for all the diatonic chords found within the major modes in all keys across all strings.

Part 2: Write Melody/Improv

Next I want you to next write a simple melody combining scale fragments along with the upper approach pattern.

Use your melody as a starting point for your own improvisations. Again, the use of a sustained drone or related chord is important as it gives you a great reference so you can hear the concept in question clearly.

Play your melody and improvisations over a variety of tempos, slow to fast, all over the fretboard. It is a good idea to play your improvisations for 2-3 minutes at each tempo. Make sure you are comfortable at the tempos before moving on.

For example, you can use a drum groove or a metronome on beats 2 and 4 starting at 60 bpm increasing the tempo increments by 5 degrees each time. Work your way up to a fast challenging tempo like 160bpm, 200bpm or even 240bpm.

If you are using a metronome on beats 2 and 4, remember that 60bpm is equivalent to 120bpm.

Here is an example of a melody using the scale fragments plus upper approach concept.

Example using C^{maj7} (I^{maj7}) (Ionian)

Repeat this concept for all the chords found within the major modes in all keys.

ESSENTIAL
BASS LIBRARY

MARK EGAN

Pat Metheny Group
(Pat Metheny)
ECM, 1978

Part 3: Diatonic Cycle of 5ths Progression

This study concept involves playing the upper approach pattern over a diatonic cycle of 5ths chord progression. It covers each of the chords found within the major modes and is a great way to practise the exercise.

Halve the duration of the chord progression and randomly apply two of the upper approaches instead of all four. Practise this concept again at various tempos, slow to fast and repeat the cycle 2-3 times covering as much of the fretboard as possible. Also, once completed, try improvising the upper approach concept over the progressions.

Here is the upper approach pattern over a diatonic cycle of 5ths progression.

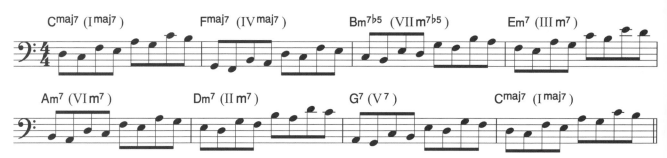

Halve the duration of the chord progression and randomly play any 2 of the upper approach patterns over each chord within the form.

Practise these progressions in all keys, and then afterwards improvise over these progressions with the upper approach concept.

Part 4: IIm7–V7–Imaj7 in all keys

For the final part of the 4-part study exercises we will use the II–V–I chord movement as the platform.

The most common progression in jazz and popular music is the II–V–I chord structure. So for this last exercise I want you to play the upper approach pattern over a IIm^7–V^7–I^{maj7} in every key.

Play this cycle at various tempos, slow to fast and repeat 2 to 3 times before increasing the tempo increment.

Try these concepts over some standards.

ESSENTIAL
BASS LIBRARY

LARRY GALES

Nonet: Live!
(Thelonious Monk)
Le Jazz, 1967

LOWER APPROACH (CHROMATIC)

The lower approach always uses a half-step below the target note (chord tone), moving chromatically.

Having practised the upper approach concept we will next look at practising the lower approach concept.

We will apply the concept to the four different chord types found within the major modes.

The same system works for the Ionian and Lydian.

The same system works for all three of the minor chords. [?]

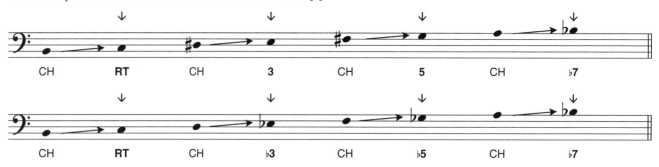

Again we will study the lower approach concept in four ways.

Part 1: Single String

The order for the lower approach concept using C^maj7 on the E string will be

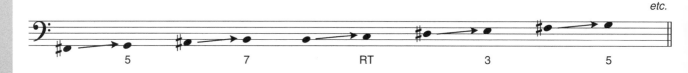

Move from the lowest available lower approach note in sequence up to the highest available lower approach note (resolving onto the chord tone), then returning back down to the lowest. Repeat this exercise on each string and for each of the diatonic chords found within the major modes.

The use of a sustained chord or drone is recommended to play these exercises. Remember that the single string exercise is more of an ear training exercise than a technical one.

Part 2: Melody/Improv

Here is an example of a melody over C^maj7 using scale fragments and the lower approach concept.

Use this melody or your own as a basis for your own improvisations. Repeat for all chords found within the major modes, in all keys.

Part 3: Diatonic Cycle of 5ths Progression

Here is the lower approach concept over a diatonic cycle of 5ths progression.

Next, halve the duration of the chord progression and randomly choose two of the chromatic lower approaches for each chord.

Practise these diatonic cycle of 5ths progressions in all keys.

Try improvising over this progression using both scale fragments and the approach concept.

Part 4: IIm7–V7–Imaj7 in all keys

Chromatic approach to chord tone over IIm^7–V^7–I^{maj7} in all keys.

Practise this idea over some standards.

ESSENTIAL BASS LIBRARY

JIMMY GARRISON

Afro Blue Impressions
(John Coltrane)
Pablo, 1963

UPPER-LOWER APPROACH

The next approach concept is a combination of the first two we looked at.

The upper approach note (diatonic) of a chord tone is immediately followed by the lower approach note (chromatic), before resolving onto the chord tone. The scale approaches will be different depending on the function of the chord in question.

Here are the approaches over the available diatonic chords found within the major modes.

Part 1: Single String

The concept applied across the whole range of a single string. Using a C major 7 chord, the order for the upper-lower approach for the whole range of the E string will be:

Move from the lowest note pattern, in order, up to the highest available note pattern, and back down. Repeat this process across each string for each of the chord types and in all keys.

Part 2: Melody/Improv

Here is an example of a melody incorporating scale fragments and the upper-lower approach concept.

Use the melodies as a starting point for your improvisations.

Practise your melody/improvisations as explained in the previous exercise.

Part 3: Diatonic Cycle of 5ths Progression

Next, I want you to play the upper-lower approach concept over this diatonic cycle of 5ths chord progression.

ESSENTIAL BASS LIBRARY

JIMMY GARRISON

Live in Antibes
(John Coltrane)
France's Concert, 1965

Halve the duration of the progression and randomly choose two of the target note approaches.

Practise both of these cycle of 5ths progressions in all keys at various tempos.

Part 4: IIm7–V7–Imaj7 in all keys

Next practise the upper-lower approach concept over the IIm⁷–V⁷–I^maj7 progression in all keys.

Also try mixing up the order of the II–V–I progressions—here they are in descending whole steps.

LOWER-UPPER APPROACH

For both the upper-lower and lower-upper approach concepts, the lower approach note remains chromatic and the upper approach note remains diatonic.

We can reverse the previous pattern, and so instead of starting with the upper approach, you can start with the lower approach. This gives us the lower-upper approach concept.

Here are the approaches over the diatonic chords found within the major modes.

Part 1: Single String

Again, we will study and practise this exercise in four ways.

Firstly, we will apply the concept across the whole range of a single string. Again, using C major 7 across the whole range of the E string, the order for the lower-upper approach concept will be:

Move from the lowest note pattern, in order, up to the highest available note pattern, and back down. Repeat this process across each string for each of the chord types and in all keys.

Part 2: Melody/Improv

Here is an example of a melody using the lower-upper approach concept.

Cmaj7 (Imaj7)

Use this or your own written melody as a starting point for your improvisations.

Repeat this process for all chord types in all keys.

Part 3: Diatonic Cycle of 5ths Progression

Here is the lower-upper approach over a diatonic cycle of 5ths chord progression.

Halve the duration of the progression and randomly choose two of the target note approaches.

Practise these diatonic cycle of 5ths progression in all keys.

Part 4: IIm7–V7–Imaj7 in all keys

Practise the lower-upper approach concept over this ascending minor 3rd, IIm^7–V^7–I^{maj7} progression in all keys.

DOUBLE-UPPER APPROACH (CHROMATIC)

The next approach we will be looking at is the double-upper chromatic approach. This approach pattern only works when the scale degree above the chord tone is a whole step away. I will simply miss out the double-upper chromatic approaches that do not apply to the particular chords.

Here are the double-upper chromatic approach patterns over all the available diatonic chords found within the major modes. For the maj7 chords we replace the seventh degree with the sixth.

The most common use of these approaches used over any major chord is from the Lydian chord scale.
The most common use of the approaches used over any minor chord is from the Dorian chord scale.
All the upper structure tensions can be used on these two chord types.

Part 1: Single String

Here is the Cm⁷ (Dorian) with double-upper chromatic approach over the E string.

Work your way from the lowest available chord tone (with the double-upper chromatic approach) moving up, in order, to the highest available double-upper chromatic approach, and then back down.

Repeat this process across each string for all chord types found within the major modes in all keys.

Part 2: Melody/Improv

Here is an example of a melody using the double-upper chromatic approach, over C^maj7. Remember to swap the sixth degree for the seventh. We will use the tensions found within the Lydian chord scale—C^maj7 (I^maj7, IV^maj7)

Use this or your own melody as a basis for your improvisations.

Part 3: Diatonic Cycle of 5ths Progression

For both the major chords we will use the Lydian approach as it is the most common and colourful, and for all the minor chords we will use the approach based on the Dorian mode.

For the 7 chord we'll use the scale above approach for now. In the melodic minor study I'll introduce you to the ♯II to this sound, making available the double-upper chromatic approach to the third degree.

Also for the m7♭5 we will use the upper (diatonic) approach. Again in the melodic minor study we will introduce the natural 9 in the chord scale giving us the double-upper chromatic approach.

Here is the double-upper chromatic approach concept applied to this diatonic cycle of 5ths progression.

Please be aware that these approaches for the major and minor chords generally work over any given major or minor chord unless the song or progression you are working with dictates a particular sound. For example, the IIIm⁷ sometimes requires a Phrygian sound—always check and learn the melody for a piece of music you are working on. A lot of the time the melody will dictate the appropriate sound needed.

Next halve the duration of the chord progression and randomly pick two of the double-upper chromatic approaches.

Practise these diatonic cycle of 5ths progressions in all keys.

Part 4: IIm7–V7–Imaj7 in all keys

Practise the double-upper chromatic approach over this descending IIm^7–V^7–I^{maj7} progression. For now, the V^7 chord will use the upper approach method.

In the melodic minor study, we will introduce the Lydian ♭7 chord scale which introduces the ♯4 which will give us the double-upper chromatic approach to the third degree.

Practise and improvise this concept over some standards.

DOUBLE-UPPER LOWER APPROACH (CHROMATIC)

The next approach we'll look at is a double-upper lower chromatic approach. This approach pattern only works when the scale degree above the chord tone is a whole step away.

As before, we will miss out this concept when it does not apply to particular chords. Here are the double-upper lower chromatic approach patterns over all the diatonic chords found within the major modes.

For the maj7 chords we replace the seventh degree with the sixth.

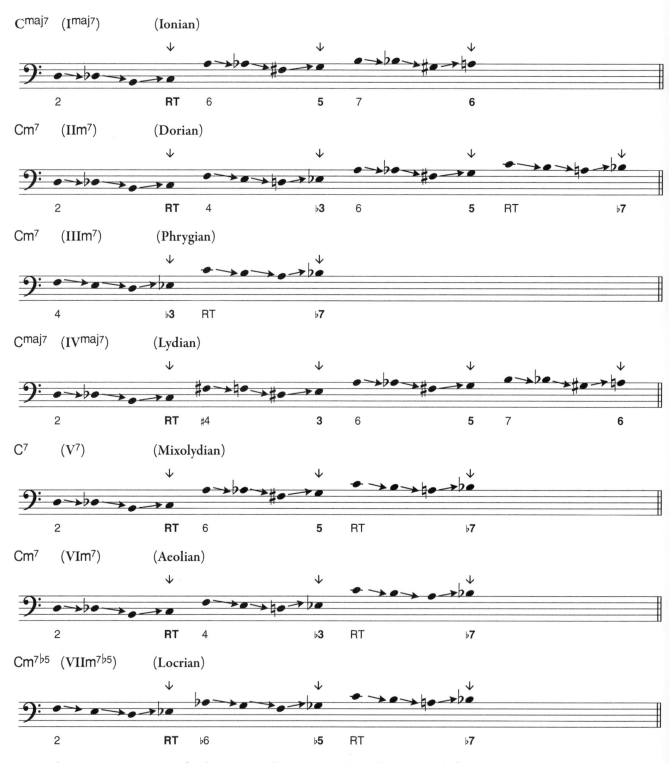

Again, the most common usage for these approach patterns is the Lydian approach for the major chords and the Dorian approach for the minor chords.

Part 1: Single String

The order for the double-upper lower chromatic approach using C^{maj7} (IVmaj7) on the E string will be:

Move from the lowest available double-upper lower chromatic approach (allowing for the bottom lower approach) in sequence, up to the highest available double-upper lower chromatic approach, on each string, and then back down. Repeat this exercise for each of the diatonic chords found within the major modes across each string in all keys.

Part 2: Melody/Improv

Here is a melody over C^{maj7} (IVmaj7), using a combination of scale fragments and the double-upper lower chromatic approach patterns.

Use this or your own melody as a basis for your own improvisations.

Part 3: Diatonic Cycle of 5ths Progression

Again, for both of the major chords we use a Lydian approach, giving us approaches to all chord tones. The Lydian is the more common scale over a maj7 chord, as the Ionian has a natural fourth degree (an avoid note).

For the minor chords, like the Lydian, the Dorian approach gives us all the available tensions.

However, let the music and melody from the piece of music you are working on dictate the choices you make. Let your ears be the judge.

For the 7 chord we will use the upper-lower approach to the third degree.

The Lydian ♭7 (♯II) chord will be discussed and analysed later.

For the m7♭5 chord we will use the upper-lower approach to the root. The Aeolian (♭5) m7♭5 chord and scale gives us a natural second degree and is a great alternative.

Both of these chords and chord scales are derived from the melodic minor modes and will be discussed later.

ESSENTIAL BASS LIBRARY

TONY GREY

Brain
(Hiromi)
Telarc Digital, 2004

Halve the duration of the chord progression and randomly choose two of the target note approaches.

Practise these cycle of 5ths progressions in all keys.

Part 4: IIm7–V7–Imaj7

Practise the double-upper lower chromatic approach over this cycle of 5ths, IIm⁷–V⁷–Iᵐᵃʲ⁷ progression.

Again, for now the V⁷ chord will use the upper-lower approach. More options for the dominant 7 chord will be discussed later.

LOWER DOUBLE-UPPER APPROACH (CHROMATIC)

The last approach exercise that we will look at is a variation on the previous approach concept.

As with previous double-upper or diatonic upper approaches, this approach pattern only works when the scale degree above the chord tone is a whole step away. We will miss out the lower double-upper chromatic approaches that do not apply to these particular chords.

Here are the lower double-upper chromatic approach patterns over all the diatonic chords found within the major modes.

For the maj7 chords we replace the seventh degree with the sixth.

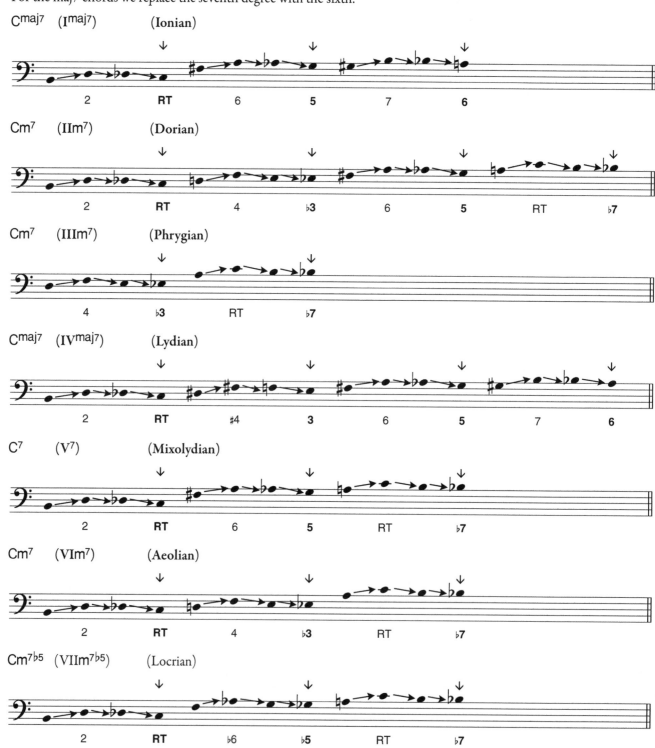

Again regarding approach patterns for major chords, the Lydian approach is more common; for the minor chords the Dorian approach is more common.

Part 1: Single String

The order of the lower double-upper chromatic approach using C^maj7 (IVmaj7) on the E string will be:

Move from the lowest available lower double-upper chromatic approach, in sequence up to the highest available lower double-upper chromatic approach, on each string, and then back to the lowest. Repeat this exercise for each of the diatonic chords within the major modes, across each string and in all keys.

Part 2: Melody/Improv

Here is a melody over C^maj7 (IVmaj7) using a combination of scale fragments and the lower double-upper chromatic approaches.

Use this or your own melody as a basis for your own improvisations.

Part 3: Diatonic Cycle of 5ths Progression

Again, for the major chords use the Lydian approach and for the minor chords use the Dorian approach. Be aware this can change depending on the musical situation you are dealing with. The Dorian approach would not work if the minor chord required a strong Phrygian sound. These are all options so that you can make the right choices.

For the dominant 7 chord we use the lower-upper approach to the third degree. Later in the melodic minor study I will introduce the Lydian ♭7, which gives us the double-upper chromatic approach to the third degree.

For the m7♭5 chord we approach the root with a lower-upper sequence. Again, in the melodic minor modes I will introduce the m7♭5 chord with a natural second degree.

Here is the lower double-upper chromatic approach over a cycle of 5ths chord progression.

ESSENTIAL
BASS LIBRARY

TONY GREY

Chasing Shadows
(Tony Grey)
Abstractlogix, 2008

Halve the duration of the chord progression and randomly choose two of the target note approaches.

Practise these diatonic cycle of 5ths progressions in all keys.

Part 4: IIm7–V7–Imaj7 in all keys

Practise the lower double-upper chromatic approach over this cycle of 5ths IIm^7–V^7–I^{maj7} progression.

Again for the V^7 chord I will be using the lower-upper approach.

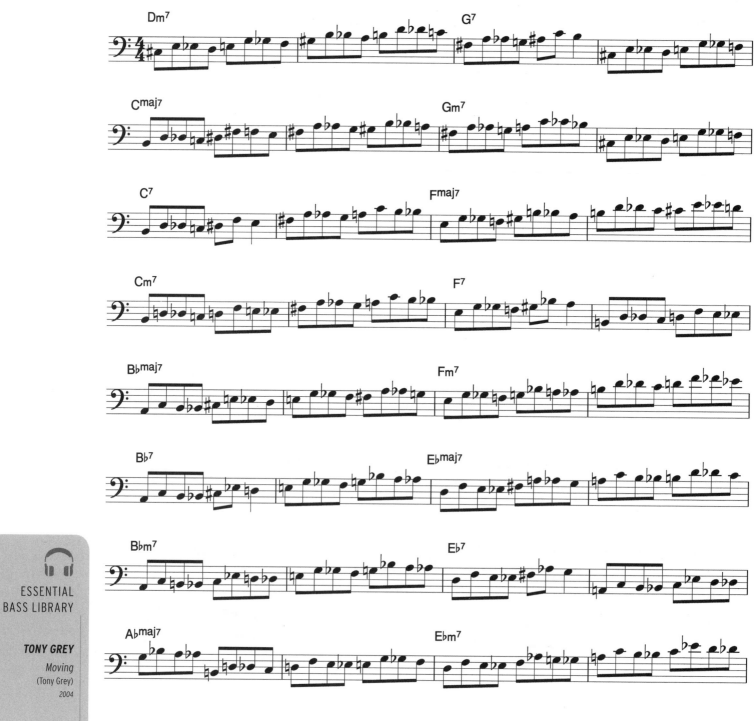

APPROACH TO TARGET NOTE REVIEW

In this segment of the book we have looked at 7 different approach patterns and 4 ways to practise each of them. These are:

1. Upper—approaching from a scale degree above (diatonic).

2. Lower—approaching from a half-step below (chromatic).

3. Upper-Lower—approaching from a scale degree above (diatonic), followed by a half-step below (chromatic).

4. Lower-Upper—approaching from a half-step below (chromatic), followed by a scale degree above (diatonic).

5. Double-upper chromatic—approaching with two half-steps above (chromatic).

6. Double-upper lower chromatic—approaching with two half-steps above (chromatic), followed by a half-step below (chromatic).

7. Lower double-upper chromatic—approaching with a half-step below (chromatic), followed by two half-steps above (chromatic).

It is important once you have completed the exercises to try and imply these concepts into your playing.

Create your own progressions along with some Jazz Standards and improvise using a combination of these exercises.

DECISIONS IN CHORD APPROACH DURING IMPROV

When soloing (improvising) we need to make choices about how we are going to approach the particular passage or chord progression in front of us. Here are some things to consider:

1. Playing completely free and reacting spontaneously

2. Understanding the chord structure and related chord scales—using a combination of the linear concept, intervals, scale fragment patterns, etc.

3. Applying arpeggios (triads and 4-note chords), shifting the base note each time in a stepwise, modal fashion, with the direct arpeggio related to the chord in question. Also applying upper structure extensions against the chords and suitable approaches to target notes.

4. Combining scales and chord tones.

5. Quoting melodies, making phrases, repeating/modulating them to build tension, and developing a melody.

Really, the choices are overwhelming and endless. It also defies the point of improvising to be thinking so much whilst soloing.

The goal is to really play what you hear in the moment, rather like how we interact with each other. When we are comfortable, the words just come out of our mouths creating engaging conversation. It is like we are improvising spontaneously but really we do not think like that.

To me, music can be like that too. If we spend time learning our instrument to the point where we forget what we are doing and just let go so we can react to what is going on around us, we can really create an individual approach to music and melody.

Don't forget music is a conversation between musicians and the audience/environment we are in. As in our interactions with each other, no-one really likes arrogant, self-centred, selfish people. Always try to be open to another point of view musically. The soloist or band leader is not always the leader of the moment. A soloist may react to a drummer playing a certain rhythm or a chord voicing, even a mistake. Just let the moment show you the way to go.

Part 3

Melodic Minor Modes:
Fingering Patterns
Linear Solo Concepts
Triads and Inversions

3.1

CHAPTER 3.1

Melodic Minor Modes

Like the major modes the melodic minor modes are a group of scales built off each degree of the melodic minor scale. The melodic minor scale is made up of a series of steps.

They are: W, H, W, W, W, W, H. (W= whole step, H= half-step)

Each scale built off the melodic minor has its own set of intervals and characteristics.

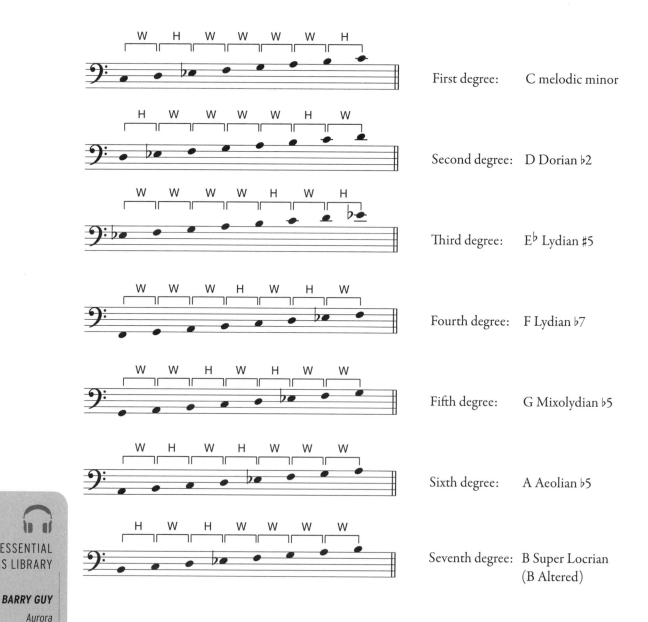

First degree: C melodic minor

Second degree: D Dorian ♭2

Third degree: E♭ Lydian ♯5

Fourth degree: F Lydian ♭7

Fifth degree: G Mixolydian ♭5

Sixth degree: A Aeolian ♭5

Seventh degree: B Super Locrian
                 (B Altered)

C Melodic Minor

One way of considering the melodic minor scale is as an Ionian ♭3 scale (the third degree lowered by a half-step). The scales built from each degree of the melodic minor scale form a group of new scales called the melodic minor modes, the first mode being the melodic minor scale. The minor 3rd, perfect 5th, major 7th degrees make the melodic minor a minor-major scale.

The correct way of considering the melodic minor scale is as an Aeolian scale (the natural minor scale) with sharpened sixth and seventh degrees. Using C melodic minor as an example, you can see that the A♭ and B♭ of the C Aeolian scale have been sharpened to an A♮ and B♮.

D Dorian ♭2

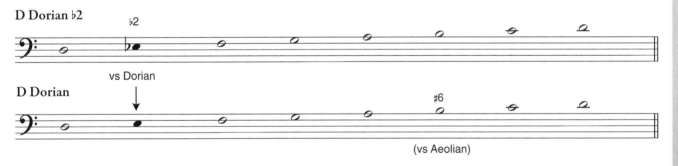

The D Dorian ♭2 scale is built off the second degree of the C melodic minor scale.

When we compare the D Dorian ♭2 scale to the D Dorian you will notice its second degree has been lowered by a half-step, therefore we can consider the Dorian ♭2 scale to be similar to a natural minor scale with a flattened 2nd and sharpened 6th.

The minor 3rd, perfect 5th and minor 7th degrees make the D Dorian ♭2 a minor scale.

Although a minor-major scale is essentially a minor scale but with a sharpened 7th, the 4-note chord that is formed from this scale is a m(maj7), hence the name 'minor-major'.

ESSENTIAL
BASS LIBRARY

CHARLIE HADEN

Night And The City
(Kenny Barron &
Charlie Haden)
Verve, 1996

E♭ Lydian ♯5

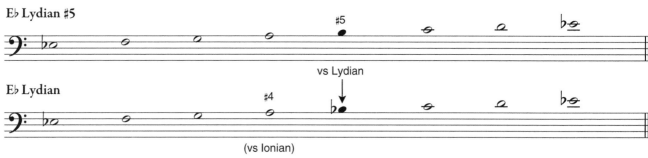

The E♭ Lydian ♯5 scale is built off the third degree of the C melodic minor scale.

Compared to the E♭ Lydian, you will notice the fifth degree is raised a half-step, and so the E♭ Lydian ♯5 is similar to an Ionian scale (a major scale) with a sharpened 4th and 5th. The major 3rd, augmented 5th and major 7th degrees make the E♭ Lydian ♯5 an augmented major scale.

F Lydian ♭7

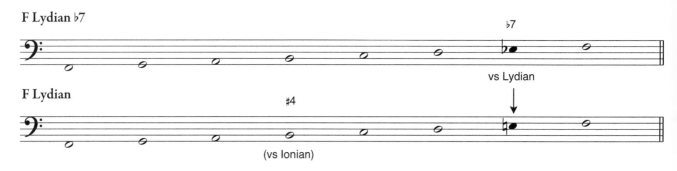

The F Lydian ♭7 scale is built off the fourth degree of the C melodic minor scale.

Comparing to the F Lydian, you will notice the seventh degree is lowered a half-step, making the F Lydian ♭7 similar to an Ionian scale with a sharpened 4th and flattened 7th. The major 3rd, perfect 5th and minor 7th degrees make the F Lydian ♭7 a dominant scale.

G Mixolydian ♭6

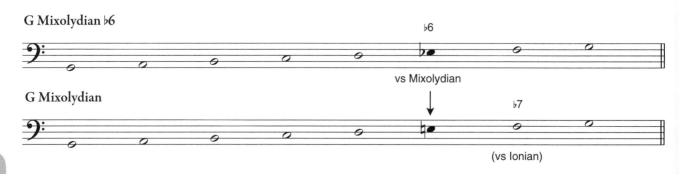

The G Mixolydian ♭6 scale is built off the fifth degree of the C melodic scale.

Comparing to the G Mixolydian, you will notice the sixth degree is lowered a half-step, and so the G Mixolydian ♭6 is similar to an Ionian scale with a flattened 6th and 7th. The major 3rd, perfect 5th and minor 7th degrees make the G Mixolydian a dominant scale.

A Aeolian ♭5

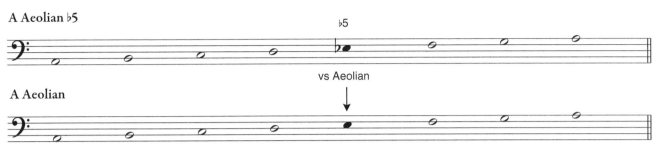

The A Aeolian ♭5 scale is built off the sixth degree of the C melodic minor scale.

Compared to the natural minor scale, the A Aeolian has a flattened fifth degree. The minor 3rd, diminished 5th and minor 7th degrees make the A Aeolian ♭5 a half diminished scale.

B Super Locrian (B Altered)

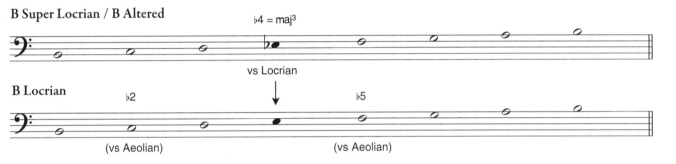

The seventh mode of the melodic minor scale is a very important and frequently used scale in jazz music. It has two commonly used names: Super Locrian or Altered.

One way of constructing an Altered scale is to start with an Aeolian scale and flatten the 2nd, 4th and 5th, however this isn't really the proper way to consider the scale, as I will explain...

Compared to the Locrian, we can see the flattened fourth degree. Interestingly, this fourth degree (diminished 4th) is an E♭. Enharmonically it can be called a D♯, which is coincidentally the major third degree of the B scale. This gives the scale the option to change between having a minor 3rd and a major 3rd (actually the diminished 4th).

When you look at the written scale it looks like some kind of minor scale with the third and seventh degrees both flattened. In fact this scale is most commonly used as an altered dominant scale, with chords often being formed to include the diminished 4th instead of the minor 3rd. This gives the derived chord a dominant sound.

Play the scale against this root, 3rd and 7th:

3.2

CHAPTER 3.2

Intervals and Diatonic Whole Range Fingering Patterns for the Melodic Minor Modes

This chapter focuses on fingering patterns for the C melodic minor modes and their intervals.

INTERVALS

We have already looked at all the intervals found within the major modes. Here are all the available intervals found within the melodic minor modes. These are diatonic intervals found within the C melodic minor scale.

C melodic minor

| Perfect unison | maj 2nd | min 3rd | Perfect 4th | Perfect 5th | maj 6th | maj 7th | Perfect octave |

D Dorian ♭2

| P unison | min 2nd | min 3rd | P 4th | P 5th | maj 6th | min 7th | P octave |

E♭ Lydian ♯5

| P unison | maj 2nd | maj 3rd | aug 4th | aug 5th | maj 6th | maj 7th | P octave |

F Lydian ♭7

| P unison | maj 2nd | maj 3rd | aug 4th | P 5th | maj 6th | min 7th | P octave |

G Mixolydian ♭6

| P unison | maj 2nd | maj 3rd | P 4th | P 5th | min 6th | min 7th | P octave |

A Aeolian ♭5

| P unison | maj 2nd | min 3rd | P 4th | dim 5th | min 6th | min 7th | P octave |

B Super Locrian

| P unison | min 2nd | min 3rd | dim 4th | dim 5th | min 6th | min 7th | P octave |

DIATONIC FINGERING PATTERNS

As with the major modes, we will go through exercises that cover the whole range of the melodic minor modes, from the lowest note up to the highest note on the instrument.

Firstly, I have written out the whole range of C melodic minor starting with the lowest note available which is an (F) on the E string up to a (G) on the 24th fret of the G string. The idea of this exercise is to find the perfect fingering pattern to play across the whole instrument with ease.

Next, I took the C melodic minor from the lowest C on the lowest string (E) up to the highest available C on the highest string (G). Again, I found and wrote out the perfect fingering pattern. I continued this exercise throughout all the modes of the C melodic minor modes:

C melodic minor, D Dorian ♭2, E♭ Lydian ♯5, F Lydian ♭7, G Mixolydian ♭6, A Aeolian ♭5 and B Super Locrian. There is a different fingering pattern, position and range for each exercise.

Practise these exercises with the metronome on beats 2 and 4, starting at 40bpm. Repeat 5 times, up and down the fretboard without stopping then raise the tempo by 2bpm and repeat.

I perform these exercises until the metronome is at 120bpm on beats 2 and 4. However, play up to whatever tempo is comfortable for you. Speed is not the point for this exercise. I recommend practising these exercises for no more than 30 minutes a day. Once your time is up make a note of your bpm and continue from that point next time.

C MELODIC MINOR MODES

Whole Range

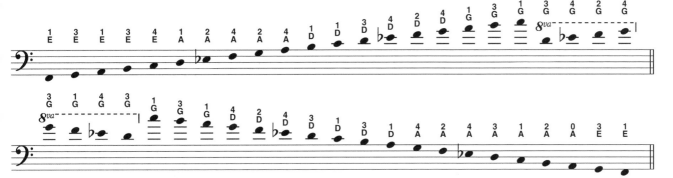

This exercise covers the whole range of the C melodic minor scale, starting on the lowest available note on the E string (F) up to the highest note available on the G string (G).

C Melodic Minor

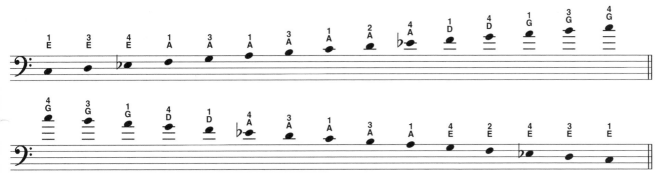

This exercise covers the C melodic minor scale from the lowest root (C) on the E string to the highest root (C) on the G string.

ESSENTIAL
BASS LIBRARY

CHARLIE HADEN

Michael Brecker
(Michael Brecker)
Impulse, 1987

D Dorian ♭2

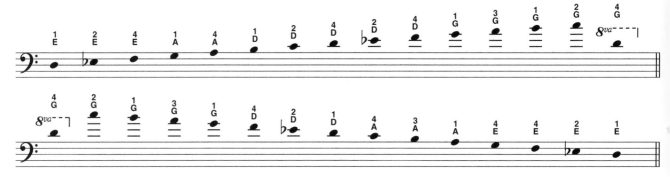

This exercise covers the D Dorian ♭2 scale from the lowest root (D) on the E string to the highest root (D) on the G string.

E♭ Lydian ♯5

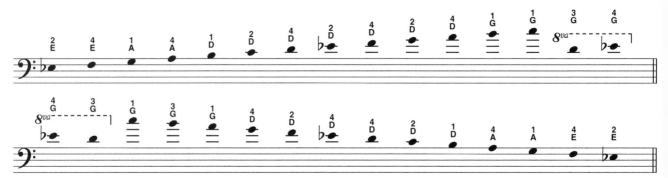

This exercise covers the E♭ Lydian ♯5 scale from the lowest available root (E♭) on the E string up to the highest available root (E♭) on the G string.

F Lydian ♭7

This exercise covers the F Lydian ♭7 scale from the lowest available root (F) on the E string to the highest available root (F) on the G string.

G Mixolydian ♭6

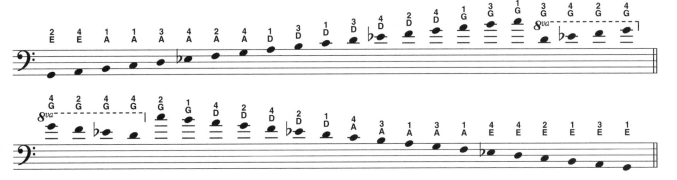

This exercise covers the G Mixolydian ♭6 scale from the lowest available root (G) on the E string to the highest available root (G) on the G string.

A Aeolian ♭5

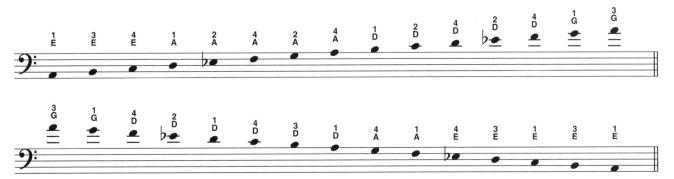

This exercise covers the A Aeolian ♭5 scale from the lowest available root (A) on the E string to the highest available root (A) on the G string.

B Super Locrian/Altered

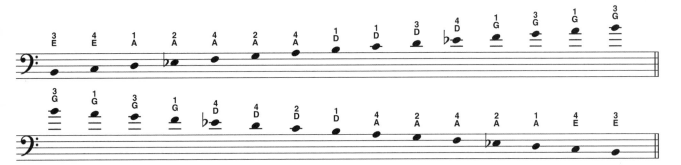

This exercise covers the B Super Locrian scale from the lowest available root (B) on the E string to the highest available root (B) on the G string.

ESSENTIAL
BASS LIBRARY

CHARLIE HADEN

*The Shape of Jazz
Jazz to Come*
(Ornette Coleman)
Atlantic, 1959

SCALES IN 3RDS

Whole Range 3rds

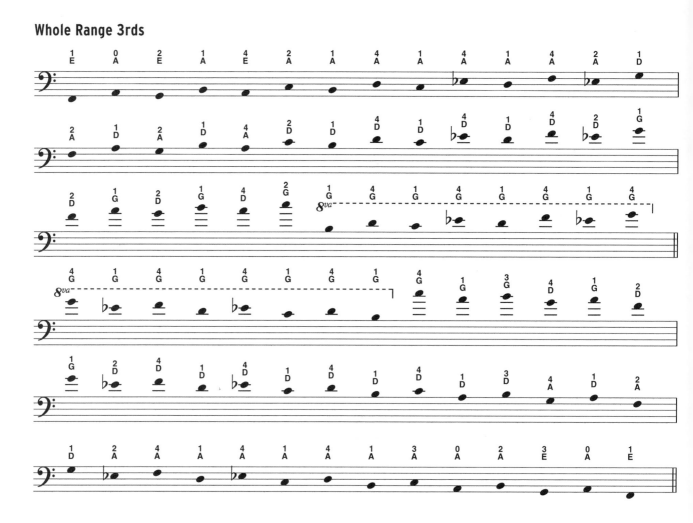

This exercise covers the whole range of the C melodic minor scale in 3rds moving from the lowest note on the E string (F) to the highest note on the G string (G).

C Melodic Minor 3rds

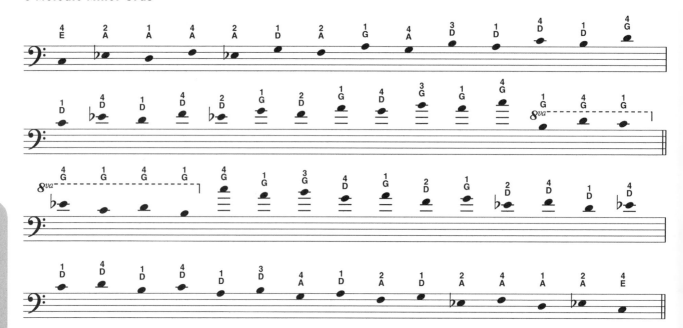

This exercise covers the C melodic minor scale in 3rds from the lowest root (C) available on the E string to the highest available interval from the root (Eb) on the G string.

D Dorian ♭2 3rds

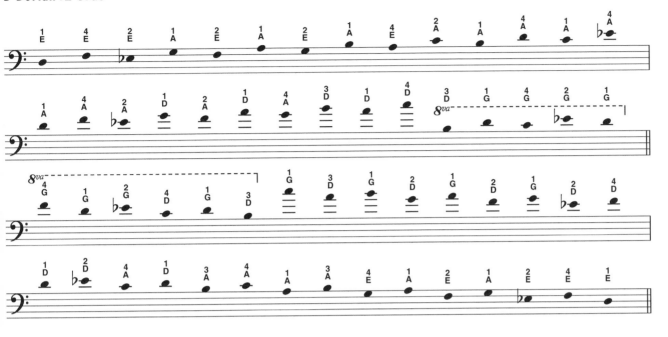

This exercise covers the D Dorian ♭2 scale in 3rds from the lowest available root (D) on the E string to the highest available interval from the root (F) on the G string.

E♭ Lydian ♯5 3rds

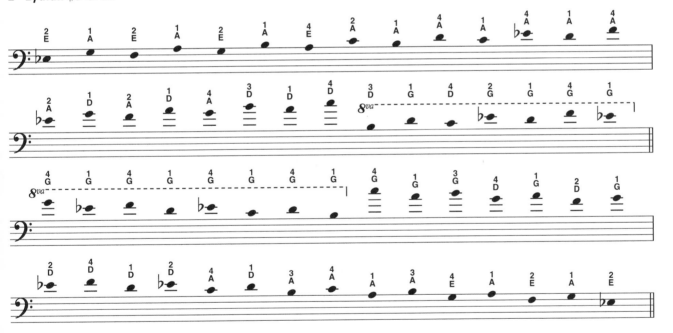

This exercise covers the E♭ Lydian ♯5 scale in 3rds from the lowest root (Eb) on the E string to the highest available interval from the root (G) on the G string.

F Lydian ♭7 3rds

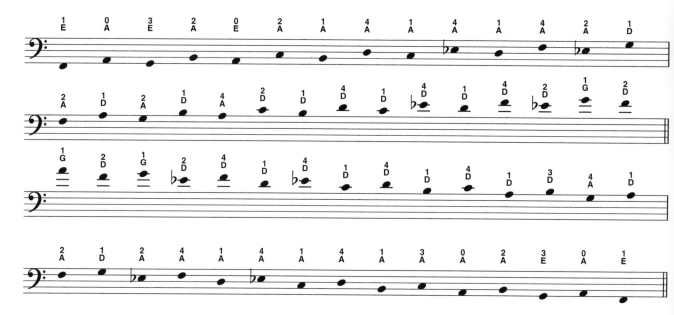

This exercise covers the F Lydian ♭7 scale in 3rds from the lowest root (F) on the E string to the highest available interval from the root (A) on the G string.

G Mixolydian ♭6 3rds

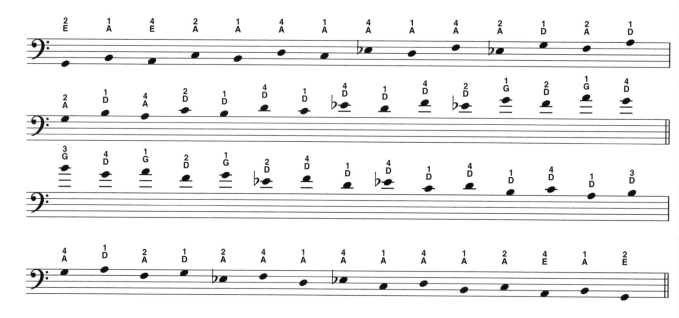

This exercise covers the G Mixolydian ♭6 scale from the lowest root (G) on the E string to the highest available interval from the root (B) on the G string.

A Aeolian ♭5 3rds

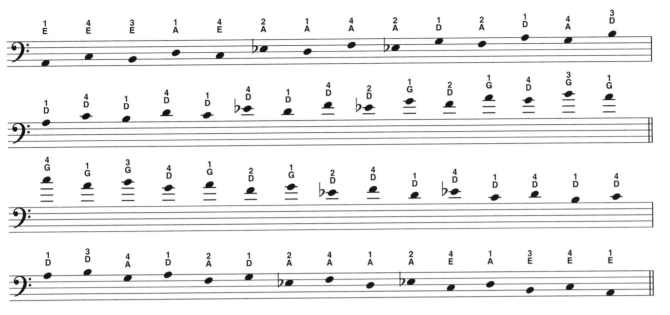

This exercise covers the A Aeolian ♭5 in 3rds from the lowest root (A) on the E string to the highest available interval from the root (C) on the G string.

B Super Locrian/Altered 3rds

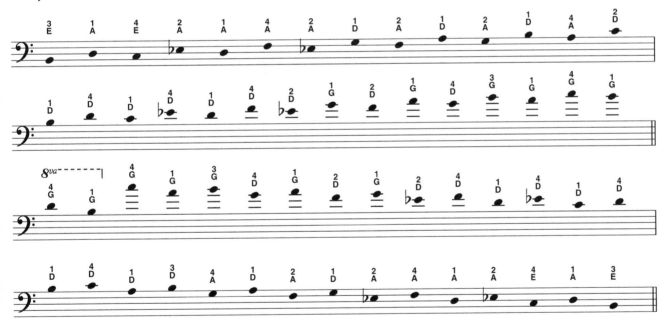

This exercise covers the B Super Locrian scale in 3rds from the lowest root (B) on the E string to the highest interval from the root (D) on the G string.

PRACTISING FINGERING PATTERNS FOR THE MELODIC MINOR MODES

Combining the use of ear training, technique, knowledge of your instrument and musical vocabulary are crucial for becoming a master of your craft.

It is important to practise the material given to you within these chapters in a straight and focused manner, but it is almost more important to apply the things you study in a musical way.

As we did with the major harmony studies, we will first go through some linear fingering patterns that you can include in your improvisations. They are a combination of fluency, ear training and technical exercises.

Next I will write out some simple melodies for each of the modes outlining the characteristics important for each scale. This will be a basis for your own improvisations helping you to instinctively create and hear melodies and colours within the harmonic boundaries.

Linear fingering patterns

These patterns are to be played and studied across the entire fretboard. They have been written out diatonic to C melodic minor, but as always you should learn them in all keys.

Practise these exercises starting at a slow tempo (perhaps 40bpm) and then gradually increase the speed when you become more fluent. It is important to play these exercises steadily and accurately. They will help improve your sound, touch, technique and melodic development.

Exercise 1

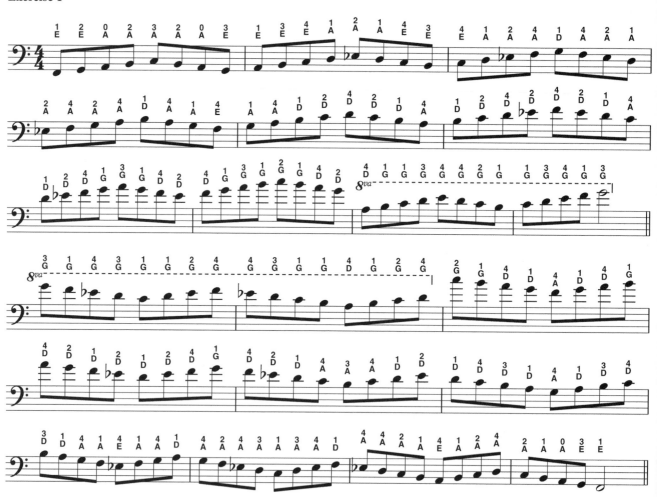

Exercise 2

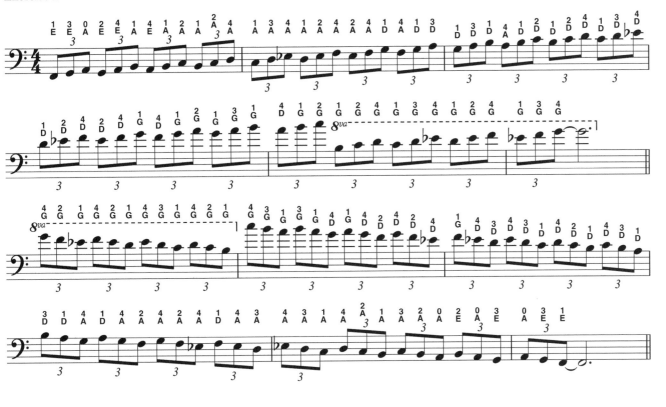

Exercise 3

ESSENTIAL
BASS LIBRARY

CALVIN HILL

Song for my Lady
(McCoy Tyner)
Original Jazz Classics, 1972

HOW TO PRACTISE AND APPLY THE LINEAR FINGERING PATTERNS

For the melodic minor modes study I want to apply the same practise concepts. Here are the following steps:

1. Write out a melody for the scale in question, trying to outline the colour of the scale. Start in sequence from the C melodic minor, D Dorian ♭2, E♭ Lydian ♯5 etc. Next, use C melodic minor 3rds, D Dorian ♭2 3rds etc. Next, try to incorporate the use of intervals into your melodies. For example, write out a melody including the C melodic minor scale fragments along with intervals of a 3rd. Do this for each mode and each interval.

2. Set up some kind of drone or sustained chord based on the scale you are studying. This will help you stay within the scale colour. Although each scale within the modes uses the same notes, each scale and adjacent chord has its own characteristics.

3. Set a timer for 3-5mins as this will help keep you moving forward. There are many keys and scales to work through, so a time limit for each tempo will give you some light at the end of the tunnel!
   For each 3-5min time slot, try working different tempos. Start slowly at about 40bpm, and each time increase the increment by 5bpm, and then repeat. Play the whole range you are working on once, as a review, then play through your short melody and improvise, staying within the boundaries of your scale study (3rds, 4ths, 5ths, etc.). Use all areas of the fretboard, practising the position shifts. Use a metronome on beats 2 and 4, or some kind of drum machine.

4. Be mindful of your practising habits. Push yourself in the areas where you struggle most. It is important not to just go through the motions—focus is also important.

5. Practise this way for 30mins. Make a note of your progress and next time you can start where you left off.

Here is an example of some melodies using different scales and intervals found within these melodic minor studies.

C melodic minor

Cm^{maj7} using scale fragments

D Dorian ♭2

Dm⁷ using 3rds and scale fragments

E♭ Lydian #5

Emaj7#5 using 4ths and scale fragments

F Lydian ♭7

F7#11 using 5ths and scale fragments

G Mixolydian ♭6

G7♭13 using 6ths and scale fragments

A Aeolian (♭5)

Am7♭5 using 7ths and scale fragments

B Super Locrian/Altered

B7alt

3.3

CHAPTER 3.3

Linear Solo Concepts Through The Changes Using Diatonic Melodic Minor Harmony

In this chapter we will look at playing through a series of non-related chords found within the melodic minor modes. We will pick and choose two or more chords from different keys all within the melodic minor modes.

LINEAR SOLOING

As with major harmony, we will learn how to solo and change keys without losing direction of your line and position on the fretboard. Again, the result of these exercises will help your knowledge and fluency within the melodic minor modes. It will also help you play through non-related chord progressions in a smooth and focused melodic fashion.

Exercise 1

For this first exercise I will choose two chords from the melodic minor modes. The two chords will be from different keys.

Play a never-ending quarter-note line through the progression. As the chord changes adjust the chord scale chromatically or in a stepwise order, depending on the flow of the line. Start the scale on any note and use the whole range of the fretboard. Mix up the direction of the line at random.

The first two chords I am using here are Cm^maj7 and A7#11. These two chords are completely unrelated and are from different chord scales and keys.

Cm^maj7 (C melodic minor)

C melodic minor is the first mode of C melodic minor

A7#11 (A Lydian ♭7)

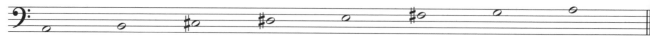

A Lydian ♭7 is the fourth mode of E melodic minor

Exercise 1 continued:

Exercise 2

In Exercise 1 the rate of the chord change is every 4 bars. In Exercise 2, I will change the rate to every 2 bars.

Exercise 3

As in the previous exercise I will double the rate of chord change. This time the chord will change every bar. You can repeat this exercise using any two chords from different keys found within the melodic minor modes.

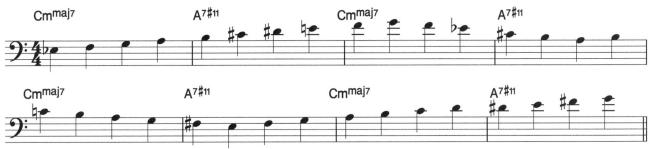

ESSENTIAL
BASS LIBRARY

MILT HINTON
The Trio: 1994
(Milt Hinton)
Chiaroscuro, 1994

Exercise 4

Exercise 4 uses six different chords all from different keys. The progression is a mixture of chords derived from the major and melodic minor modes.

The six chords are: B♭maj7, A7♭13, Dm7, D♭7♯11, Cm7 and F7alt

B♭maj7 (B♭ Lydian)

B♭ Lydian is the fourth mode of F major

A7♭13 (A Mixolydian ♭13)

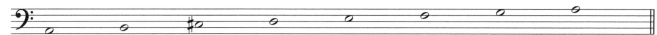

A Mixolydian ♭13 is the fifth mode of D melodic minor.

Dm7 (D Dorian)

D Dorian is the second mode of C major

D♭7♯11 (D♭ Lydian ♭7)

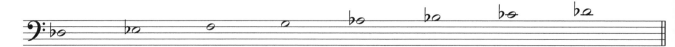

D♭ Lydian ♭7 is the fourth mode of A♭ melodic minor

Cm7 (C Dorian)

C Dorian is the second mode of B♭ major

F7alt (F Super Locrian/alt)

F7alt is the seventh mode of F♯ or G♭ melodic minor

Play each exercise starting at a slow tempo. Play the written quarter note example then continue using your own quarter note lines.

An example of how to practise is to play a quarter note line over the progression for 2½ minutes, then solo for a further 2½ minutes. If you are struggling with your quarter note line then you may want to start at a slower tempo, or continue working through it past your time limit.

Once you are comfortable, try soloing over the progression. Try to keep your solos simple and focus on playing as much

of the fretboard as possible, playing through the changes rather than stopping and starting.

Remember, the point of these exercises is to create fluidity while playing through non-related chord changes. Once you are comfortable with the tempo you are working on raise the tempo by increments of 5bpm and repeat. Practise these exercises for no more than 30mins per day. This helps you to keep your focus and gives you time to work on other things. You can continue from your last point next time you work on this exercise.

ESSENTIAL
BASS LIBRARY

DAVE HOLLAND

*Conference of
the Birds*
(Dave Holland Quartet)
ECM, 1972

131

3.4

CHAPTER 3.4

Diatonic Triads and their Inversions found within the Melodic Minor Modes

DIATONIC TRIADS WITHIN THE MELODIC MINOR MODES

The triads found within the melodic minor modes are constructed in exactly the same way as we did for the diatonic triads found within the major modes.

C melodic minor scale

If you stack two diatonic 3rds related to the scale of C melodic minor, for each degree you will find each of the seven related diatonic triads found within the melodic minor modes.

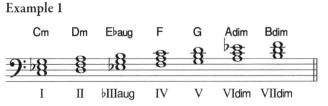

Once you analyse these triads you will notice there are four different chord quality types. They are: minor, augmented, major and diminished.

The I and II chords are minor:

The bIII chord is augmented:

The IV and V chords are major:

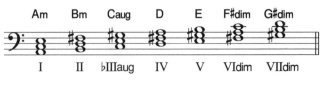

The VI and VII chords are diminished:

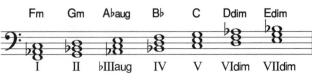

Review of Diatonic Triads found within the Melodic Minor Modes in Various Keys

Example 1

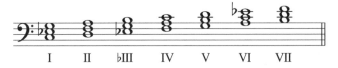

Example 2

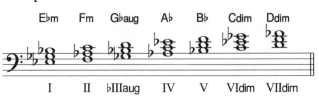

Example 3

Example 4

Reviewing and Practising Triads from the Melodic Minor Modes

After you have studied all the diatonic triads from the melodic minor modes in all keys and inversions, try these sequential patterns. All these written exercises are in the key of C.

1. Ascending diatonic broken triads (melodic minor modes) across the whole range of the instrument followed by descending diatonic broken triads back down to the starting note.

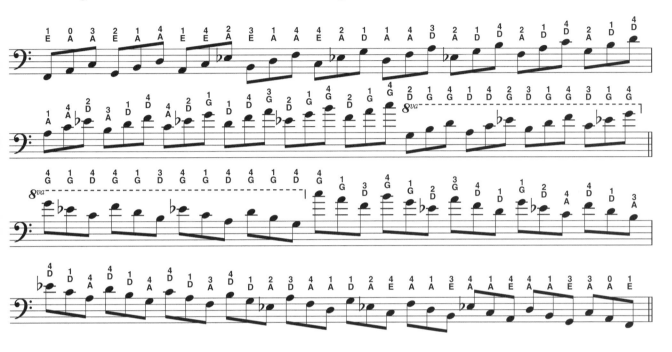

Learn this pattern in all keys.

2. Ascending up one diatonic broken triad from the melodic minor modes followed by a descending diatonic broken triad across the whole range of the instrument. Reverse the pattern on the way back down the octave.

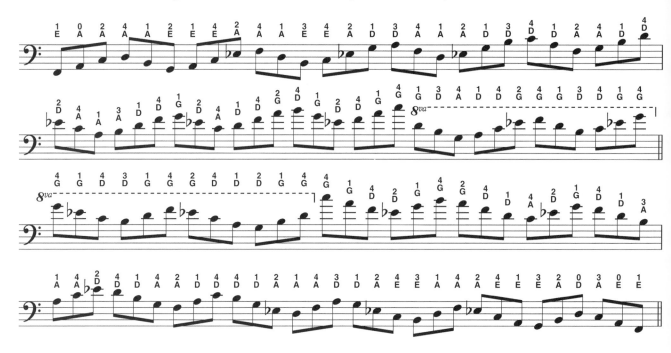

Learn this pattern in all keys.

Recap of Whole Range Triad Patterns from the Melodic Minor Modes

As we did with the triad patterns for the major modes, practise these whole range exercises from a slow tempo.

Make sure you memorise the fingering pattern, and as you play the sequence you should always be mindful of which triad you are playing and your position on the fretboard.

As always, practise at a slow tempo, repeating a few times without stopping (for maybe 5mins or so), and then gradually increase the tempo and repeat again. Play up to a challenging tempo, e.g. 120 bpm (on beats 2 and 4) , then move to the next exercise. Once you have played through

and studied each exercise, return to each and apply the concept in a musical way, repeating in all keys.

Set up a sustained drone or chord progression related to the key you are working with, and use a drum machine groove or metronome. Play once through the sequence along with the groove or metronome then improvise using the idea of the pattern along with scale fragments.

Practising in this way helps you to be musical and in control of your lines.

ESSENTIAL BASS LIBRARY

DAVE HOLLAND
Bitches Brew
(Miles Davis)
Columbia, 1969

Part 4

Melodic Minor Modes
4-Note Chords
Chord Changes
Tensions & Approaches To Chord Tones

4.1

CHAPTER 4.1

The Construction Of 4-Note Chords And Their Inversions For The Melodic Minor Modes

In this chapter we will discuss the construction of 4-note chords and their inversions found within the melodic minor modes.

The diatonic 4-note chords found within the melodic minor modes are built in the same way as the diatonic 4-note chords found within the major modes, by stacking three notes a diatonic 3rd above each other from the root.

C melodic minor

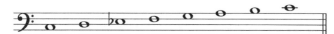

By stacking three diatonic 3rds related to the C melodic minor on each degree of the scale we can make each of the seven related diatonic 4-note chords found within the melodic minor modes.

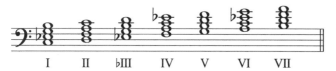

I   II   ♭III   IV   V   VI   VII

Once you analyse these 4-note chords you will notice there are five different chord quality types. They are minor (maj7), minor 7, major 7♯5, dominant 7 and minor 7♭5.

The I chord is a minor(maj7):

The II chord is a minor 7:

The ♭III chord is a major 7(♯5):

The IV and V chords are dominant 7:

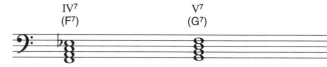

The VI and VII chords are minor 7(♭5):

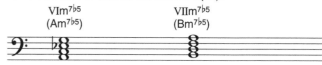

The VII chord can vary due to the minor and major 3rd intervals found within the scale.

B Super Locrian/Altered

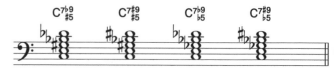

| 1 | ♭9 | ♯9 | 3 | ♯11 | ♭13 | ♭7 | 1 |
| 1 | ♭2 | ♭3 | 4 | ♭5 | ♭6 | ♭7 | 1 |

Here are a few chord voicings most commonly used for the 7alt chord. I am building the chords from the root C so you can clearly see the concept of altered tensions. Also, I am using 5-note chords so you can hear the tension.

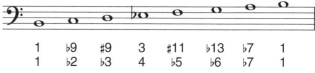

The most common use of the 7th chord of the melodic minor modes is the VII7alt. The alt implies the altered tensions ♭9, ♯9, ♯11, ♭13, ♭5, ♯5.

Review of Diatonic 4-Note Chords found within the Melodic Minor Modes in Various Keys

Example 1

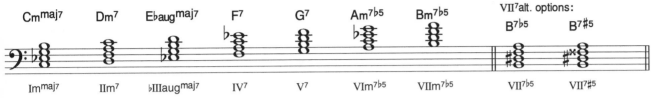

Example 2

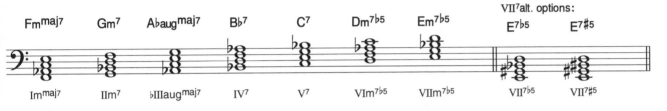

Example 3

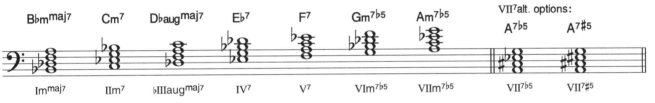

Example 4

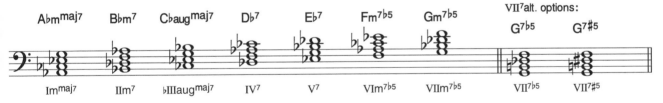

Reviewing and Practising 4-Note Chords from the Melodic Minor Modes

After you have studied and learned all the diatonic 4-note chords from the melodic minor modes in all keys try putting together sequences. This will help you be more fluent and melodic with these chords and scales.

We will use the m7b5 chord for the seventh mode. It is stacked in diatonic 3rds and fits with the sequence more fluently. The uses for the 7alt chords will be explained in a later chapter. All these exercises are written in the key of C.

1. Ascending diatonic 4-note broken chords related to the melodic minor modes across the whole range of the instrument followed by descending diatonic 4-note broken chords back down to the starting note. Begin this exercise moving from the lowest note available within the key up to the highest note then returning back down the fretboard.

Learn this pattern in all keys.

2. Ascending up one diatonic 4-note broken chord from the melodic minor modes followed by a descending diatonic 4-note broken chord across the whole range of the instrument. Reverse the pattern on the way back down to the starting note.

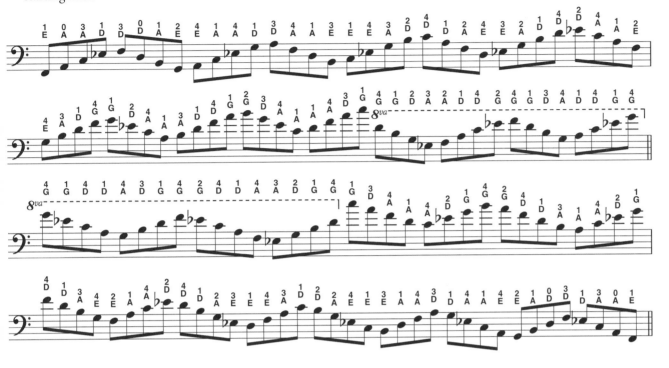

Learn this pattern in all keys.

Practise these fluency exercises as you did for the diatonic 4-note chord patterns related to the major modes. Remember these are my fingering patterns suited to my way of playing. If they are uncomfortable and unnatural to your way of playing, write out your own.

As before, repeat each of these exercises 5 times without stopping at one tempo before increasing the tempo. Work to a challenging tempo, in all keys, and then try incorporating the patterns into your improvisations.

ESSENTIAL
BASS LIBRARY

PETER IND

The Artistry Of Kenny Barron
(Peter Ind and Kenny Barron)
Wave, 1998

4.2

CHAPTER 4.2

Moving 4-Note Chords From The Melodic Minor Modes Through Non-Related Chord Changes (Melodic Minor Harmony)

In this chapter you will learn how to tackle playing through a series of non-related chords from the melodic minor modes within a progression.

We will be playing through these changes using sequential ascending and descending 4-note chords. As the chord changes within the progression, build a diatonic 4-note chord off the next available note within the related chord scale. It applies the same concept we have used in previous linear soloing chapters.

In this chapter we will also be combining chords from the major modes along with chords from the melodic minor modes. Regarding the seventh mode of the melodic minor modes, for the 7alt chord we will be using the m7♭5 chord from the sequential 4-note chord patterns.

Exercise 1

We will take two non-related chords both from the melodic minor modes (but from different keys), and play ascending and descending diatonic 4-note chords related to the particular key and set of modes.

As you reach the point of the chord change, the next available scale tone ascending or descending related to that particular chord scale will become your root or seventh degree of the chord.

The first two chords we will use for Exercise 1 are Cm(maj7) and A7#11. These two chords are both derived from the melodic minor modes but are from different keys.

For the Cmmaj7 chord I am using the C melodic minor scale which is the first mode of the C melodic minor modes. For the A7#11 chord I am using the A Lydian ♭7 chord scale which is built off the fourth mode of the E melodic minor modes.

C melodic minor (Cmmaj7)

C melodic minor modes

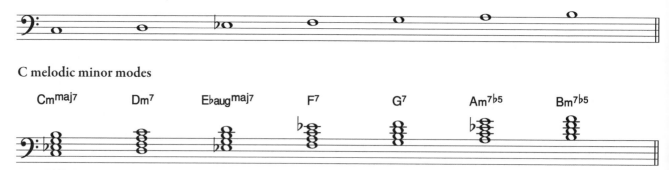

A Lydian ♭7 (A7#11)

E melodic minor modes

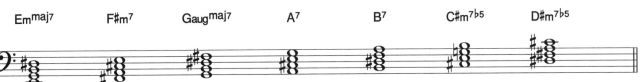

Continue this exercise for as long as you wish. Try to use as much of the fretboard as possible. Change direction of the line randomly to avoid repeating chords already used.

Exercise 2

In Exercise 1 the rate of the chord change is every two bars. In this Exercise 2 the rate of the chord change is every bar. The chords remain Cm^maj7 and A7#11.

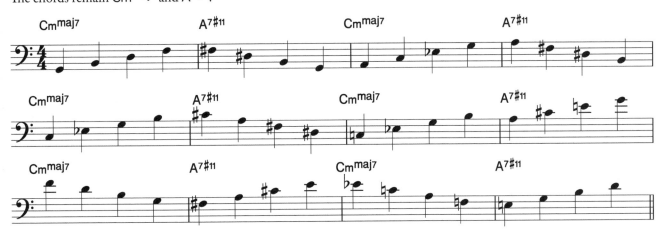

The chord progressions used in this chapter are the same ones used in the chapter Linear Solo Concepts For Diatonic Melodic Minor Harmony. However, I strongly advise you to create your own chord progressions.

ESSENTIAL BASS LIBRARY

CHUCK ISRAELS

Time To Remember (Live In Europe 1965-1972) (Bill Evans) Natasha, 1969

Exercise 3

For Exercise 3 we will use six different chords from the melodic minor modes and the major modes:
B♭maj7, A7♭13, Dm7, D♭7♯11, Cm7 and F7alt.

Here are the chord scales that will be used for each chord.

B♭maj7	B♭ Lydian which is the fourth mode of F major.
A7♭13	A Mixolydian ♭6 which is the fifth mode of D melodic minor.
Dm7	D Dorian which is the second mode of C major.
D♭7♯11	D♭ Lydian ♯11 which is the fourth mode of the A♭ melodic minor.
Cm7	C Dorian which is the second mode of B♭ major.
F7alt	F Altered (Super Locrian) which is the seventh mode of G♭ melodic minor.

F major modes

B♭ Lydian (B♭maj7)

F major modes

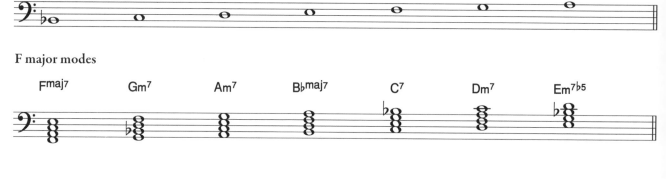

A Myxolydian ♭6 (A7♭13)

D melodic minor modes

D Dorian (Dm7)

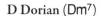

C major modes

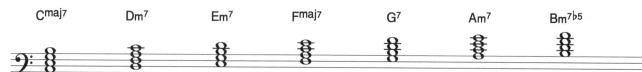

Db Lydian b7 (D7#11)

Ab melodic minor modes

Abm maj7   Bbm7   Cbaug maj7   Dbmaj7   Eb7   Fm7b5   Gm7b5

C Dorian (Cm7)

Bb major modes

Bbmaj7   Cm7   Dm7   Ebmaj7   F7   Gm7   Am7b5

F Altered (Super Locrian) (F7alt)

Gb melodic minor modes

Gbm7   Abm7   Bbbmaj7   Cb7   Dbm7   Ebm7b5   Fbmaj7

Bbmaj7   A7b13

Dm7   Db7#11   Cm7   F7alt.

Bbmaj7   A7b13

Dm7   Db7#11   Cm7   F7alt.

143

4.3

CHAPTER 4.3

Tensions And Upper Structures For The Chords Found Within The Melodic Minor Modes

The harmony and colour with the melodic minor modes is very different to the major modes. There is a lot more tension and dissonance found in the upper structures, which makes for some interesting sounds.

Cm(maj7)—C melodic minor

Here is the first mode C melodic minor built in diatonic 3rds.

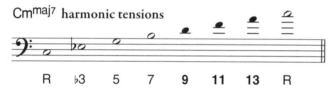

Cm^{maj7} harmonic tensions

R ♭3 5 7 9 11 13 R

Once we arrive back at C the cycle begins again. Each of these tensions is a harmonic tension and a whole step above a chord tone.

Tension 9 is a D which is a whole step from the Root (C).

Tension 11 is an F which is a whole step from the ♭3 (Eb).

Tension 13 is an A which is a whole step from the 5th (G).

If you look at the sequence of notes you can see the different arpeggios which include the harmonic tensions.

E♭maj7♯5	gives us the tension 9.
G7	gives us the tensions 9 and 11.
Bm7♭5	gives us the tensions 9, 11 and 13.
Dm7	gives us the tensions 9, 11 and 13.
F7	gives us the tensions 9, 11 and 13.
Am7♭5	gives us the tensions 9, 11 and 13.

You can superimpose these chords over a Cm^{maj7} to provide colour for the harmony.

As mentioned in the Major Harmony Upper Extensions section, a bassist, guitarist or pianist accompanying a soloist would cover the chord tones, and so playing and arpeggiating these upper structures would add a lot of separation and colour to the solo.

You can practise these tensions along with a sustained drone or Cm^{maj7} chord so that you can clearly hear the sound of the chord with tensions. Remember that this is

an ear training exercise and not a technical one. Make sure you play along with a sustained drone or chord so that you can hear the chord tones and upper structures. As before, try starting on a single string.

Play in order the lowest available chord tone or tension up to the highest available chord tone or tension then return back in order to the lowest.

On the E string the lowest available chord tone or tension for Cm^{maj7} is F which is tension 11. In order the chord tones and tensions on the E string will be:

11 13 RT ♭3 5 7 9 11 etc.

Ascend all the way up the string to the highest tension or chord tone available and from there descend back to where you started.

Next, repeat this exercise starting from the 2nd lowest chord tone or tension available. After F the next available chord tone or tension will be a G which is the 5th of the chord.

The 2nd pattern on the E string is as follows:

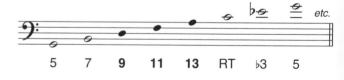

5 7 9 11 13 RT ♭3 5 etc.

Again, ascend up in order to the highest chord tone or tension back to where you started. From here, repeat this 2 part exercise across each string.

Remember to play along with a drone or sustained chord to help you hear the colours you are creating. Remember this is not a technical exercise. It is an ear training and awareness exercise.

D13sus4♭9 (D Dorian ♭2)

The second mode of the C melodic minor modes is a D Dorian ♭2 chord. The diatonic 4-note chord for this scale is a Dm⁷. If we keep building the Dm⁷ up in diatonic 3rds related to the C melodic minor we will see the tensions that are created.

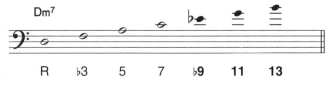

The natural tensions on this chord are ♭9, 11 and 13. The ♭9 in this chord sounds harsh and dissonant but tensions 11 and 13 sound fine and are acceptable. However, this is very similar to the tensions we chose to use in the Dm⁷ from the C major modes and does not reflect the special sound of the melodic minor tonality.

A common and interesting chord commonly used to represent the second mode of the melodic minor modes is a sus ♭9 13 chord. Here is a good voicing for the D¹³♭⁹ˢᵁˢ⁴ chord.

Here is the D¹³♭⁹ˢᵁˢ⁴ chord spelt out in order.

Apply these chord tones and tensions to the single string exercise. Start in order from the lowest available chord tone or tension up to the highest available chord tone or tension and descend back down in order.

In order the chord tones and tensions for the D¹³♭⁹ˢᵁˢ⁴ chord on the E string will be:

There is no need to repeat this exercise from the next lowest chord tone or tension as it is an A, which (like G) is a chord tone and the sequence it creates is the same as the first one.

However, on the A string the 2-part exercise applies as the lowest chord tone or tension available is an (A), which is the 5th. The next available chord tone or tension is a (B) which is tension (13).

The order for the D¹³♭⁹ˢᵁˢ⁴ on the A string is:

From the next lowest the order will be:

Repeat this exercise across all strings. If you look at the sequence of notes you can see the different arpeggios which include the harmonic tensions.

Here are the different upper structure arpeggios you can superimpose over this chord D¹³♭⁹ˢᵁˢ⁴:

Am⁷♭⁵	gives us tensions ♭9 and 11
Cm^maj7	gives us tensions ♭9, 11 and 13
E♭maj7♯5	gives us tensions ♭9, 11 and 13
G	gives us tensions 11 and 13

You can superimpose these arpeggios over D¹³♭⁹ˢᵁˢ⁴ to create colour and tension.

Ebmaj7♯5 (E♭ major ♯5♯11)

The next chord we will look at is built off the third mode and is an augmented major 7 chord. In the C melodic minor modes the diatonic 4-note chord is E♭maj7♯5. If we keep building the 4-note chord in diatonic 3rds we can see the upper structure tensions it creates.

E♭maj7♯5 built in diatonic 3rds related to the C melodic minor.

1   3   ♯5   7   9   ♯11   13

The natural tensions are 9, ♯11 and 13.

While the 9 and ♯11 sound pleasant and interesting to the ear, the tension 13 sounds a little more dissonant.

However, is played in the right order this chord with all added natural tensions can work well. Listen to these two voicings for E♭maj7♯5 with all added tensions.

In the second example tension 13 is buried in the middle of the voicing and adds a nice interesting sound.

The first example with the C on top sounds a little more dissonant.

On the E string the lowest available tension or chord tone for the chord E♭maj7♯5 is F. In order the chord tones and tensions available on the E string will be:

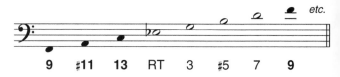

9   ♯11   13   RT   3   ♯5   7   9

Next you can repeat this exercise starting from the second available chord tone or tension. After F, the next available chord tone or tension will be a G which is the 3rd of the chord.

The 2nd pattern on the E string will be as follows:

3   ♯5   7   9   ♯11   13   RT   3

Repeat these exercises across all strings.

Beware: the tension 13 (C) on the maj7♯5 chord in this case is E♭maj7♯5 creates a high level of dissonance, so try the following superimpositions out and apply them the way you hear them.

Here are the different upper structure arpeggios you can superimpose over this chord E♭maj7♯5:

Gmaj7	gives us the tension 9
Bm7♭5	gives us tensions 9 and ♯11
Dm7	gives us tensions 9, ♯11 and 13
F7	gives us tensions 9, ♯11 and 13
Am7♭5	gives us tensions 9, ♯11 and 13
Cmmaj7	gives us tension 13

F7#11 (F Lydian ♭7)

The next chord we will look at is built off the fourth mode of melodic minor and is a dominant 7 chord.

In the C melodic minor modes the diatonic 4-note chord built off the fourth degree is an F⁷. If we keep building the 4-note chord in diatonic 3rds we can see the upper structure tensions it creates.

F⁷ built in diatonic 3rds related to the C melodic minor

RT   3   5   ♭7   **9**   **#11**   **13**

The natural tensions are 9, #11 and 13.

This chord F⁷#11 is a great and very commonly used chord in jazz harmony. These tensions can be used to outline any dominant 7 chord.

On the E string the lowest available tension or chord tone for the F⁷#11 is an F (root).

In order the chord tones and tensions available on the E string will be:

RT   3   5   ♭7   **9**   **#11**   **13**   RT

Next repeat this exercise from the second lowest available chord tone or tension.

After F the next available chord tone or tension will be a G which is tension 9.

The second pattern on the E string will be as follows:

9   **#11**   **13**   RT   3   5   ♭7   **9**

Repeat these exercises across all strings.

Here are the different upper structure arpeggios you can superimpose over this chord F⁷#11.

Am⁷♭5	gives us tension 9
Cm^maj7	gives us tensions 9 and #11
E♭maj7#5	gives us tensions 9, #11 and 13
G⁷	gives us tensions 9, #11 and 13
Bm⁷♭5	gives us tensions 9, #11 and 13
Dm⁷	gives us tension 13

ESSENTIAL
BASS LIBRARY

PAUL JACKSON

Headhunters
(Herbie Hancock)
Columbia, 1973

G7♭13 (G Mixolydian ♭13)

The next chord we will look at is built off the fifth mode of melodic minor and is a dominant 7 chord.

In the C melodic minor modes the diatonic 4-note chord built off the fifth degree is a **G⁷**. If we keep building the 4-note chord in diatonic 3rds we can see the upper structure tensions it creates.

G⁷ built in diatonic 3rds related to the C melodic minor

The natural tensions are 9, 11 and ♭13.

Tension 11 is considered an avoid note due to the clash and contradiction of functionality with the third degree. As with all major 7 or dominant 7 chords the tension 11 is usually avoided in the chord structure and functions as a scale or passing tone.

The **G⁷(♭13/9)** chord is not so commonly used due to the high level of dissonance. 7 ♭9/♭13, 7 9/13, ♭9/13, 7alt chords are more commonly used. However, **G⁷(♭13/9)** also functions as an extended dominant chord and will be discussed later.

The diatonic tensions available on the V⁷ chord related to the melodic minor modes are 9 and ♭13.

Am7♭5 (A Aeolian ♭5)

The next chord we will look at is built off the sixth mode of melodic minor and is a minor 7♭5. In the C melodic minor modes the diatonic 4-note chord built off the sixth degree is an **Am⁷♭⁵**.

If we keep building the 4-note chord in diatonic 3rds we can see the upper structure tensions it creates. **Am⁷♭⁵** built in diatonic 3rds related to the C melodic minor.

The natural tensions are 9, 11 and ♭13. All of these diatonic tensions sound great when stacked on top of one another. These tensions work great over any m7♭5 chord, providing the melody allows for it.

On the E string the lowest available tension or chord tone for the **Am⁷♭⁵** is an F (♭13). In order, the chord tones and tensions available on the E string will be:

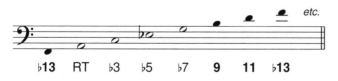

On the E string the lowest available tension or chord tone for the **G⁷♭¹³** is an F (7th).

In order the chord tones and tensions available on the E string will be:

After F the next available chord tone or tension will be a G which is the root.

The second pattern on the E string will be as follows:

Repeat these exercises across all strings.

Here are the different upper structure arpeggios you can superimpose over the chord **G⁷♭¹³**:

Bm⁷♭⁵	gives us tension 9
Dm	gives us tension 9
E♭maj7♯5	gives us tension ♭13

After F the next available chord tone or tension will be a G (♭7). The second pattern on the E string will be:

Repeat these exercises across all strings.

Here are the different arpeggios you can superimpose over the chord **Am⁷♭⁵**:

Cm^maj7	gives us tension 9
E♭maj7♯5	gives us tensions 9 and 11
G⁷	gives us tensions 9, 11 and ♭13
Bm⁷♭⁵	gives us tensions 9, 11 and ♭13
Dm⁷	gives us tensions 11 and ♭13
F⁷	gives us tension ♭13

ESSENTIAL
BASS LIBRARY

PAUL JACKSON

*Everybody Come
On Out*
(Stanley Turrentine)
Fantasy, 1976

B7alt (B Super Locrian/B Altered)

The last chord we will look at is built off the seventh mode of the C melodic minor modes.

This mode is a little different from the others in that when you build it in diatonic 3rds it spells out a Bm7♭5 chord which does not really give us the true colour of the altered sound.

As we saw in the chord construction chapter the altered scale has both the intervals of a minor 3rd and a major 3rd giving us the choice of chords.

In the diatonic fluency exercises I am using the m7♭5 chord as that is the chord which is spelt out in the stacked diatonic 3rds.

This works well in sequential patterns. For these exercises we will focus on the diatonic chords and their upper structure tensions that represent the colour and characteristics of the modes in question.

For the B7alt we will use two different altered 4-note chords to represent this chord scale.

The first consists of a root, 3rd, ♭5 and ♭7.

The second consists of a root, 3rd, ♯5 and ♭7

Here are the two altered 4-note chords.

Here are the two B7alt chords with tensions.

The natural tensions are ♭9, ♯9 and ♭13. All of these tensions are available and make an interesting dominant functioning altered chord.

On the E string the lowest available chord tone or tension for the B7alt (with ♭5) is an F (♭5). In order, the chord tones and tensions available on the E string will be:

After F the next lowest available chord tone or tension will be a G (♭13). The 2nd pattern on the E string will be:

Repeat these exercises in all keys.

Here is the 2nd B7alt chord using the ♯5 with tensions B7alt.

The natural tensions this time are ♭9, ♯9 and ♯11. Again, all tensions are available and make an interesting dominant functioning altered chord.

On the E string the lowest available chord tone or tension for the B7alt (with ♯5) is an E♯ (♯11). In order, the chord tones and tensions available on the E string will be:

After E♯ the next available chord tone or tension will be an F♯♯ (♯5). F♯♯ is an enharmonic (same note) as G. In order the chord tones and tensions available on the E string will be:

Here are the different arpeggios you can superimpose over the B7alt.

Fmaj	gives us tension ♭9
Fmaj6	gives us tensions ♭9 and ♯9
G7♯5	gives us tension ♭13

Here is a recap of all the 4-note chords and commonly used tensions discussed so far:

Major 7	9, ♯11, 13
Minor 7	9, 11, 13
Dominant 7	♭9, ♯9, ♯11, ♭13
Minor 7♭5	9, 11, ♭13
Major 7♯5	9, ♯11, 13
Dominant 7Sus4 ♭9/13	♭9, 11, 13

Practise playing the upper structure tensions over these cycle of 5ths m(maj7) chords.

Cycle of 5ths minor (maj7) chords with tensions (9, 11, 13), in all keys, from root

Cycle of 5ths 7sus4 ♭9/13 chords (♭9, 11, 13), in all keys, from root

Cycle of 5ths maj7#5 chords with tensions (9, #11, 13), in all keys, from root

ESSENTIAL
BASS LIBRARY

**ALPHONSO
JOHNSON**

Mysterious Traveller
(Weather Report)
Columbia, 1974

Cycle of 5ths 7#11 chords with tensions (9, #11, 13), in all keys, from root

Cycle of 5ths 7♭13 chords with tensions (9, ♭13), in all keys, from root

Cycle of 5ths m7♭5 chords with tensions (9,11, ♭13), in all keys, from root

ESSENTIAL
BASS LIBRARY

BILL JOHNSON

*The Complete
Johnny Dodds*
(Johnny Dodds)
RCA, 1929

Cycle of 5ths 7alt chords with tensions (chord tones R, 3, ♭5, ♭7; tensions ♭9, ♯9, ♭13), in all keys, from root

Cycle of 5ths 7alt chords with different tensions (chord tones R, 3, ♯5, ♭7; tensions ♭9, ♯9, ♯11), in all keys, from root

Practise playing diatonic 4-note chords plus upper structure tensions from the melodic minor modes from the third degree of the chord.

Cycle of 5ths m(maj7) chords with tensions (9, 11, 13), in all keys, from third degree

ESSENTIAL
BASS LIBRARY

MARC JOHNSON

Bass Desires
(Marc Johnson)
ECM, 1985

Cycle of 5ths 13sus4♭9 chords with tensions (♭9, 11, 13), in all keys, from fourth degree

Cycle of 5ths maj7♯5 chords with tensions (9, ♯11, 13), in all keys, from third degree

Cycle of 5ths 7♯11 chords with tensions (9, ♯11, 13), in all keys, from third degree

ESSENTIAL
BASS LIBRARY

MARC JOHNSON

*Turn Out The Stars:
The Final Village
Vanguard Recordings*
(Bill Evans)
Dreyfus, 1980

Cycle of 5ths 7♭13 chords with tensions (9, ♭13), in all keys, from third degree

Cycle of 5ths m7♭5 chords with tensions (tensions 9, 11, ♭13), in all keys, from third degree

Cycle of 5ths 7alt chords with tensions (chord tones R, 3, ♭5, ♭7; tensions ♭9, #9, ♭13), in all keys, from third degree

Cycle of 5ths 7alt chords with different tensions (chord tones R, 3, #5, ♭7; tensions ♭9, #9, #11), in all keys, from third degree

Only diatonic tensions over this cycle of 5ths m(maj7) progression

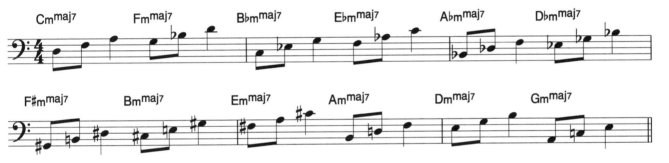

Only diatonic tensions over this cycle of 5ths 7sus4 ♭9/13 progression

Only diatonic tensions over this cycle of 5ths maj7#5 progression

Only diatonic tensions over this cycle of 5ths 7♯11 progression

Only diatonic tensions over this cycle of 5ths 7♭13 progression

Only diatonic tensions over this cycle of 5ths m7♭5 progression

Only diatonic tensions over this 7alt progression (♭9, ♯9, ♯11, ♭13)

ESSENTIAL
BASS LIBRARY

SAM JONES
Eastern Rebellion,
Vol. 1
(Eastern Rebellion)
Timeless, 1975

Play the available diatonic tensions over this cycle of 5ths diatonic chord progression from the melodic minor modes.

For the alt 7 chord choose between the two chords or repeat the exercise and use both.

Play the exercise in all keys.

Play the available diatonic tensions from the 3rd of the chord, over this cycle of 5ths diatonic chord progression from the melodic minor modes.

Play the exercise in all keys.

Only play the available diatonic tensions over this cycle of 5ths diatonic chord progression from the melodic minor modes. Use all tensions for the 7alt chord.

Play the exercise in all keys.

MELODIC MINOR TENSIONS RECAP

Now we have looked at harmonic, diatonic, available and avoid note tensions for major harmony and melodic minor harmony. I really do not like the term avoid note as it implies that note is to be avoided. All 12 notes are available; it is just about understanding how they sound and how they can be applied. The modes of melodic minor carry a lot more tension and dissonance.

Understanding and applying the exercises discussed in this chapter can really help you learn how to control the sound and be free to make any choices you may wish to make. I recommend you use all these exercises primarily as ear training exercises. You have to be able to hear these upper structures and how they work. Get them inside your ears and hands to open up your options.

ESSENTIAL
BASS LIBRARY

DARYL JONES
Live In Tokyo 1986
(Steps Ahead)
NYC, 1986

4.4

CHAPTER 4.4

Approach to Target Note Exercises for Chords found within the Melodic Minor Modes

As we did for the chords found within the major modes we will apply different approach techniques for the chords found within the melodic minor modes. When improvising or writing melodies, the strongest reference we have is the chord we are playing or writing on, and the strongest way to outline a chord in through its chord tones.

We have looked at the upper structure tensions which help us add colour to the chords and harmony. Now let us look at different ways to approach the different chord tones with use of scale and chromatic notes. This is another great tool to have when creating tension and pattern to your lines.

The following exercises are related to the ones we studied for the chords found within the major modes. This approach can be heard in jazz and be bop by some of the greats. With care and diligence you can expand your ears and knowledge of harmony with these exercises helping you to create some great and interesting solos.

UPPER APPROACH (DIATONIC)

Here are all the upper approaches for all the diatonic chords found within the melodic minor modes. I am building each chord off the root C.

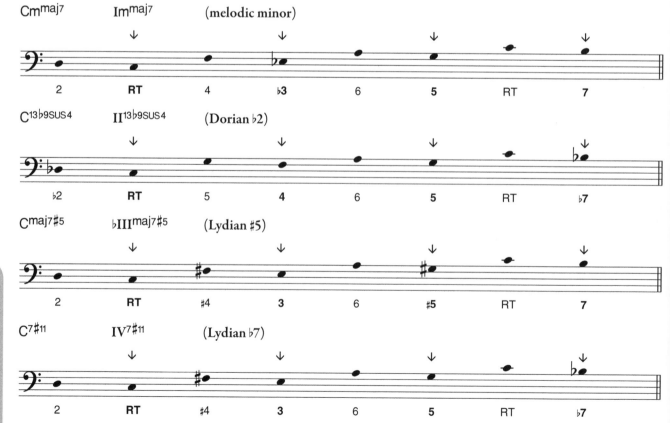

ESSENTIAL
BASS LIBRARY

TOM KENNEDY
Basses Loaded
(Tom Kennedy)
TKM, 1996

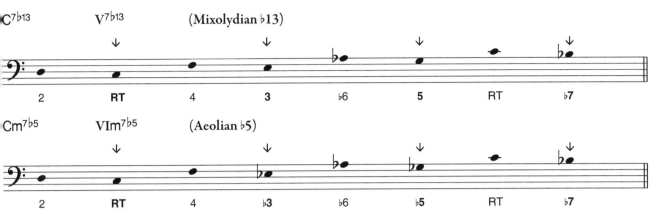

C7b13 — V7b13 — (Mixolydian b13)

2 — RT — 4 — 3 — b6 — 5 — RT — b7

Cm7b5 — VIm7b5 — (Aeolian b5)

2 — RT — 4 — b3 — b6 — b5 — RT — b7

For the 7alt chord, as with the upper structure exercise, we will use two variations:

(RT, 3, b5, b7) and (RT, 3, #5, b7)

We will analyse both in these exercises.

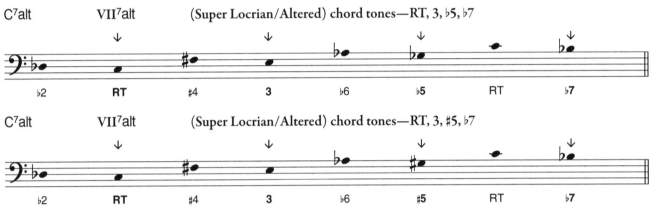

C7alt — VII7alt — (Super Locrian/Altered) chord tones—RT, 3, b5, b7

b2 — RT — #4 — 3 — b6 — b5 — RT — b7

C7alt — VII7alt — (Super Locrian/Altered) chord tones—RT, 3, #5, b7

b2 — RT — #4 — 3 — b6 — #5 — RT — b7

As with the major harmony exercises we will practise these target note chord exercises in four ways.

Part 1: Single String

As before, I think it is a good idea to treat these exercises and sounds as an ear training study.

Again, playing across single strings helps to:

- play in unfamiliar areas of the fretboard;
- not approach these concepts in a patterned structure;
- play as an ear training exercise rather than a technical one due to the physical limitations of playing on a single string.

Of course, it is important to be able to play these concepts fluently all over the finger-board and as memorable shapes and patterns. However, if you only work on memorizing these shapes and patterns, this may restrict you in being able to hear and understand what you are playing. The goal of this book is to help you understand and hear things to help you make personal choices and to find your own voice as an improvising musician.

Playing these single string exercises along with a drone or sustained chord will help you reference what you are playing against the harmony you are playing against.

The upper approach exercise across the whole range of the E string using Cm maj7 (melodic minor)

Move from the lowest available upper approach note (resolving onto the chord tone), play in sequence up to the highest available upper approach note, and back down.

The order will be:

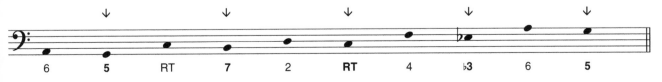

6 — 5 — RT — 7 — 2 — RT — 4 — b3 — 6 — 5

Practise for all the diatonic chords found within the melodic minor modes in all keys across all strings. For the 7alt chord use both of the chord structure variations.

ESSENTIAL
BASS LIBRARY

JOHN KIRBY

The Biggest Little Band
(John Kirby Sextet)
Smithsonian, 1937-1941

Part 2: Write Melody/Improv

Next, I want you to write a simple melody consisting of the target note exercise you are working on along with scale fragments from the related scale. I then want you to use your melody as a starting point of reference for your own improvisations.

This is the part where you can create your own style as a writer and improviser. Once you learn any of the exercises or patterns in this book I feel it is really important to express the studied concept in a musical context. For now, try to keep as much of the concept as possible in your improvisations—this will engrain the sound of the shape into your playing. Again, the use of a sustained drone or related chord is important as it gives you a great reference so you can hear the concept in question clearly.

Play your melody and improvisations over a variety of tempos, slow to fast, over the entire range of the fretboard.

Again, use the same study methods as discussed before. Do not try to perfect your improvisations before moving on. Just make sure you are comfortable applying the concept. There are many chords and scales to work through and you will improve as you advance.

It is really an ongoing study. Just remember to focus on your goal as you practise. Do not over do it and limit your study time on one particular lesson type to 30 minutes a day. This will help you stay fresh and give yourself the time to absorb the information you are working on. Just remember to keep some sort of study diary so when you stop you can continue from that point next time you resume the particular study lesson.

Here is an example of a melody using scale fragments and the upper approach pattern.

Example using Cm^{maj7} (Im^{maj7}) (melodic minor)

Repeat this concept for all the chords found within the melodic minor modes in all keys.

Part 3: Diatonic Cycle of 5ths Progression

The cycle of 5ths progression covers each of the chords found within the melodic minor modes and is a great way to practise the approach exercise.

Next, halve the duration of the chord progression and randomly apply two of the chord tone approaches instead of all four. Practise this concept again at various tempos, slow to fast and repeat the cycle 2 to 3 times covering as

much of the fretboard as possible. Also once completed, try improvising scale fragments along with the approach concept over the progressions.

Here is the upper approach pattern over a diatonic cycle of 5ths progression from the melodic minor harmony in the key of C. Again choose one of the two 7alt chords.

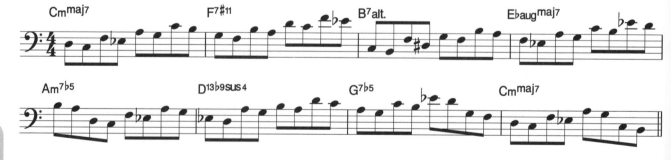

Halve the duration of the chord progression and randomly play any two of the patterns over each chord within the form.

Practise these progressions in all keys. Once finished improvise over these progressions with the approach to chord tone in question as your concept.

Part 4: IIm7♭5-V7alt-Im(maj7)

Lastly, we will use the minor II–V–I progression as a platform to practise these approach exercises. Practise these approach exercises in all keys, again at various tempos. As with the Linear Exercises, each chord comes from a different key. The m7♭5 uses the Aeolian (♭5) scale, 7alt uses the Super Locrian/Altered scale and the m(maj7) uses the melodic minor scale.

For this exercise I will alternate the choice of V^7 alt chord, but you should repeat the progression so you can use both variations.

Practise this concept over some standards.

ESSENTIAL
BASS LIBRARY

SCOTT LaFARO

*Newport Jazz
Festival*
(Stan Getz)
Raretone, 1961

LOWER APPROACH (CHROMATIC)

We will now to look at practising lower (chromatic) approaches. Here are all the lower approach patterns for all the diatonic chords found within the melodic minor modes, each chord build from the root (C).

Part 1: Single String

The order for the lower approach using Cm^{maj7} on the E string will be:

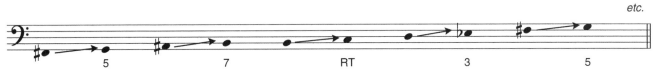

Move from the lowest available lower approach note, in sequence up to the highest available lower approach note, then returning back down to the lowest. Repeat this exercise on each string and for each of the diatonic chords found within the melodic minor modes, and practise in all keys. Remember the single string exercise is more of an ear training exercise rather than a technical one—use a sustained chord or drone.

Part 2: Melody/Improv

Here is an example of a melody over C^{7#11} using scale fragments and the lower approach pattern.

Repeat for all chord types in all keys found within the melodic minor modes.

Use this or your own melody as a basis for your own improvisations.

Part 3: Diatonic Cycle of 5ths Progression

Here are the lower approach patterns over a diatonic cycle of 5ths progression from the C melodic minor modes.

Next halve the duration of the chord progression and randomly choose two of the chromatic approaches for each chord.

Practise these diatonic cycle of 5ths progressions found within the melodic minor modes in all keys.

Try improvising over this progression using scale fragments and the approach patterns you are working on.

Part 4: IIm7♭5-V7alt-Im(maj7) in all keys

Lower approach over a minor II–V–I progression from the melodic minor modes in all keys.

Practise and improvise this concept over some standards.

UPPER-LOWER APPROACH

This next approach concept is a combination of the first two we look at, using both the upper (diatonic) approach and the lower (chromatic) approach to the chord tone. Here are the approaches over all the available diatonic chords found within the melodic minor modes.

Part 1: Single String

The order for the upper-lower approach using $C^{maj7\#5}$ across the E string will be:

6   **5**   RT   **7**   2   **RT**   4   ♭**3**

Move from the lowest available target note pattern in order up to the highest available target note pattern and back down. Repeat this process across each string for each of the chord types found within the melodic minor modes in all keys.

Part 2: Melody/Improv

Here is an example of a melody over $Cm^{7♭5}$ using a combination of scale fragments and the upper-lower approach pattern.

Repeat for all chord types in all keys found within the melodic minor modes, and use this or your own melody as a basis for your improvisations.

Part 3: Diatonic Cycle of 5ths Progression

Here are the upper-lower approach patterns over a diatonic cycle of 5ths progression from the melodic minor modes.

ESSENTIAL
BASS LIBRARY

RALPH LAIRD

*Visions Of The
Emerald Beyond*
(Mahavishnu Orchestra)
Columbia, 1975

Halve the duration of the progression and randomly play any two of the upper-lower approach patterns over each chord within the form.

Practise both these diatonic cycle of 5ths progressions found within the melodic minor modes in all keys.

Try improvising over these progressions combining the use of scale fragments and the approach to target note exercise you are working with.

Part 4: IIm7♭5–V7alt–Im(maj7) in all keys

Upper-lower approach over a minor II–V–I progression from the melodic minor modes in all keys.

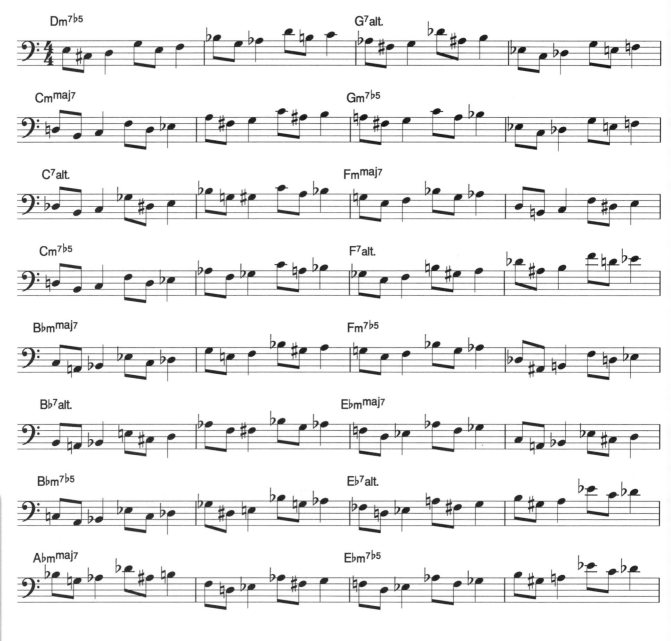

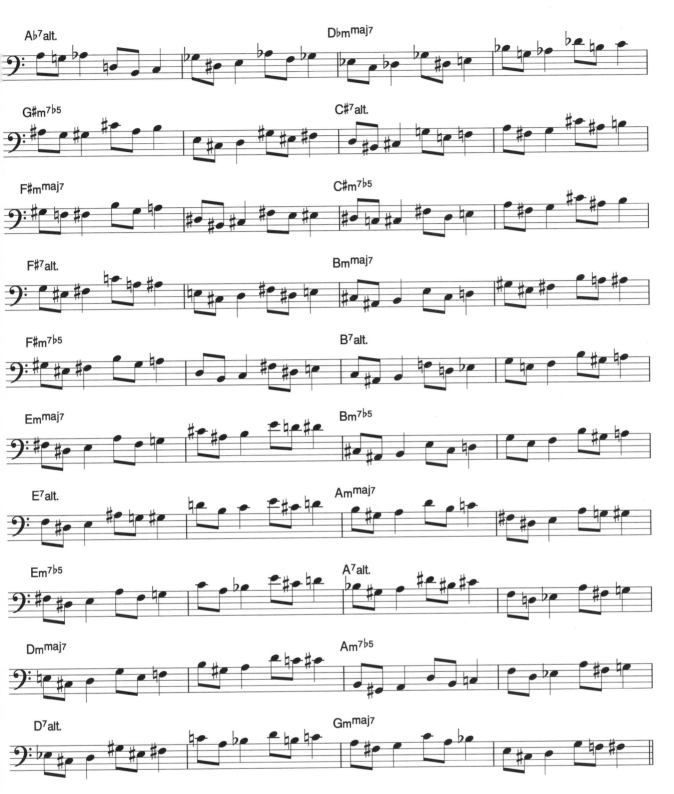

Practise and improvise this concept over some standards.

LOWER-UPPER APPROACH

This next approach is a variation of the previous one, combining the lower (chromatic) approach with the upper (diatonic) approach to the chord tone.

Part 1: Single String

The order for the lower-upper approach to chord tone using Cm^{maj7} across the E string will be:

Move from the lowest available target note pattern in order up to the highest available target note pattern and back down. Repeat this process across each string for each of the chord types found within the melodic minor modes in all keys.

Part 2: Melody/Improv

Here is an example of a melody over Cm^{maj7} using a combination of scale fragments and the lower-upper approach pattern.

Repeat for all chords types in all keys found within the melodic minor modes. Use this or your own melody as a basis for your own improvisations.

Part 3: Diatonic Cycle of 5ths Progression

Here are the lower-upper approach patterns over a diatonic cycle of 5ths progression from the C melodic minor modes.

ESSENTIAL
BASS LIBRARY

JYMIE MERRITT

Night In Tunisia
(Art Blakey)
Blue Note, 1960

Halve the duration of the progression and randomly play two of the lower-upper approaches patterns over each chord within the form.

Practise both these diatonic cycle of 5ths progressions found within the melodic minor modes in all keys.

Try improvising over these progressions combining the use of scale fragments and the approach to target note exercise you are working with.

Part 4: IIm7♭5-V7alt-Im(maj7) in all keys

Lower-upper approach over a minor II–V–I progression from the melodic minor modes in all keys.

Practise and improvise this concept over some standards.

ESSENTIAL
BASS LIBRARY

JYMIE MERRITT

Live At The Lighthouse
(Lee Morgan)
Blue Note, 1970

173

DOUBLE-UPPER APPROACH (CHROMATIC)

This next chord tone approach pattern is the double-upper chromatic approach. This approach pattern only works when the scale degree above the chord tone is a whole step away—as before, we will miss out approaches that do not apply.

Here are all the approaches over all the available diatonic chords found within the melodic minor modes. For the Cm^{maj7} chord we replace the seventh degree with the sixth.

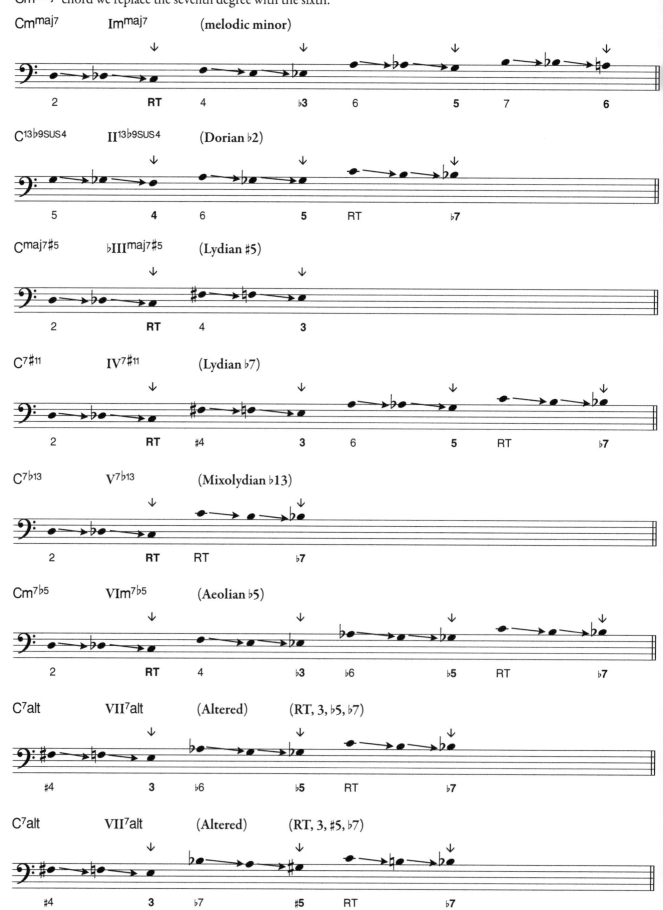

Part 1: Single String

The order for the double-upper chromatic approach using Cm^{maj7} across the E string will be:

Move from the lowest available target note pattern in order up to the highest target note pattern and back down. Repeat this process across each string for each of the chord types found within the melodic minor modes in all keys.

Part 2: Melody/Improv

Here is an example of a melody over C^{7alt} using a combination of scale fragments and the double-upper approach patterns.

Repeat for all chords types in all keys found within the melodic minor modes. Use this or your own melody as a basis for your own improvisations.

Part 3: Diatonic Cycle of 5ths Progression

Here are the double-upper approach patterns over a diatonic cycle of 5ths progression from the C melodic minor modes. We use the upper approach where the double-upper approach is not available.

Halve the duration of the progression and randomly play two of the double-upper chromatic approach patterns over each chord found within the form.

Practise both these diatonic cycle of 5ths progressions found within the melodic minor modes in all keys. Try improvising over these progressions combining the use of scale fragments and the approach to target note exercise you are working with.

Part 4: IIm7♭5–V7alt–Im(maj7) in all keys

Double-upper approach over a minor II–V–I progression from the melodic minor modes in all keys.

Again, we use the upper approach where the double-upper approach is not available.

Practise and improvise this concept over some standards.

DOUBLE-UPPER LOWER APPROACH (CHROMATIC)

As with the previous pattern (double-upper chromatic) this approach pattern only works when the scale degree above the chord tone is a whole step away, and so we will miss out the approach patterns that do not apply to these particular chords.

Here are all the double-upper lower chromatic approaches over all the available diatonic chords found within the melodic minor modes. As before, the seventh degree of the C^maj7 chord is replaced with the sixth.

Part 1: Single String

The order for the double-upper lower chromatic approach using Cm^maj7 across the E string will be:

Move from the lowest available target note pattern in order up to the highest available target note pattern and back down. Repeat this process across each string for each of the chord types found within the melodic minor modes in all keys.

Part 2: Melody/Improv

Here is an example of a melody over C7#11 using a combination of scale fragments and the double-upper lower chromatic approach pattern.

Repeat for all chords types in all keys found within the melodic minor modes. Use this or your own melody as a basis for your own improvisations.

Part 3: Diatonic Cycle of 5ths Progression

Here are the double-upper lower chromatic approach patterns over a diatonic cycle of 5ths progression from the C melodic minor modes.

We use the upper-lower approach patterns where the double-upper lower chromatic approach pattern is not available.

ESSENTIAL
BASS LIBRARY

MARCUS MILLER
Tutu
(Miles Davis)
Warner Brothers, 1986

Halve the duration of the progression and randomly play two of the double-upper lower chromatic approach pattern over each chord within the form.

Practise both these diatonic cycle of 5ths progressions found within the melodic minor modes in all keys. Try improvising over these progressions combining the use of scale fragments and the approach to target note exercise you are working with.

Part 4: IIm7♭5-V7alt-Im(maj7) in all keys

Double-upper lower chromatic approach over a minor II–V–I progression from the melodic minor modes in all keys. Again, I am using the scale above, chromatic below approach where the double-upper lower chromatic approach is not available.

Practise and improvise this concept over some standards.

LOWER DOUBLE-UPPER APPROACH (CHROMATIC)

The next and last chord tone approach pattern we will look at is the lower double-upper chromatic approach. As before, the approach pattern will only apply when the scale degree above the chord tone is a whole step away.

Here are all lower double-upper chromatic approach patterns over all the available diatonic chords found within the melodic minor modes.

For the Cm maj7 chord I am replacing the seventh degree with the sixth.

Part 1: Single String

The order for the lower double-upper approach using Cm^{maj7} across the E string will be:

Move from the lowest available target note pattern in order up to the highest available target note pattern and back down. Repeat this process across each string for each of the chord types found within the melodic minor modes in all keys.

Part 2: Melody/Improv

Here is an example of a melody over Cm^{maj7} using a combination of scale fragments and the lower double-upper approach pattern.

Repeat for all chords types in all keys found within the melodic minor modes. Use this or your own melody as a basis for your own improvisations.

Part 3: Diatonic Cycle of 5ths Progression

Here are the lower double-upper approach patterns over a diatonic cycle of 5ths progression from the C melodic minor modes. We will use the lower-upper approach pattern where the lower double-upper approach pattern is not available.

Halve the duration of the progression and randomly play two of the lower double-upper approach patterns over each chord within the form.

Practise both these diatonic cycle of 5ths progressions found within the melodic minor modes in all keys. Try improvising over these progressions combining the use of scale fragments and the approach to target note exercise you are working with.

Part 4: IIm7♭5–V7alt–Im(maj7) in all keys

Lower double-upper approach over a minor II–V–I progression from the melodic minor modes in all keys. Again, we use the lower-upper approach where the lower double-upper chromatic approach is not available.

Practise and improvise this concept over some standards.

ESSENTIAL
BASS LIBRARY

CHARLES MINGUS

Money Jungle
(Duke Ellington)
Blue Note, 1962

Part 5

Passing Tones

5.1

CHAPTER 5.1

Commonly Used Scales With Passing Tones

In this chapter I will be discussing the use of two commonly used scales with an added passing tone:

- Major Ionian scale
- Mixolydian scale

Each of these scales contains 7 notes

C major

C mixolydian

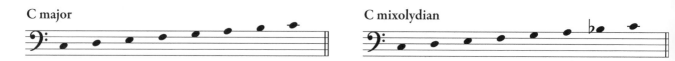

Let us now see each of these scales played as eighth-notes over 2 measures...

MAJOR SCALE WITH PASSING TONE

C major scale

As you can see the C major scale works perfectly over a C^maj7 chord. However, due to the odd number of scale degrees (seven) each time you change measure the scale will shift up one degree. By adding a passing tone to this 7-note scale will create a certain symmetry and flow to your phrasing.

In a major scale the passing tone is added between the fifth and sixth degrees.

C major scale with passing tone

Now let us look at this 8-note scale over 2 measures.

As you can see and hear in that example the major scale has a more musical flow to it. Because of the even number of scale degrees (eight) it repeats itself from the root every bar.

These scales with an added passing tone are commonly used in jazz and bebop.

Practise the ascending major scale with a passing tone over this cycle of 5ths maj7 progression.

Repeat the process this time using the descending major scale with a passing tone over this cycle of 5ths maj7 progression.

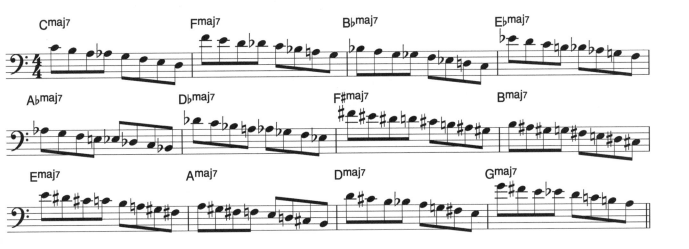

Next, play the whole major scale with passing tone ascending and descending over this cycle of 5ths maj7 progression Either use sixteenth-notes to create a double-time feel or continue using eighth-notes and elongate the rate of chord change to 2 measures each.

Here is the ascending and descending major scale with passing tone over this cycle of 5ths maj7 chord progression.

There are three different fingering patterns I want you to observe for the one octave major scale with passing tone.

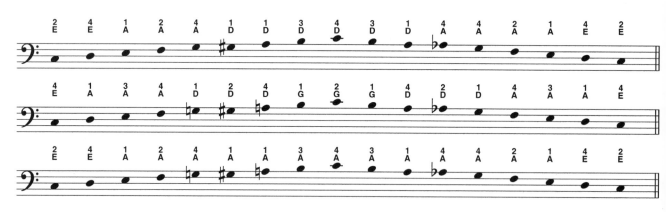

MIXOLYDIAN SCALE WITH PASSING TONE

The next scale we will look at is the Mixolydian scale with passing tone.

C Mixolydian

As you can see the C Mixolydian scale works perfectly over a C⁷ chord. However, again due to the odd number of scale degrees (seven) each time you change measure the scale will shift up one degree.

As before, the solution is to add a passing tone to this 7-note scale. In a Mixolydian scale the passing tone is added between the ♭7 and root.

C Mixolydian with passing tone

1   2   3   4   5   6   ♭7   7   8 (RT)

Now let us look at this 8-note scale over 2 measures.

As you can see and hear in the second example, the Mixolydian scale with passing tone has a more musical flow to it. Because of the even number of scale degrees (eight) it repeats itself from the root every bar. You will notice the Mixolydian scale contains the same notes as the key related Dorian scale with passing tones—they just start from different chord tones.

D Dorian scale with passing tone and G Mixolydian scale with passing tone contain the same notes. Practise the ascending Mixolydian scale with passing tone over this cycle of 5ths dominant 7 progression.

Repeat the process this time using the descending Mixolydian scale with passing tone over this cycle of 5ths dominant 7 progression.

Next, play the Mixolydian scale with passing tone ascending and descending over this cycle of 5ths dominant 7 progression. Again, either use sixteenth-notes to create a double-time feel or continue playing eighth-notes and elongate the rate of chord change to 2 measures each.

There are three different fingering patterns you should observe for the one-octave Mixolydian scale with passing tone.

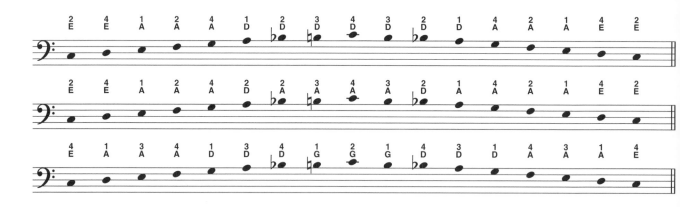

ESSENTIAL
BASS LIBRARY

*CHARNETT
MOFFETT*

*Black Codes From
The Underground*
(Wynton Marsalis)
Columbia, 1985

Part 6

Harmonic Minor Modes:
Fingering Patterns
Linear Solo Concepts
Tensions and Approaches To Chord Tones

6.1

CHAPTER 6.1

Harmonic Minor Modes

Like the major and melodic minor modes, the harmonic minor modes are a group of scales built from each degree of the harmonic minor scale. The harmonic minor scale was created for harmonic reasons, specifically to give minor harmony a dominant 7 chord (built from the fifth degree). The fifth mode (Spanish Phrygian) is a commonly used and very important mode in Western contemporary music. The other modes are rarely used but also have a very interesting colour and sound. I feel they are useful to study and play.

The harmonic minor scale is built off a series of intervals which are: W, H, W, W, H, W/H, H.

Notice between the sixth and seventh degrees there is an interval of a minor 3rd. Due to this large intervallic leap and for melodic purposes the melodic minor scale and its modes were created. The harmonic minor modes have a very Spanish flavor and can be heard in Latin and flamenco music. There are many names out there for each mode of harmonic minor, but here are the names I have chosen for them.

W = whole step, H = half-step, W/H = minor 3rd (whole plus half)

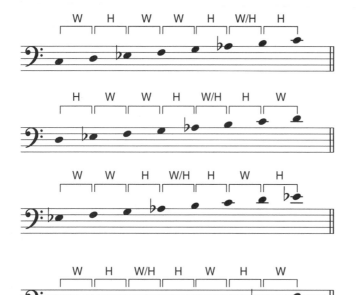

First degree: C harmonic minor

Second degree: D Locrian ♮6

Third degree: E♭ Ionian ♯5

Fourth degree: F Dorian ♯4

Fifth degree: G Phrygian dominant
or Spanish Phrygian

Sixth degree: A♭ Lydian ♯2

Seventh degree: B Super Locrian diminished

As I already mentioned, the harmonic minor exists so that chord V (the dominant) is able to form a dominant 7 chord, with a sharpened third, which leads onto chord I (the tonic). As we know, this V–I chord movement is the strongest harmonic progression, and so it is important for us to understand these two chords within each mode.

C Harmonic Minor

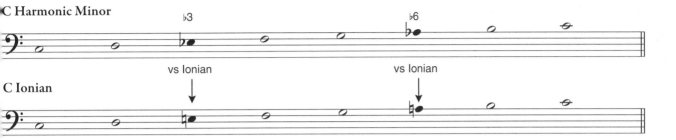

The C harmonic minor is like the Aeolian scale with a sharpened seventh degree. The minor 3rd, perfect 5th and major 7th degrees make the harmonic minor scale a minor/major scale.

G Spanish Phrygian

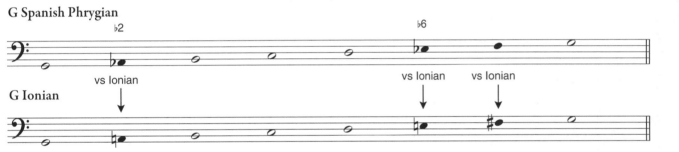

The G Spanish Phrygian scale is built from the fifth degree of the C harmonic minor. Compared to a G Phrygian, you will notice the G Spanish Phrygian has a sharpened third degree. The major 3rd, perfect 5th and minor 7th degrees make the G Spanish Phrygian a dominant scale.

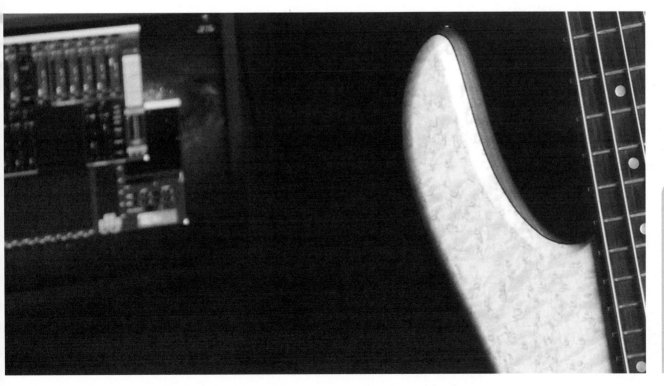

ESSENTIAL
BASS LIBRARY
**MONK
MONTGOMERY**

*Jazz Showcase
Introducing The
Mastersounds*
(The Mastersounds With
Monk Montgomery)
World Pacific, 1957

6.2

CHAPTER 6.2

Diatonic Fingering Patterns For The Harmonic Minor Modes

This chapter focuses on fingering patterns for the C harmonic minor modes and their intervals, specifically the tonic (I) and dominant (V) scales, in order to find the perfect fingering pattern to play across the whole instrument with ease and efficiency

DIATONIC FINGERING PATTERNS—C HARMONIC MINOR MODES

As before, I have written out the fingering patterns—practise and study these fingering patterns in the same way, using the same methods.

Whole Range

This exercise covers the whole range of the C harmonic minor scale. Starting on the lowest note on the E string (F) up to the highest note available on the G string (G).

C Harmonic Minor

This exercise covers the C harmonic minor scale from the lowest root (C) on the E string to the highest root (C) on the G string.

ESSENTIAL
BASS LIBRARY

**MONK
MONTGOMERY**

The King And I
(The Mastersounds)
World Pacific, 1957

G Spanish Phrygian

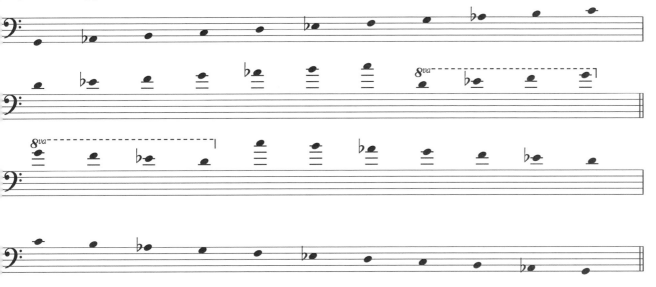

This exercise covers the G Spanish Phrygian scale from the lowest root (G) on the E string to the highest root (G) on the G string.

SCALES IN 3RDS

Whole Range in 3rds

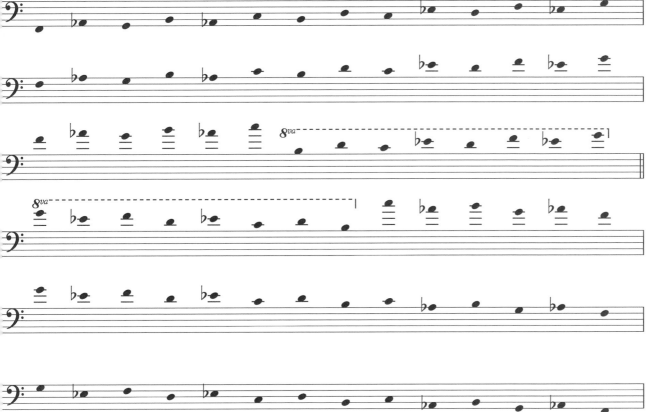

This exercise covers the whole range of the C harmonic minor scale in 3rds moving from the lowest note on the E string (F) to the highest note on the G string (G).

ESSENTIAL BASS LIBRARY

GEORGE MORROW

Brown and Roach, Inc.
(Clifford Brown & Max Roach)
EmArcy, 1954

C Harmonic Minor in 3rds

This exercise covers the Harmonic minor scale in 3rds from the lowest root (C) available on the E string to the highest available interval from the root (E♭) on the G string.

G Spanish Phrygian in 3rds

This exercise covers the G Spanish Phrygian in 3rds from the lowest root (G) on the E string to the highest available interval form the root (B) on the G string.

PRACTISING FINGERING PATTERNS FOR THE HARMONIC MINOR MODES

Now, as we did for the major and melodic minor modes we will go through some linear fingering patterns which you can include in your improvisations. I feel once you have studied and understood the different modes it is vital to be able to use your knowledge in a musical way. After the linear fingering patterns I will write out some simple melodies for each of the modes outlining the characteristics important for each scale. This will be a basis for your own improvisations helping you to instinctively create and hear melodies and colours within the harmonic boundaries.

Linear Fingering Patterns

These patterns are to be played and studied across the entire fretboard. They have been written out diatonic to C harmonic minor and learn them in all keys.

It is important to play these exercises steadily and accurately. They will help improve your sound, touch, technique and melodic development.

Exercise 1

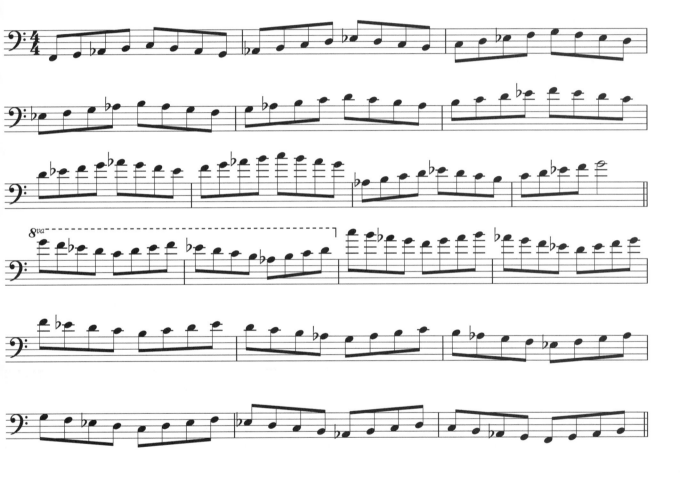

ESSENTIAL
BASS LIBRARY

JACO PASTORIUS

Jaco Pastorius
(Jaco Pastorius)
Columbia, 1976

Exercise 2

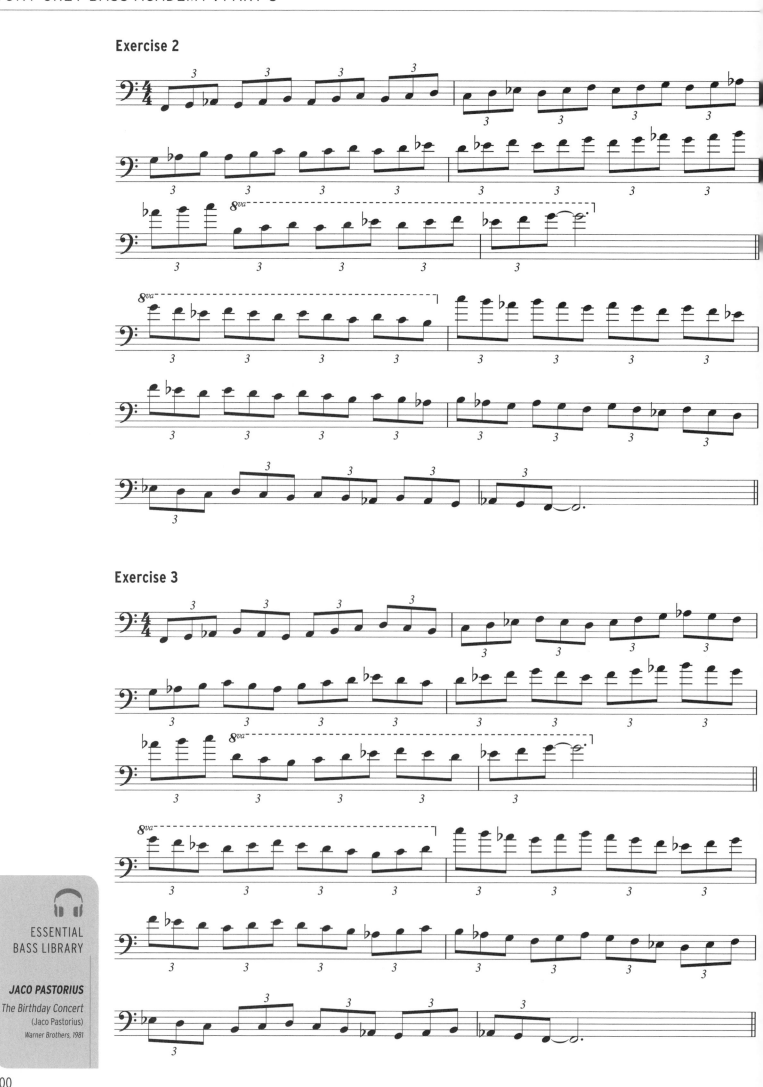

Exercise 3

HOW TO PRACTISE AND APPLY THE LINEAR FINGERING PATTERNS

For the harmonic minor modes study I want to recap the methods we used to apply the linear fingering patterns to the major and melodic minor modes.

1. I want you to write out a simple melody for each of the harmonic minor modes. Try to outline the colour and characteristics for each mode. Also try to incorporate the intervals we studied. Use these melodies as a basis for your own improvisations. For example, write out a melody for C harmonic minor only using scale fragments. Next, write out a melody incorporating scale fragments and the use of 3rds, etc.

2. Set up a drone or sustained chord to outline the scale you are working on. It is important to use these exercises to get the true sound of the mode into your playing. Although each mode contains the same notes they all create a different sound. So, playing along with a related chord to the mode will help you stay within the characteristics of the modes.

3. Set a timer for 3 to 5 minutes. This will help you keep moving forward. You will improve as you go. There are many keys and scales to work through so a time limit for each tempo will give you the willpower to get through them all! Follow the same practising techniques as mentioned before.

4. Be mindful of your practice habits. Push yourself in the areas in which you struggle most. Remember you will sound like how you practise. Being lazy or skipping corners will reflect in your playing and attitude.

5. Practise this lesson for 30mins a day and make a note of your progress as next time you practise this lesson you can carry on where you left off.

Here is an example of some melodies using different scales and intervals found within the harmonic minor mode studies.

C Harmonic minor (using scale fragments)

G Spanish Phrygian (using 6ths and scale fragments)

6.3

CHAPTER 6.3

Linear Solo Concepts through the Changes Using Diatonic Harmonic Minor Harmony

In this chapter we will look at playing through a series of non-related chords found within the major, melodic minor and harmonic minor modes.

LINEAR SOLOING

The harmonic minor gives us only one chord that is commonly used in Western contemporary music. That chord is built off the fifth mode (Spanish Phrygian). The chord that it produces is a $V^{7\flat9}$. Although there are other chords that can be built from these modes they are not really in use as there are better options from the other modes we have looked at.

In this chapter we will focus on the addition of Im^{maj7} and the $V^{7\flat9}$ chords, along with other chords found within the major and melodic minor modes.

Exercise 1

For this exercise I will choose four chords, one of which is taken from the harmonic minor modes. The chord we will use from the harmonic minor mode is from the fifth mode. We will play a quarter-note line through the progression. As the chords change, adjust the chord scale chromatically or in a stepwise manner to fit the new appropriate chord scale. Start the whole sequence on any note within the chord scale. Use the whole range of the fretboard and mix up the direction of the line.

The four chords will be: Cm^7, $F^{7\sharp11}$, Dm^7 and the $G^{7\flat9}$. All four chords are taken from a different group of modes.

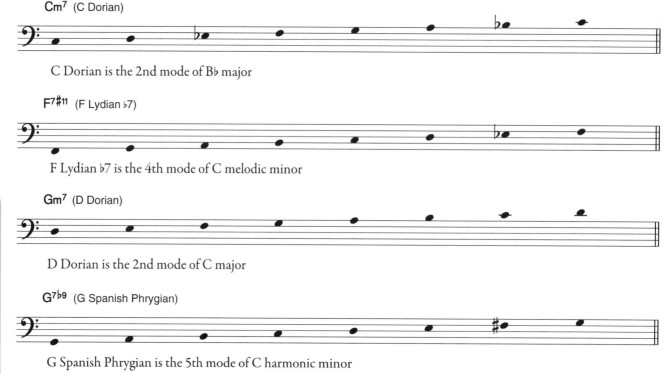

Cm^7 (C Dorian)

C Dorian is the 2nd mode of B♭ major

$F^{7\sharp11}$ (F Lydian ♭7)

F Lydian ♭7 is the 4th mode of C melodic minor

Gm^7 (D Dorian)

D Dorian is the 2nd mode of C major

$G^{7\flat9}$ (G Spanish Phrygian)

G Spanish Phrygian is the 5th mode of C harmonic minor

CHAPTER 6.4

Tensions and Upper Structures for the V7♭9 Chord found within the Harmonic Minor Modes

As I have already discussed the harmonic minor modes only produce one commonly used chord and chord scale—the V7♭9 chord and the Spanish Phrygian chord scale. In this segment we will only analyse the V7♭9 chord. To find the available tensions for the V7♭9 chord we need to build the Spanish Phrygian in diatonic 3rds.

G7♭9—G Spanish Phrygian

In the C harmonic minor modes the diatonic 4-note chord built off the fifth degree is G7. If we keep building the 4-note chord in diatonic 3rds we can see the upper structure tensions it creates. G7 is built in diatonic 3rds related to the harmonic minor modes:

| RT | 3 | 5 | ♭7 | ♭9 | 11 | ♭13 |

The natural tensions are 9, 11 and ♭13.

Tension 11 is considered an avoid note due to the clash and contradiction of functionality with the third degree. As with all major 7 or dominant 7 chords the tension 11 is usually avoided in the chord structure and functions as a scale or passing tone. The diatonic tensions available on the V7 chord related to the harmonic minor modes are ♭9 and ♭13. The most common symbol used for the V7 chord related to the harmonic minor modes is V7♭9. V7 ♭9/♭13 is also a valid symbol choice.

As with the chords found within major and melodic minor harmony, you can practise these upper structure tensions across single strings. Play in order the lowest available chord tone or tension up to the highest available chord tone or tension, then return back in order to the lowest. Remember to uese a sustained drone or chord so you can hear the chord tones and upper structures.

On the E string the lowest available chord tone or tension for G7♭9 is F which is the ♭7th degree. In order the chord tones and tensions available on the E string will be:

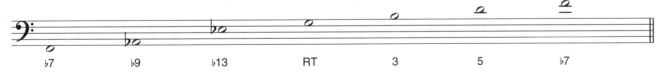

| ♭7 | ♭9 | ♭13 | RT | 3 | 5 | ♭7 |

Ascend all the way up the string to the highest tension or chord tone available and from there descend back to where you started.

Next, repeat this exercise starting from the second-lowest chord tone or tension available. After F, the next available chord tone or tension will be a G which is the root of the chord.

ESSENTIAL BASS LIBRARY

JACO PASTORIUS

Bright Size Life
(Pat Metheny)
ECM, 1975

The second pattern on the E string is as follows:

RT 3 5 ♭7 ♭9 ♭13 RT

Again, ascend up in order to the highest chord tone or tension then descend back to the starting point. From here repeat this 2-part exercise across each string. If you look at the sequence of notes you can see the different arpeggios which include the harmonic tensions.

Here are the different upper structure arpeggios you can superimpose over this chord $G^{7\flat9}$:

$Bdim^7$	gives us tension ♭9
$Ddim^7$	gives us tension ♭9
$Fdim^7$	gives us tension ♭9
$A^\flat dim^7$	gives us tension ♭9
$Fm^{7\flat5}$	gives us tensions ♭9, ♭13
$A^\flat m^{maj7}$	gives us tensions ♭9, ♭13
$E^{\flat maj7\sharp5}$	gives us tension ♭13

You can superimpose these arpeggios over $G^{7\flat9}$ to create colour and tension. You can see in the analysis of the $G^{7\flat9}$ chord that there is a strong connection with the diminished chord. The half whole diminished scale sounds great over this $V^{7\flat9}$ chord. More will be discussed later about diminished chords and its harmony.

Tony Grey and Reb Beach live on stage

ESSENTIAL BASS LIBRARY

JACO PASTORIUS

Heavy Weather
(Weather Report)
Columbia, 1977

Practise playing the upper structure tensions over these cycle of 5ths V⁷♭⁹ chords (tensions ♭9, ♭13).

Practise playing the V⁷♭⁹ with upper structure tensions from the third degree in a cycle of 5ths progression.

Play only available diatonic tensions over the V⁷♭⁹ chord over this cycle of 5ths progression.

I recommend that these exercises are used primarily as ear training exercises. You have to be able to hear these upper structures to see how they work.

ESSENTIAL
BASS LIBRARY

JACO PASTORIUS

Night Passage
(Weather Report)
Columbia, 1980

6.5

CHAPTER 6.5

Approach To Target Note Exercises For The V7♭9 Chord (Harmonic Minor Harmony)

As we did for chords found within the major and melodic minor modes we will apply different approach techniques for the V7♭9 chord from the harmonic minor modes. When improvising or writing melodies, the strongest reference we have is the chord we are working with, through its chord tones.

We already looked at the upper structure tensions that colour the sound of the V7♭9 chord. Now let us look at the different ways to approach the different chord tones with the use of scale and chromatic notes. This is another great way to create colour, tension and pattern to your lines. The following exercises are related to the ones we studied for the chord found within the major and melodic minor modes.

UPPER APPROACH (DIATONIC)

Here are the upper approaches for the V7♭9 chord.

The chord scale we will use for the V7♭9 chord is the Spanish Phrygian, the fifth mode of the harmonic minor scale.

($\downarrow$ = target note)

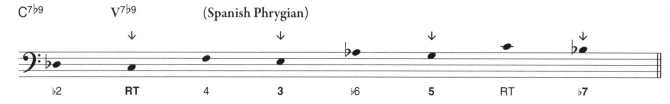

For the major and melodic minor modes we practised the approach to target note exercises in four ways:

1. Across a single string.
2. Writing a melody and improvising.
3. Across a cycle of 5ths progression.
4. Over a II–V–I progression.

For the harmonic minor modes we are only working with the V7♭9 chord, and so for this chord we will only study it in two ways:

1. Across a single string, and
2. Writing a melody/improvising.

You can add these concepts to your own progressions.

Part 1: Single String

As with the upper structure exercises I think it is important to treat these exercises as ear training exercises. It is also important to be able to hear and understand what you are playing—remember to play with a sustained chord or drone.

The upper approach exercise across the whole range of the E string using the $G^{7\flat9}$ chord from the Spanish Phrygian

Moving from the lowest available upper approach note (resolving onto the chord tone), play in sequence up to the highest available upper approach, and back down. The order will be:

Practise this exercise across each string and each key.

Part 2: Melody/Improv

Next, write a simple melody consisting of the target note exercise you are working on along with scale fragments from the related scale. I then want you to use your melody as a starting point of reference for your own improvisations.

It is very important to turn these exercises in to musical statements. Writing melodies or improvising is the best way to develop your own voice in music. Again, the use of a sustained drone or related chord is important as it gives you a great reference so you can hear the concept in question more clearly.

Play your melody and improvisations over a variety of tempos, slow to fast, all over the fretboard.

Here is an example of a melody using scale fragments and the upper approach pattern:

G7♭9   V7♭9   (Spanish Phrygian)

Use this or your own melody as a basis for your own improvisations. Repeat this concept in all keys.

LOWER APPROACH (CHROMATIC)

Here is the lower approach for G$^{7\flat9}$:

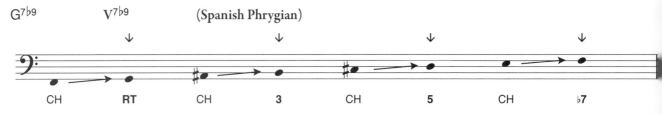

Part 1: Single String

The order for the lower approach concept using G$^{7\flat9}$ on the E string will be:

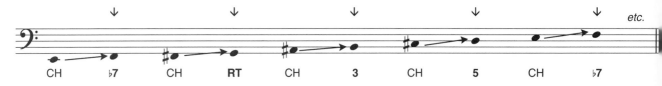

Move from the lowest available lower approach note, in sequence up to the highest available lower approach note, then returning back down to the lowest.

Repeat this exercise across each string and in all keys.

Part 2: Melody/Improv

Here is an example of a melody over G$^{7\flat9}$ using scale fragments and the chromatic approach to chord tone pattern.

Repeat this for all keys and use this or your own melody as a basis for your own improvisations.

ESSENTIAL
BASS LIBRARY

JOHN PATTITUCCI

John Pattitucci
(John Pattitucci)
GRP, 1987

UPPER-LOWER APPROACH

Here is the upper-lower approach for G⁷♭⁹:

Part 1: Single String

The order for the upper-lower approach using G⁷♭⁹ on the E string will be:

Move from the lowest available target note pattern in order up to the highest available target note pattern and back down.

Repeat this exercise across each string and in all keys.

Part 2: Melody/Improv

Here is an example of a melody over G⁷♭⁹ using a combination of scale fragments and the upper-lower approach pattern.

As always, repeat in all keys and use this or your own melody as a basis for your own improvisations.

LOWER-UPPER APPROACH

Here is the lower-upper approach concept for G$^{7\flat9}$:

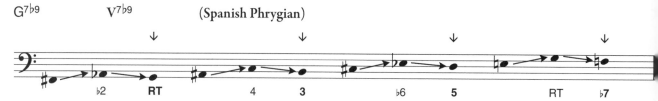

Part 1: Single String

The order for the lower-upper using G$^{7\flat9}$ on the E string will be:

Move from the lowest available target note pattern in order up to the highest available target note pattern and back down.

Repeat this exercise across each string and in all keys.

Part 2: Melody/Improv

Here is an example of a melody over G$^{7\flat9}$ using a combination of scale fragments and the lower-upper approach pattern.

Use this or your own melody as a basis for your own improvisations. Repeat in all keys.

There are 3 more approach to target note patterns we have studied for the chords found within the major and melodic minor modes.

The other approach to target note patterns are:

- Double-upper chromatic approach
- Double-upper lower chromatic approach
- Lower double-upper chromatic approach

These approach patterns do not really apply to the V$^{7\flat9}$ chord as the only double chromatic approach is from the root to the $\flat$7th degree.

Part 7

Advanced Harmony:
Functions, Progressions, Secondary Dominants, Substitutions, and Further Chords & Scales

7.1

CHAPTER 7.1

A Recap Of Diatonic Major And Minor Harmony—Chords, Scales And Functions

So far we have looked in detail at the major modes, the natural minor modes, the melodic minor modes and the harmonic minor modes. Now we will look at the function of the chords that are derived from these modes, and how they relate to one another.

DIATONIC MAJOR HARMONY

Firstly, let us re-visit the major modes and their related diatonic chords.

Basic chords within C major:

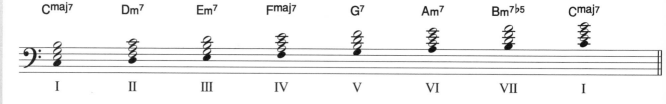

In traditional music theory, this progression of V-I is often called a perfect cadence.

Each of the diatonic chords found within the major modes relate to one another in a certain way. Some are harmonically grounded—without the 'urge' to move to another chord—and some are unstable, with an inclination to resolve to another chord. It is the way in which these chords relate to one another that dictates the flow of the harmony, and by considering some basic principles we can understand how chord progressions are put together.

These principles are rooted in the last few centuries of Western classical music, which we won't attempt to cover in depth here; for the purposes of learning about common jazz techniques there are only a handful of concepts that you really need to know.

If you try playing a chord at one end of a harmony instrument and then another chord at the other end, it will sound as if the chords bear no relation to each other at all, even if the chord progression should theoretically work.

Play the chords from the example above, and then consider the following:

- The first degree chord (I) has the strongest harmonic identity and stability, and is known as the tonic. Any movement away from this chord will create tension, and so almost every overall progression will eventually return to the tonic. Therefore, the tonic will usually be the chord that a piece starts and/or ends on.

- The furthest departure from the tonic is fifth degree chord (V), known as the dominant. The vast majority of music involves a movement from chord I (stable) to chord V (unstable), and then back again (stable). Try playing this now—it will be a very familiar sound.

- As chords change within a progression, the individual notes of one chord will often sound as if they need to follow a linear movement to the closest chord tones of the next chord. This is known as voice-leading and is one of the fundamental concepts of harmony.

- Scale degree 7 is only a half-step away from the tonic degree (8, but more often referred to as 1), and so there is a great deal of tension that requires a movement to the tonic degree to resolve. This must follow a stepwise fashion and move upwards to resolve.

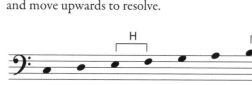

🎧

ESSENTIAL BASS LIBRARY

JOHN PATTITUCCI

Footprints Live!
(Wayne Shorter)
Verve, 2002

- The dominant chord contains scale degree 7, which in the key of C major is a B. This B has a very strong urgency to move to the C, the root of the tonic.

- Almost every genre of music, especially Jazz, employs a number of additional notes to the standard triads of the scale, all of which add character and tension to the harmony. We have already encountered many of these chords. One of the most fundamental of these chords is the dominant 7. The 7th of this chord is only a half-step from the 3rd of the tonic, and so in keeping with the concept of voice-leading it will resolve in this way.

- The combination of the 3rd and 7th of the dominant (initially a very dissonant tritone apart) resolving to the root and 3rd of the tonic gives the V^7–I progression a very strong sense of resolution, making it one of the keystones of diatonic harmony. Try playing a dominant 7 chord in isolation—you will probably find that you will naturally want to hear the resolution to the tonic!
- This V^7–I shape can be applied across the range of chords, even remaining diatonic to C major (or using the related modes). Essentially all of the chords are somewhat unstable, except for the tonic chord, I. This instability gives each chord the tendency to move to another, until the progression eventually reaches chord I.

Having considered these principles, we can now go about finding some of the best ways of building and resolving tension through typical jazz chord progressions.

If we only use the diatonic chords of C major, the effective dominant of chord V^7 (G^7) is chord IIm^7 (Dm^7). This II–V–I progression is one of the most common progressions used in traditional Western harmony.

This movement from chord IIm^7 to chord V^7 in C Ionian is very similar to a V^7–I^7 progression in G Mixolydian (or Vm^7–I^7 in G Ionian).

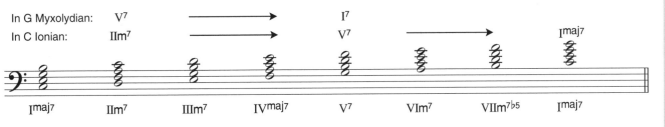

We can apply this 'V–I shape' principle a number of times with different chords to form a longer progression, such as the widely-used $IIIm^7$–VIm^7–IIm^7–V^7–I^{maj7} sequence. Notice how it uses the II–V–I progression at the end.

In the key of C:

$IIIm^7$	VIm^7	IIm^7	V^7	I^{maj7}
Em^7	Am^7	Dm^7	G^7	C^{maj7}

Again this progression effectively moves down in 5ths.

When we string together a number of these progressions, it is known as a cycle of 5ths progression, and this can be used to sustain a feeling of movement within a key or to modulate to a different key altogether. This concept will be further explained when we get to extended dominants.

DIATONIC MINOR HARMONY

The functions of the chords within the minor modes are not too dissimilar to that of the major modes, however there are still some distinct characteristics.

The natural minor, which is the same as the Aeolian mode, has a flattened leading note (not a half-step below the tonic) and so its dominant chord V is actually a minor 7 chord. This chord V doesn't have the same inclination to resolve to chord I.

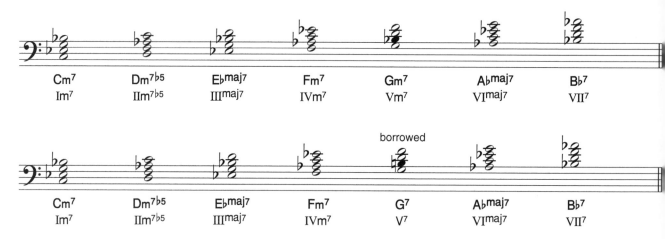

For the harmonic minor modes, this Vm7 was replaced with the chord V7 from the major mode. However, this is not an isolated instance of exchanging chords between the various parallel major and minor harmonies. The borrowing of chords from the parallel modes is called modal interchange.

Here is an example of a II–V–I major mode resolution which uses the IIm7b5 chord from the minor modes:

This modal interchange makes the harmonic progression of the chords far more interesting. Here is a longer example, using chords from the C major modes and its parallel minor modes the C natural minor modes.

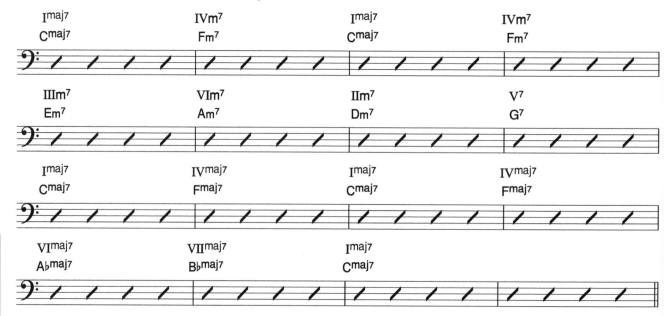

This is a very simple progression to demonstrate the use of modal interchange chords.

The IIm⁷♭⁵ is also used in a minor II–V–I cadence but more often than not the IIm⁷♭⁵ chord is borrowed from the Aeolian or the melodic minor modes. Here is a progression using the minor II–V–I taken from the harmonic minor modes.

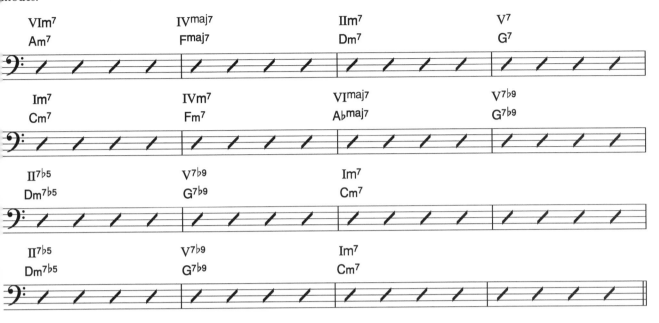

This progression borrows chords from the major modes, the natural minor modes and the harmonic minor modes. You should experiment with your own progressions.

The melodic minor modes and diatonic chords found within them are widely used in modern and traditional jazz music and give us some very interesting chords and scales.

C melodic minor — Cm^maj7 (Im^maj7)

D Dorian (♭2) — Dm⁷ (IIm⁷)

E♭ Lydian (#5) — E♭aug^maj7 (♭IIIaug^maj7)

F Lydian (♭7) — F⁷ (IV⁷)

G Mixolydian (♭6) — G⁷ (V⁷)

A Aeolian (♭5) — Am⁷♭⁵ (VIm⁷♭⁵)

B Superlocrian/Altered — Bm⁷♭⁵ (VIIm⁷♭⁵)

The second mode, D Dorian ♭2, gives us the diatonic chord Dm^7, but another dark and interesting chord that can be found within this mode is a D$^{13♭9sus4}$.

The seventh mode, B Super Locrian (also known as the B altered scale), gives us a Bm$^{7♭5}$. However, the most common use from this mode is the B^{7}alt chord. The altered scale contains a minor 3rd and a major 3rd, which gives us some interesting and tense-sounding chords.

Another popular chord found within these modes is the dominant 7♯11, built off the fourth mode—the Lydian ♭7. This great sounding scale and chord is very characteristic of the melodic minor modes.

All these scales and modes give us so many colours and choices. There are only 12 notes used in Western harmony but the permutations and choices are endless. The more you understand through hearing the more colours and sounds you can use to paint your own pictures.

This part gives you a basic outline of how harmony works. Once you've given yourself time to absorb these principles you should be able to react naturally, without having to break down and analyse each chord progression first.

Here are some of the popular modal interchange and chords from the major modes:

I chords:	I^{maj7}	Im^{maj7}	Im^7	I^6	
II chords:	IIm^7	♭II^{maj7}	IIm$^{7♭5}$	II$^{13♭9sus4}$	
III chords:	IIIm^7	♭III^{maj7}	♭III$^{maj7♯5}$		
IV chords:	IV^{maj7}	IV^7	IVm^7	♯IVm$^{7♭5}$	
V chords:	V^7	V9	V$^{7♭9}$	V^{7}alt	Vm^7
VI chords:	VIm^7	♭VI^{maj7}	VIm$^{7♭5}$		
VII chords:	VIIm$^{7♭5}$	♭VII7	♭VII^{maj7}	VIIdim^7	

Experiment, mixing these chords to make interesting progressions.

CHAPTER 7.2

Further Harmony

SECONDARY DOMINANTS AND THEIR RELATED II CHORDS

Secondary Dominants

The primary function of a dominant 7 chord is to resolve down a perfect 5th. For example, in the key of C major the G[7] chord is usually followed by a C^maj7.

As we have seen, the V[7] contains a tritone between its 3rd and 7th, causing a need for resolution. Using C major and its V[7] chord as an example, the tritone is found between the B and F of the G[7] chord.

The 3rd of G[7] (B) pulls towards the root of C^maj7 (C) and the 7th of G[7] (F) pulls towards the 3rd of C^maj7 (E).

The preceding progression of II–V is similar to a V–I resolution, however if we only use chords that are diatonic to C major, then there is a lack of a tritone resolution. By altering chord II so that it is relative to G major, we introduce another dominant 7 chord. This gives us another tritone to maintain the momentum of resolving harmonies. This new dominant 7 chord is known as a secondary dominant.

Secondary
dominant

Notice that the F♯ of the D[7] chord is conflicted by the F♮ of the G[7] chord. This shift in harmony is one of the main characteristics of secondary dominants.

The resolution of this short chain of tritones offers a far more interesting alternative to the usual diatonic II–V–I progression, however there are a couple of things that you need to bear in mind.

To effectively use a secondary dominant:

1. The root must always be diatonic to the key;

2. One of the notes within the chord will be non-diatonic.

For example, approaching chord II of C major (Dm) with a secondary dominant would require an A[7] chord. The A (root) is diatonic to the key of C, and C♯ (3rd) is non-diatonic to the key of C.

Approaching chord VII of C major (Bm♭5) is not possible in this way because the V[7] chord would need to be based on F♯, which is not diatonic to the key of C.

The available secondary dominant progressions in the key of C are:

A[7]	-	Dm[7] (II)
B[7]	-	Em[7] (III)
C[7]	-	Fmaj[7] (IV)
D[7]	-	G[7] (V)
E[7]	-	Am[7] (VI)

**ESSENTIAL
BASS LIBRARY**

GARY PEACOCK

Oracle
(Ralph Towner and
Gary Peacock)
ECM, 1993

Here is a progression in the key of C that incorporates the use of secondary dominants.

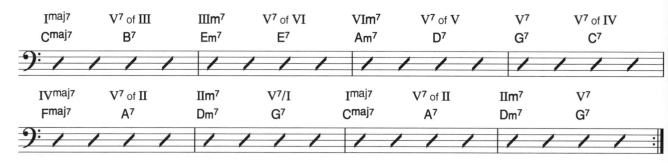

The use of secondary dominants adds colour and variation to harmony and chord progressions. The chord scales used over these secondary dominants are formed in two steps. Firstly, build the secondary dominant chord using only chord tones.

Example: V⁷ of II (A7)

RT 3 5 ♭7

Secondly, fill in the scale tones with diatonic notes related to the key, which in this case is C major.

RT 3 5 7♭

If we related these scale tones to the root of the dominant chord (A) we can see how these notes relate to that scale.

Example: V⁷ of II   A7

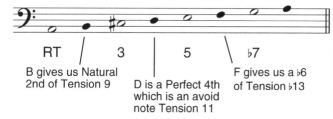

RT / 3 | 5 \ ♭7

B gives us Natural 2nd of Tension 9

D is a Perfect 4th which is an avoid note Tension 11

F gives us a ♭6 of Tension ♭13

The resulting chord scale is a Mixolydian ♭6 or ♭13. The chord symbol may be written as A⁷♭¹³.

The secondary dominant chords containing the tension ♭9 can also include the tension #9 as it is also diatonic to the key. This will give us an 8-note scale.

Here are the five secondary dominant chord scales we will find in the key of C major:

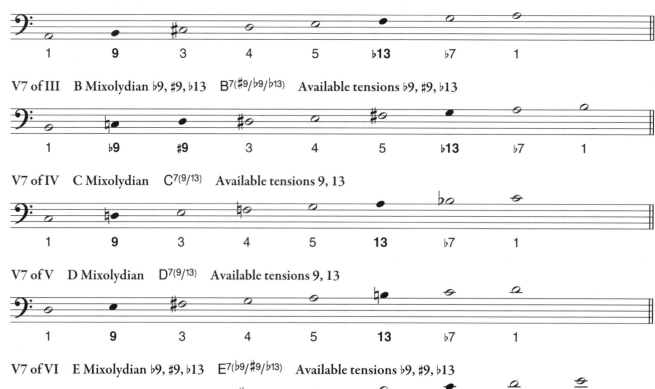

V7 of II   A Mixolydian ♭13   A⁷♭¹³   Available tensions 9, ♭13

1   9   3   4   5   ♭13   ♭7   1

V7 of III   B Mixolydian ♭9, #9, ♭13   B⁷⁽#⁹/♭⁹/♭¹³⁾   Available tensions ♭9, #9, ♭13

1   ♭9   #9   3   4   5   ♭13   ♭7   1

V7 of IV   C Mixolydian   C⁷⁽⁹/¹³⁾   Available tensions 9, 13

1   9   3   4   5   13   ♭7   1

V7 of V   D Mixolydian   D⁷⁽⁹/¹³⁾   Available tensions 9, 13

1   9   3   4   5   13   ♭7   1

V7 of VI   E Mixolydian ♭9, #9, ♭13   E⁷⁽♭⁹/#⁹/♭¹³⁾   Available tensions ♭9, #9, ♭13

1   ♭9   #9   3   4   5   ♭13   ♭7   1

A secondary dominant can also be preceded by its related IIm chord. This will give the progression a complete II–V–I cadence. Here is a simple chord progression using secondary dominant 7 chords and their related II chords.

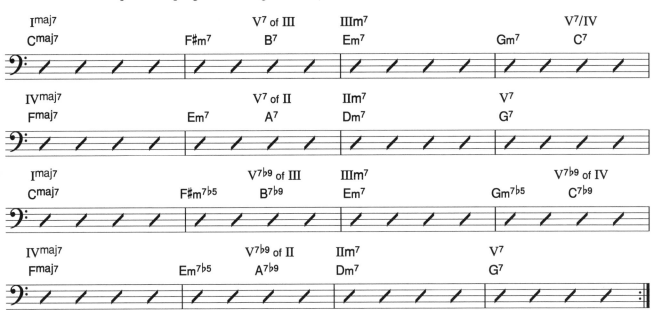

As you can see in the 2nd half of this progression, the related IIm⁷ chord has been replaced with a IIm⁷ᵇ⁵ followed by a V⁷ᵇ⁹ chord. This implies a harmonic minor sound. This kind of minor IIm⁷ᵇ⁵–V⁷ᵇ⁹ sequence is usually relative to a diatonic minor chord like IIm⁷, IIIm⁷ or VIm⁷. However, it is quite acceptable to resolve down to a maj7 chord, so that the progression is IIm⁷ᵇ⁵–V⁷ᵇ⁹–Imaj7.

It is important with related II–V chords to understand what the target chord is and the function of the preceding chords. A related II–V sequence suggests a temporary change of key.

For example: Em⁷ᵇ⁵ A⁷ᵇ⁹ Dm⁷

Dm⁷ is the suggested target chord following the related II–V progression, and the continuation of this key or modulation from this key will determine its overall importance within the larger harmonic structure of key changes.

In the previous progression, the Dm⁷ becomes part of another II–V–I in the key of C major.

Here are some choices for Em⁷ᵇ⁵ A⁷ᵇ⁹ Dm⁷:

Em⁷ᵇ⁵	A⁷ᵇ⁹	Dm⁷
IIm⁷ᵇ⁵	V⁷ᵇ⁹ of II	IIm⁷
(second mode of D Aeolian)	(fifth mode of D harmonic minor)	(second mode of C major)

You could play D harmonic minor over the whole sequence, unless the Dm⁷ becomes the new Im⁷ chord, in which case you could play D Aeolian over it. Over the V⁷ᵇ⁹ you could play a combination of altered tensions or a symmetrical half/whole diminished scale (which will be explained later).

Here is another option using the melodic minor modes:

Em⁷ᵇ⁵	A⁷ᵇ⁹	Dm⁷
IIm⁷ᵇ⁵	V⁷ of II	IIm⁷
(sixth mode of G melodic minor)	(seventh mode of Bᵇ melodic minor)	(D melodic minor)
(E Aeolian ♭5)	(A Altered)	

If you use a simple A⁷ chord, then you may have the following options:

Em⁷	A⁷	Dm⁷
	V⁷ of II	IIm⁷
(E Dorian)	(A Mixolydian ♭13)	(D Dorian)

Here, the related II chord actually functions as a temporary II chord in a new key and takes on a Dorian scale. The V chord can take on a variety of Mixolydian possibilities—Altered, Mixolydian ♭13, Mixolydian, diminished, and so on. You have many choices, but again the target chord is the most important, determining the functionality of the preceding chords.

Tritone Substitution

It can be argued that the tritone between the 3rd and 7th of a dominant 7 chord is primarily what causes the harmonic tension and inclination for resolution to the tonic. Therefore, any chord which contains this same tritone can be considered to have a similar function.

Using C major as an example:

The only other chord that both has a different root and includes the B and F tritone is a D♭⁷ chord. The C♭ is an enharmonic of B, but it still resolves to the C, and likewise the F still resolves to the E. The only difference is that the F is now the 3rd of the 7 chord, resolving downwards, and the C♭ (B) is now the 7th of the 7 chord, resolving upwards.

Therefore, replacing the chord V of the basic II–V–I progression would give us this:

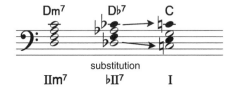

Replacing the chord V with another chord containing the same tritone is known as tritone substitution. Because of this tritone relationship the G⁷ is interchangeable with a D♭⁷.

The chord scale that is normally used for a tritone substitution is a Lydian ♭7, in this case the fourth mode of A♭ melodic minor. Conveniently, if we play a G altered scale over G⁷ it gives us the same notes, as it is the seventh mode of A♭ melodic minor.

A tritone substitution can replace any secondary dominant chord. For example, V⁷ of VI in the key of C major is E⁷. A tritone away would give us B♭⁷.

The II–V–I progression would change from:

Bm⁷	E⁷	Am7
	V⁷ of VI	VIm⁷

to:

Bm⁷	B♭⁷	Am7
	subV of VI	VIm⁷

There are some progressions that effectively use the 'sound' of a tritone substitution, but combined with a modal interchange. One popular modal interchange chord is from the Phrygian minor—a ♭II^maj7.

Here is a commonly used cadence incorporating modal interchange chords.

Dm⁷♭5	D♭maj7	Cmaj7
IIm⁷♭5	♭II^maj7	I^maj7

Instead of a D♭⁷ (which would be the normal tritone substitution chord of G⁷), a D♭maj7 chord is borrowed from the Phrygian minor.

The ♭VI^maj7 chord can also be borrowed to replace the original II chord. This gives us an effective V–I progression to the new middle chord, before the resolution to the tonic.

A♭maj7	D♭maj7	Cmaj7
♭VI^maj7	♭II^maj7	I^maj7

There are other possibilities for modal interchange within this progression. Here are a few:

Dm⁷	D♭⁷	Cmaj7
A♭m⁷	D♭⁷	Cmaj7
A♭m⁷	G⁷	Cmaj7

Here is a chord progression demonstrating all we have looked at so far in this segment.

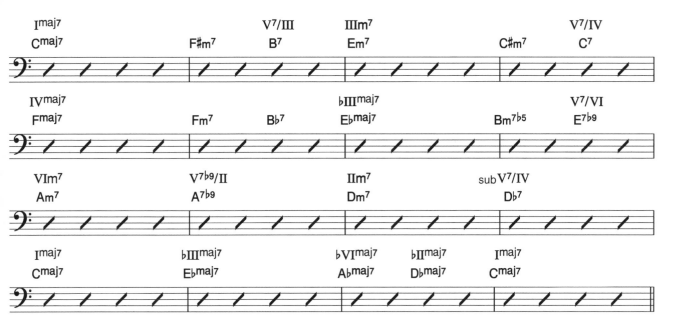

There is a transitory modulation to E♭ major in bars 6 and 7, which helps its retrospective function as ♭III^{maj7}. Experiment with different chord progressions and write melodies using appropriate chord scales.

Here is a summary of all the diatonic chords in the key of C major, their specific dominants (which, besides chord I, will be secondary dominants) and substitutions.

Target chord	Relative dominant chord	Substitution of relative dominant chord
C^{maj7} (I^{maj7})	G^7 (V^7)	D$^{♭7}$ (subV)
Dm^7 (IIm^7)	A^7 (V^7 of II)	E$^{♭7}$ (subV of II)
Em^7 (IIIm^7)	B^7 (V^7 of III)	No sub available
F^{maj7} (IV^{maj7})	C^7 (V^7 of IV)	G$^{♭7}$ (subV of IV)
G^7 (V^7)	D^7 (V^7 of V)	A$^{♭7}$ (subV of V)
Am^7 (VIm^7)	E^7 (V^7 of VI)	B$^{♭7}$ (subV of VI)

ESSENTIAL BASS LIBRARY

NIELS HENNING-ORSTED PEDERSON

The Trio
(Oscar Peterson)
Pablo, 1973

Extended Dominants

An extended dominant is essentially a series of dominant 7 chords moving down in perfect 5ths or down in ½ steps until they reach their tonic chord. This includes using a cycle of 5ths progression, as we've seen before.

Extended dominants are very common in jazz music and a good example is the bridge of Rhythm Changes.

Example 1
Key of B♭ major

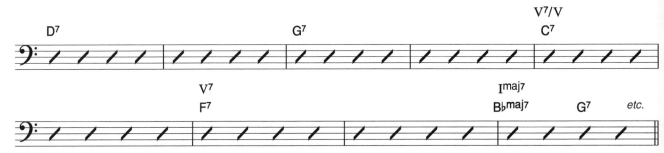

The first chord of this sequence, D^7, appears to be resolving to a G, but instead resolves to a G^7. From the G^7 the cycle of dominant 7th chords continues, next to the C^7 and then the F^7.

The F^7 now functions as the V^7 of the tonic, and resolves down to the I^{maj7} ($B♭^{maj7}$), ending the cycle. All extended dominants can be analysed as a V^7 of V, as they each resolve to another V^7 chord. Therefore a Mixolydian scale (with natural tensions 9 and 13) can be used over the top. You can add related IIm chords to these extended dominant cycles.

Here again is the bridge of rhythm changes, this time with the related IIm^7 chords included.

Example 2

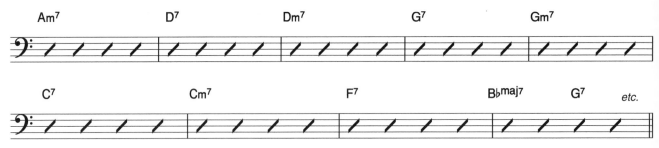

Another variation would be to use tritone substitutions.

Example 3

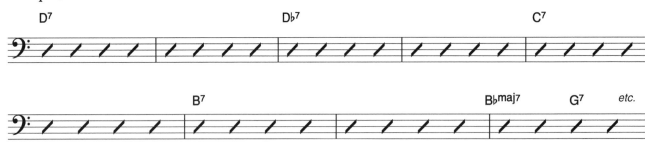

See if you can get used to identifying substitution chords from the sound of the progression, rather than over-analysing the harmony. As we have seen previously, substitution chords take on a Lydian ♭7 chord scale.

As in Ex.2 the subV chords can take on their relative IIm chords.

Example 4

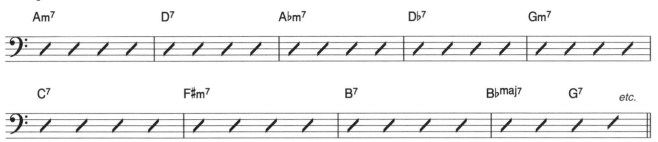

In fact, all the choices that we have been discussing throughout the previous sections are possible.

Here are some examples of a chord progression using extended dominants, along with some of the possible variations.

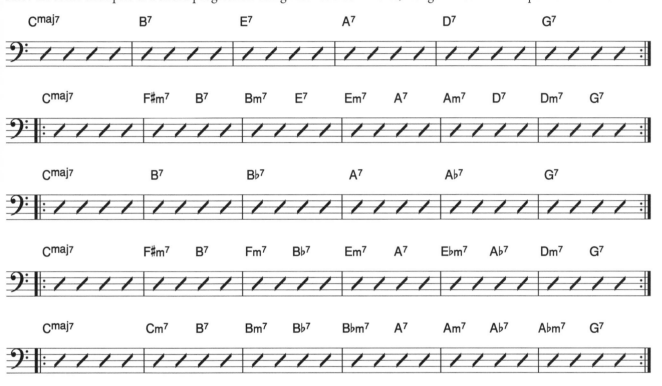

Extended dominants can also be used to modulate within a progression.

Here is an example of a progression starting in the key of C major and ending up in D major.

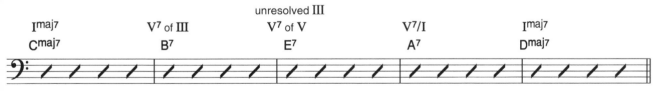

The variations are almost endless. You could use the A⁷ as a subV, resolving down a half-step to A♭maj7.

Alternatively, the A⁷ could resolve to a minor key:

I recommend that once you have grasped how functional harmony works, you should just have fun and experiment with your own progressions.

Here is a summary of chord scales for the Primary, Secondary, Extended and Substitute Dominant 7 chords. The first choice in each list is the most common.

V^7 of I	Mixolydian; Mixolydian with altered tensions; Altered
V^7 of II	Mixolydian ♭13; Altered; Mixolydian ♭9, ♯9, ♭13
V^7 of III	Mixolydian ♭9, ♯9, ♭13; Altered
V^7 of IV	Mixolydian; Mixolydian with altered tensions; Altered
V^7 of V	Mixolydian; Mixolydian ♭9, ♯9, 13
V^7 of VI	Mixolydian ♭9, ♯9, ♭13; Altered
$V^{7♭9}$	Spanish Phrygian (fifth mode of harmonic minor); Altered; Mixolydian ♭9, ♯9, ♭13
subV	Lydian ♭7
Extended V^7 chord	Mixolydian; Lydian ♭7; Altered; Mixolydian with any combination of altered tensions

Here is a summary of the modal interchange chords and parallel modes:

C major modes:	C^{maj7}	Dm⁷	Em⁷	F^{maj7}	G⁷	Am⁷	Bm^{7♭5}
	I^{maj7}	IIm⁷	IIIm⁷	IV^{maj7}	V⁷	VIm⁷	VIIm^{7♭5}
C Dorian modes:	Cm⁷	Dm⁷	E♭^{maj7}	F⁷	Gm⁷	Am^{7♭5}	B♭^{maj7}
	Im⁷	IIm⁷	♭IIImaj7	IV⁷	Vm⁷	VIm^{7♭5}	♭VIImaj7
C Phrygian modes:	Cm⁷	D♭^{maj7}	E♭⁷	Fm⁷	Gm^{7♭5}	A♭^{maj7}	B♭m⁷
	Im⁷	♭IImaj7	♭III⁷	IVm⁷	Vm^{7♭5}	♭VImaj7	♭VIIm⁷
C Lydian modes:	C^{maj7}	D⁷	Em⁷	F♯m^{7♭5}	G^{maj7}	Am⁷	Bm⁷
	I^{maj7}	II⁷	IIIm⁷	♯IVm^{7♭5}	V^{maj7}	VIm⁷	VIIm⁷
C Mixolydian modes:	C⁷	Dm⁷	Em^{7♭5}	F^{maj7}	Gm⁷	Am⁷	B♭^{maj7}
	I⁷	IIm⁷	IIIm^{7♭5}	IV^{maj7}	Vm⁷	VIm⁷	♭VIImaj7
C Aeolian modes:	Cm⁷	Dm^{7♭5}	E♭^{maj7}	Fm⁷	Gm⁷	A♭^{maj7}	B♭⁷
	Im⁷	IIm^{7♭5}	♭IIImaj7	IVm⁷	Vm⁷	♭VImaj7	♭VII⁷
C melodic minor modes:	Cm^{maj7}	Dm⁷ / Dsus^{♭9♭13}	E♭aug^{maj7}	F7^{♯11}	G^{7♭13}	Am^{7♭5}	Bm^{7♭5} / B⁷alt.
	Im^{maj7}	IIm⁷ / IIsus^{♭9♭13}	♭IIIaug^{maj7}	IV7^{♯11}	V^{7♭13}	VIm^{7♭5}	VIIm^{7♭5} / VII⁷alt.
C harmonic minor modes:	Cm^{maj7}	Dm^{7♭5}	E♭aug^{maj7}	Fm⁷	G^{7♭9}	A♭^{maj7}	B^{dim7}
	Im^{maj7}	IIm^{7♭5}	IIIaug^{maj7}	IVm⁷	V^{7♭9}	♭VImaj7	VII^{dim7}

ESSENTIAL BASS LIBRARY

OSCAR PETTIFORD

Tricotism
(Lucky Thompson)
GRP, 1956

CHAPTER 7.3

Diminished Harmony–Symmetrical/Functional Diminished Chords And Scales

There are two kinds of diminished scale we will look at. They both have a symmetrical pattern and have different functions.

The first of the symmetric scales I will discuss is called the whole/half diminished scale. The scale is built in a whole step/half-step pattern until it reaches its octave. Again, this diminished scale has 8 notes.

Here is the C diminished whole/half scale:

Another way of looking at the construction of this scale is by overlaying two diminished chords a whole step apart.

For example,

The next step is to then integrate them with one another, in an ascending stepwise order, to form an 8-note scale.

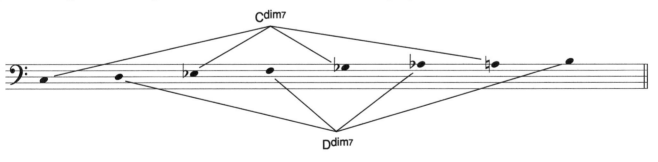

The diminished whole/half scale is often played over diminished chords that do not have root motion, e.g.:

This Idim⁷ is a delayed resolution to its Imaj⁷ chord.

If we look closer at the Idim⁷ (Cdim⁷) we can analyse the interchangeable dominant 7 chords that share the majority of the chord tones. For a Cdim⁷ chord these chords are: A♭⁷, B⁷, D⁷ and F⁷.

ESSENTIAL
BASS LIBRARY

OSCAR PETTIFORD

*Vienna Blues: The
Complete Sessions*
(Oscar Pettiford)
Black Lion, 1959

If we use all the chord tones found within these dominant 7 chords and put them in a sequential order from C we will find it spells the C whole/half diminished scale.

Due to the symmetrical pattern of this scale, there are only three different whole/half diminished scales before the pattern starts repeating from different scale degrees. Building a whole/half diminished scale from each chord tone will create the same scale.

Below is a summary of all the whole/half diminished scales.

The C whole/half diminished scale contains the same notes as the whole/half diminished scales based on E♭, G♭, and A:

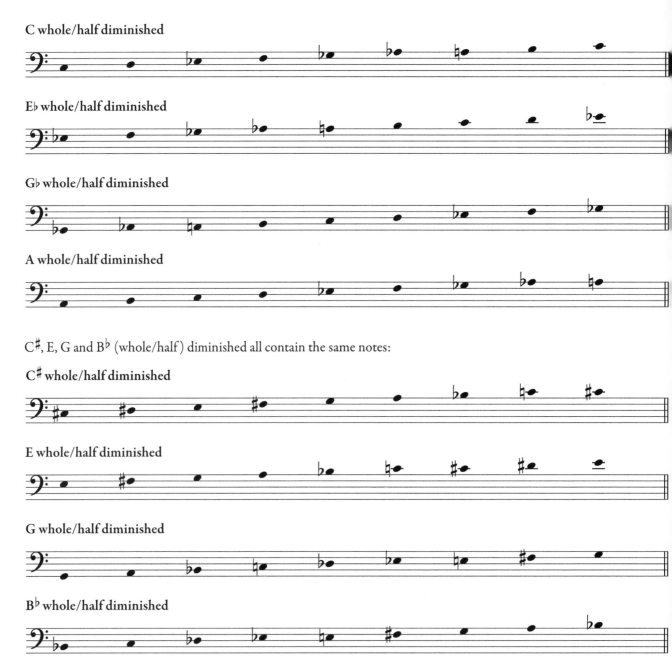

C whole/half diminished

E♭ whole/half diminished

G♭ whole/half diminished

A whole/half diminished

C♯, E, G and B♭ (whole/half) diminished all contain the same notes:

C♯ whole/half diminished

E whole/half diminished

G whole/half diminished

B♭ whole/half diminished

D, F, A♭ and B (whole/half) diminished all contain the same notes:

D whole/half diminished

F whole/half diminished

A♭ whole/half diminished

B whole/half diminished

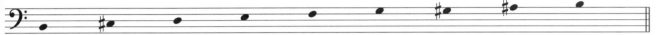

The whole/half diminished scale will work over any diminished chord, but sounds best over a 'progression' that lacks a root motion, such as Idim⁷–Imaj⁷.

The other diminished scale is a variation of the whole/half diminished scale. Again, it is a symmetrical 8-note scale, however this time the symmetrical pattern begins with a half-step followed by a whole step (continuing the sequence to form the scale). This scale is unsurprisingly called the half/whole diminished scale.

Here is a C half/whole diminished scale:

By looking closely at the scale degrees we can see that it appears to be more like a dominant scale than a diminished scale.

If the scale is reconsidered as a C Mixolydian scale then we can analyse the additional tensions that are given.

As a Mixolydian scale, the tensions are ♭9, ♯9, ♯11 and natural 13.

The C half/whole diminished scale works best on C¹³♭⁹ chords but is commonly used on all dominant 7 chords to add tension. It is a very effective scale to use over the Blues, and the half-whole pattern is frequently found within transcribed solos.

Here are some commonly used half/whole diminished patterns over a C⁷♯⁹ or C⁷♭⁹ chord:

Example 1

Example 2

Example 3

Example 4

Example 5

Example 6

Like the diminished whole/half scale there are only three different half/whole diminished scales before they start repeating from different scale degrees.

Below is a summary of all the half/whole diminished scales.

C, E♭, F♯ and A half/whole diminished scales all contain the same notes:

C half/whole diminished

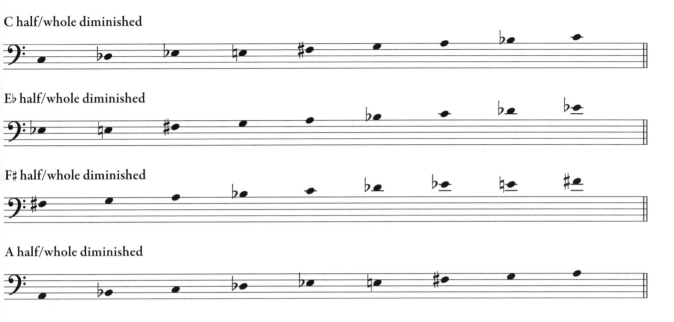

E♭ half/whole diminished

F♯ half/whole diminished

A half/whole diminished

C♯, E, G and B♭ half/whole diminished scales all contain the same notes:

C♯ half/whole diminished

E half/whole diminished

G half/whole diminished

B♭ half/whole diminished

ESSENTIAL
BASS LIBRARY

RUFUS REID

The Standard Joe
(Joe Henderson)
Red, 1991

D, F A♭ and B half/whole diminished scales all contain the same notes:

D half/whole diminished

F half/whole diminished

A♭ half/whole diminished

B half/whole diminished

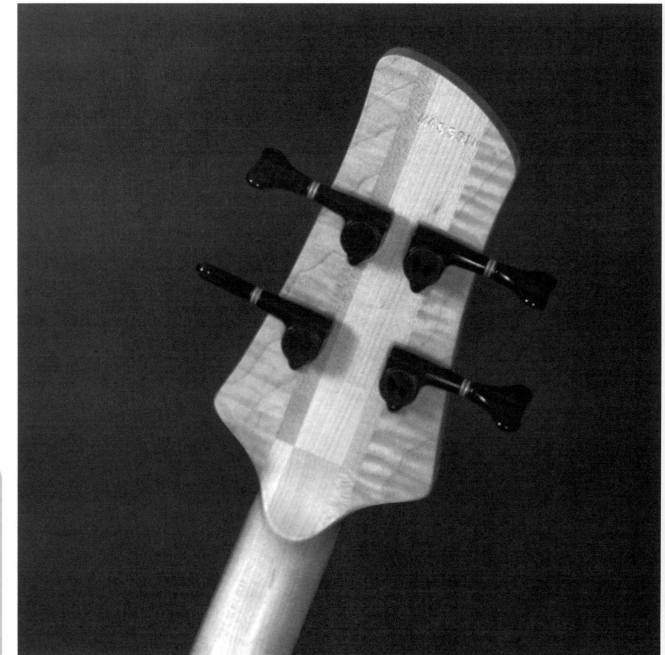

Here is Exercise 6 from the half/whole diminished patterns. Ascend up one diatonic diminished chord then return back down the scale in a stepwise manner, and then from there ascend up the next diatonic diminished chord, returning back down in a stepwise manner. Repeat the pattern over the whole range of the fretboard.

Ascending C half/whole diminished pattern:

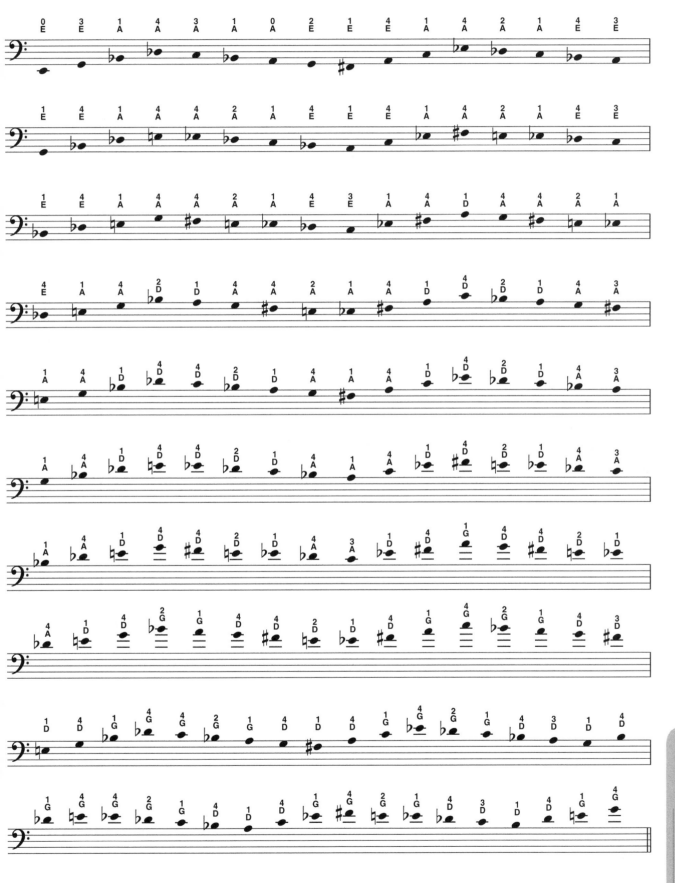

ESSENTIAL BASS LIBRARY

STEVE RODBY

Quartet
(Pat Metheny)
Geffen, 1996

Descending half/whole diminished pattern:

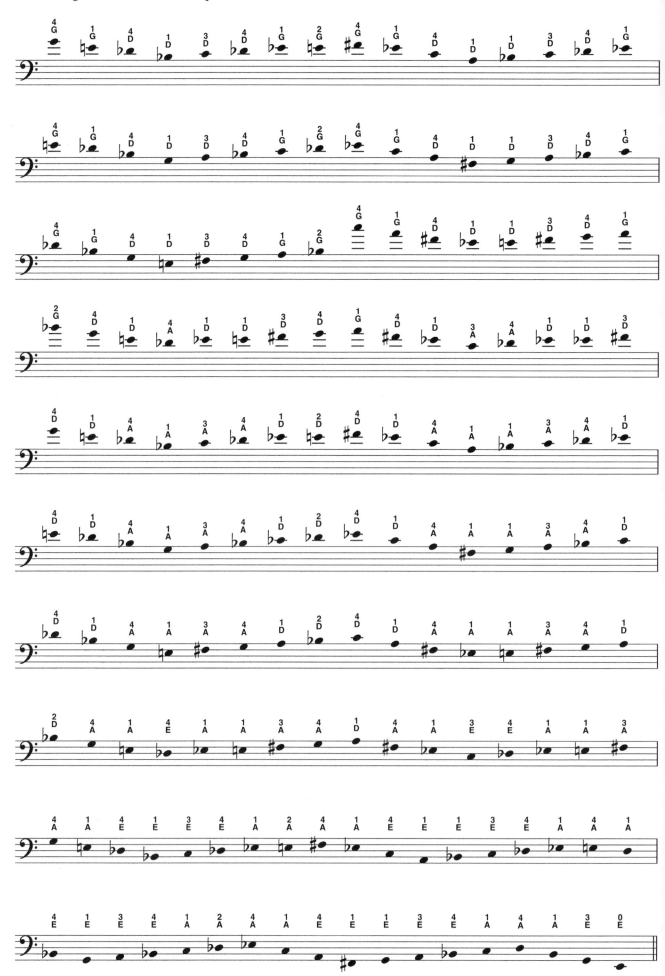

C half/whole diminished (half/whole)

Here is the C half/whole diminished scale fingering patterns over the complete range of the fretboard.

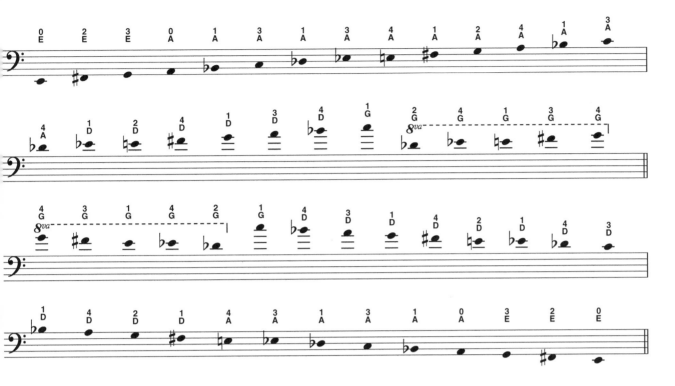

7.4

CHAPTER 7.4

Further Scales—Hexatonic Scales

A hexatonic scale is a 6-note scale. We will look at three of the more popular and common ones. The three hexatonic scales are: the whole-tone scale, the augmented scale and the Blues scale.

The Whole-Tone Scale

The whole-tone scale is a 6-note symmetrical scale constructed from a series of whole-tone intervals. Due to the symmetrical nature of the scale there are only two possible whole-tone scales consisting of different notes. Here is the C whole-tone scale:

As you can see the whole-tone scale is a series of whole tone intervals built from the root until it reaches its octave.

Another way of looking at the construction of this scale is to combine two augmented triads a whole step apart.

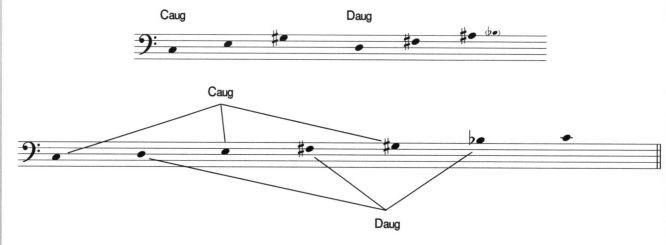

Due to the chord tones and diatonic tensions, the whole-tone scale can be played over dominant 7 and 7#5 chords.

The most common 4-note chord created from the whole-tone scale is the 7#5 chord, which is constructed from the root, 3rd, #5 and b7 degrees.

Here is C7#5 in root position:

A dominant 7♯5 chord can be built on each degree of a whole-tone scale.

C whole-tone scale contains: C7♯5, D7♯5, E7♯5, F♯7♯5, A♭7♯5 and B♭7♯5

C Whole Tone can be played over: C7, C7♯5, D7, D7♯5, E7, E7♯5, F♯7, F♯7♯5, A♭7, A♭7♯5, B♭7 and B♭7♯5

Here is the first whole-tone scale:

C whole tone

C, D , E, F♯, A♭ and B♭ whole-tone scales all contain the same notes and can all be played over:

C7, C7♯5, D7, D7♯5, E7, E7♯5, F♯7, F♯7♯5, A♭7, A♭7♯5, B♭7, B♭7♯5.

Here is the second whole-tone scale:

D♭ whole tone

D♭, E♭, F, G, A and B whole-tone scales all contain the same notes and can all be played over: D♭7, D♭7♯5, E♭7, E♭7♯5, F7, F7♯5, G7, G7♯5, A7, A7♯5, B7, B7♯5.

The symmetrical nature of the whole-tone scale allows for these kinds of phrases to be constructed over dominant 7 or 7#5 chords:

Exercise 1:

Exercise 2:

Exercise 3:

Exercise 4:

Exercise 5:

There are many possibilities for patterns and permutations using the whole-tone scale and you should experiment with your own shapes.

AUGMENTED SCALES

The next hexatonic scale we will look at is the augmented scale. Many people confuse this scale with the whole-tone scale, due to the name and the convention of playing whole-tone scales over augmented chords.

The augmented scale is also a symmetrical scale and is constructed by a minor 3rd followed by a half-step.

Here is the C augmented scale:

The most common way of constructing this scale is to integrate two augmented triads, a minor 3rd apart.

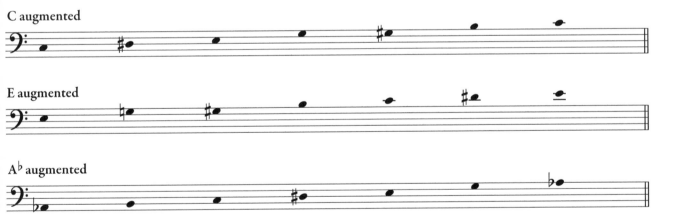

As with the previous symmetrical scales, there are only four augmented scales that contain different notes.

Below are all the augmented scales. C, E and A♭ augmented scales all contain the same notes:

C augmented

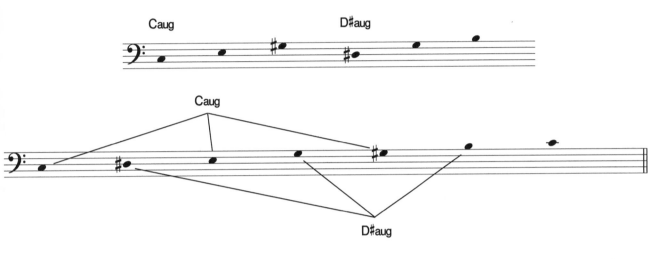

E augmented

A♭ augmented

D♭, F and A augmented scales all contain the same notes:

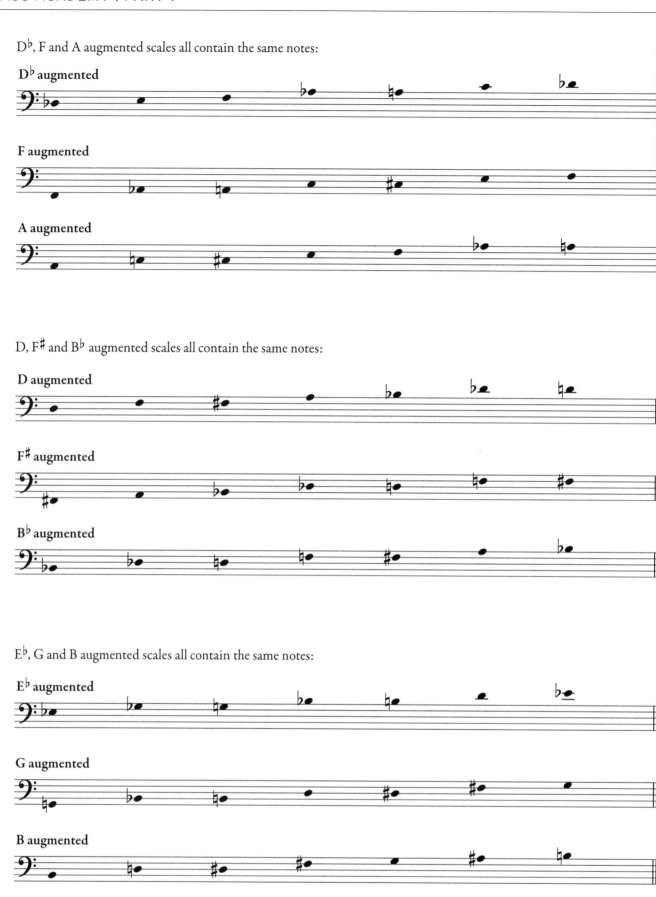

D, F♯ and B♭ augmented scales all contain the same notes:

E♭, G and B augmented scales all contain the same notes:

Like the other symmetrical scales we looked at (the half/whole diminished and the whole-tone scales), the augmented scale is most commonly used to build tension in the form of a symmetrical pattern. The augmented scale is used over chords that contain an augmented triad, and so we will now investigate which chords contain an augmented triad.

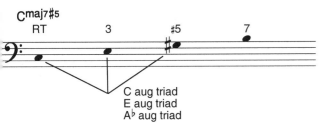

C#5 or Cmaj7#5 both contain an augmented triad. The C, E, and Ab augmented scales work well over this chord.

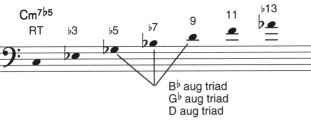

Cmmaj7 contains an augmented triad. The Eb, G, and B augmented scales work well over this chord.

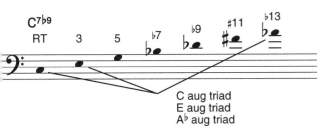

When we build the Cm7b5 (sixth mode of melodic minor) with the available diatonic tensions 9, 11 and b13 we find a D, Gb and Bb augmented triad. The D, Gb, and Bb augmented scales work well over this chord.

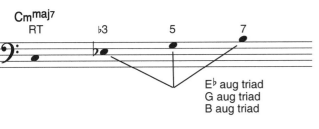

When we build a C7 chord with tensions b9, #9 and b13 we find a C, E and Ab augmented triad. The C, E and Ab augmented scales work well over C7, C7b9, C7#5 and C7alt.

Below is a recap of the chords over which you can play the augmented scale, and the relationship.

You can build an augmented scale off the root, third or fifth degrees.

C(#5) or Cmaj7#5 = C augmented, E augmented, or G# (Ab) augmented (these scales contain the same notes).

The C augmented scale contains all the chord tones for Cmaj7#5. When used in a delicate way, D# and G can be heard as approach or passing tones.

You can build an augmented scale off the root, third or fifth degrees.

Cmmaj7 = Eb augmented, G augmented, and B augmented (these scales contain the same notes).

239

Caug

RT   ♭3   5   7   RT

The C augmented scale contains all the chord tones for $C_{m}maj^7$. When used in a delicate way the E and G can be heard as approach or passing tones.

Cm7♭5

You can build an augmented scale off the fifth, seventh and ninth degrees.

$Cm^{7♭5}$ = F♯ (G♭) augmented, B♭ augmented and D augmented (these scales contain the same notes).

Daug

9   11   ♭5   ♭7   9

The D augmented scale contains the chord tones ♭5 and ♭7 and the strong characteristic tensions 9 and 11. When used in a delicate way the A and D♭ can be heard as approach or passing tones.

C7♭9

You can build an augmented scale off the root, third degree and the ♭13 tension.

$C^{7♭9}$ = C augmented, E augmented, and A♭ augmented (these scales contain the same notes).

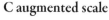

Caug

RT   **♯9**   **3**   **5**   **♭13**   **RT**

The C augmented scale contains the chord tones the root, the 3rd and the 5th. It also contains the tensions ♯9 and ♭13. The B can be heard as an approach tone to the root when used delicately.

The augmented scale works best when used over chords that contain an augmented triad. However, it can also work with chords that have many common tones.

C augmented scale

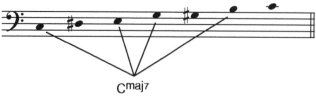

C^{maj7}

C augmented contains all the chord tones of C^{maj7}. Due to the symmetry of the scale, it can be an interesting and exotic alternative to C^{maj7}, if played with care.

C augmented scale

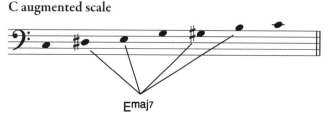

E^{maj7}

C augmented contains all the chord tones of E^{maj7}. Again, due to the symmetry of the scale, C augmented can sound interesting and exotic over E^{maj7}, if played with care.

C augmented scale

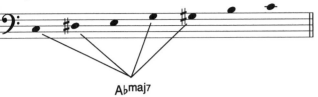

C augmented contains all the chord tones of Abmaj7.

Remember the C, E and A$\flat$ augmented scales all contain the same notes. I recommend that you experiment with some improvising or writing phrases over these chords using this augmented scale.

The C/E/Ab augmented scale also sounds very interesting and exotic over these minor II–V chord sequences.

F#m$^{7\flat5}$ to B$^{7\flat9}$ and B$\flat$m$^{7\flat5}$ to E$^{\flat7\flat9}$.

Let us analyse these chords against the augmented scale.

C augmented scale (F#m$^{7\flat5}$)

When analysed we can see the C augmented scale has a strong relationship to the F#m$^{7\flat5}$.

C augmented scale (B$^{7\flat9}$)

Again, when analysed we can see the strong relationship between the C augmented to the B$^{7\flat9}$.

Creating a symmetrical pattern over this mII–V (F#m$^{7\flat5}$–B$^{7\flat9}$) chord sequence using the C augmented scale can create a strong and interesting sound. The symmetry and relationship between the chords make the dissonance work.

One more mII–V chord sequence related to the C/E/Ab augmented scale is B$\flat$m$^{7\flat5}$–E$^{\flat7\flat5}$.

C augmented scale (B$\flat$m$^{7\flat5}$)

We can see that the C augmented scale has a strong relationship to B$\flat$m$^{7\flat5}$.

C augmented scale (E$\flat^{7\flat9}$)

Again, we can see the strong relationship between C augmented and E$^{\flat7\flat9}$.

By creating a symmetrical pattern over this mII–V (B$\flat$m$^{7\flat5}$–E$^{\flat7\flat9}$) progression using the C augmented scale, we can make a strong musical statement with a great deal of tension.

ESSENTIAL
BASS LIBRARY

STEVE SWALLOW

Real Book
(Steve Swallow)
ECM, 1993

The augmented scale can be used as a very useful tool to create controlled tension. The symmetry of the scale makes it great for creating patterns.

Here are some phrases using the augmented scale:

Experiment with your own phrases, in different keys, and remember to use as much of the fretboard as possible. Practising and writing symmetrical patterns is a valuable way of improving your melodic development and overall structure whilst soloing. Melodic development is important for a solo as it helps to build tension and properly structure your ideas. This will give a greater sense of control and stability to the overall shape and impact of your statement.

The Blues Scale

The last hexatonic scale we will look at is the Blues scale. The Blues scale is more of a melodic tool for soloing over a Blues form rather than a scale with functioning chords and modes. The Blues scale is basically a minor pentatonic scale with an added ♯4.

Here is the C Blues scale:

This scale can be used over a complete Blues form.

The ♭3, ♯4 and ♭7 are called Blue notes and create a real rootsy, traditional sound.

As the Blues scale works over a whole Blues form it is a really simple way of working on melodic and motivic development. If you listen to some old traditional Blues players and singers you will usually hear one phrase or lyric repeated over the whole progression, until the last couple of bars where it resolves. When using the Blues scale it is important to keep the simplistic nature of the scale in effect.

Here is the Blues scale in all keys:

Here is the basic Blues form in F:

Eaxmple 1

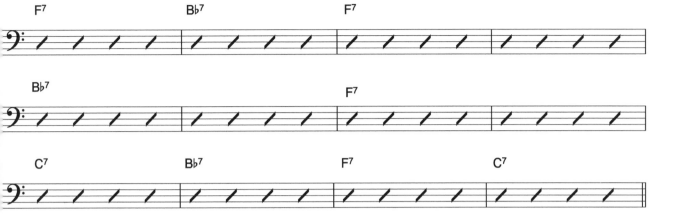

Here is another version of F Blues:

Example 2

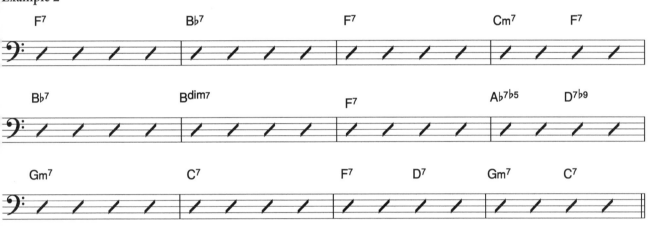

Example 2 is a common Blues progression used in a jazz setting. The F Blues scale will work over both progressions.

Let's look at ways of practising the Blues scale, using the F Blues form shown in Example 2.

1. Simply play the F Blues scale ascending and descending randomly over the F Blues.

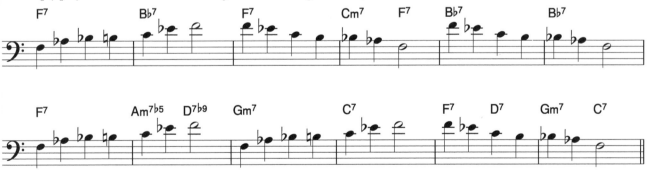

2. Create a short riff using notes from the Blues scale and repeat randomly over the Blues progression.

ESSENTIAL
BASS LIBRARY

GERALD VEASLEY

*The Electric
Mingus Project*
(Gerald Veasley)
Fanwave Media, 2011

A riff is like a musical statement. Statements in music are especially important as it gives the listener some kind of reference point within the solo or melody. However, if we only play the same riff or statement throughout a solo it can get become boring and predictable.

3. Improvising is like having a conversation through music—develop the statements you make or answer the musical questions you ask, but do so with care and consideration. Playing without any space can be extremely overwhelming to the listener, and can sound very self-indulgent and irritating. It is like talking to someone who never listens or shuts up.

Playing without strong ideas or focus can be like having a conversation that keeps jumping around and continually changes topic. Try to keep your ideas focused and concise. Use your ears and instincts to develop your statements. Do not be scared of simplicity in your solos as strong ideas and space create music.

Due to the strong sound and nature of the Blues scale it is a perfect melodic tool to work with in developing good habits for your soloing ideas. The size of the scale helps to keep your ideas concise and focused.

Here are two cycles of the Jazz Blues in F with all the above concepts discussed.

F JAZZ BLUES

Practise your own lines using the Blues scale in different keys.

Part 8

Walking Bass Lines

8.1

CHAPTER 8.1

Walking Bass Lines

The purpose of walking bass lines is to support the soloist during their solo. The idea is to outline the harmony without getting in the way of the soloist.

Feeling The Line

The exercises in this section are designed to give you ideas on how to build walking bass lines.

A walking bass line is a series of quarter notes, usually played with a strong accent placed on the 2nd and 4th beats.

An off-beat is another name for a weak beat of a bar. In a $\frac{4}{4}$ time signature, the off-beats are usually on beats 2 and 4.

These accents help to create a strong swing feel. We will later be looking at this in a little more detail, as although the rhythmic feel accents the off-beats, the chord tones still remain on beats 1 and 3. However we are simply using chord tones to start with anyway, so I will further explain this later.

During the melody of a piece of music (often jazz standards) the bassist usually plays with a 2-feel.

A 2-feel is basically when the meter feels like it is in '2' instead of '4', i.e. using half-notes instead of quarter-notes. During a 2-feel section, it is also common to use eighth-notes and quarter-notes to help give the line momentum, although half-notes still remain the focus.

2-feel examples using the Blues form

Remember that this is not only about note choice—you should also consider the feel and direction of the line.

Exercise 1
Only using half notes

Exercise 2
Some bass line adding notes and ¼ notes to give the line momentum

The Use Of Ghost Notes

A ghost note is a dead-sounding note. It helps give the line some momentum rhythmically without really committing to the harmony. A ghost note is written with an x in place of the notehead.

becomes

To achieve this sound you can place your finger as you normally would without putting pressure on the fretboard. Its usage in bass playing is very common and adds much to the feel of the bass line and indeed to the general groove of the music.

In Example 2 of the (2-feel) bass lines I used some chromatic passing tones and approaches. Later in this chapter we will discuss and play examples of all the different note choice possibilities within walking bass

lines. However, the golden rule in music is: you can play anything as long as it feels and sounds good.

The most common chord progression in jazz music is the cycle of 5ths moving up a 4th or down a 5th. I have produced a series of exercises built around the cycle of 5ths for you to analyse and play. In my own practice I like to restrict myself to one concept before moving on. It is very important to work patiently in order to grow. By studying with discipline you will gain the freedom to play what you feel in your heart and what you hear in your ears.

For these following exercises, or indeed any of the exercises, study and learn in all keys. It is very important to compose and write out your own exercises. It is also important to improvise the exercises in all keys starting with a slow tempo and after completing the exercise increase the tempo by small increments and repeat.

Exercise 1: Walking Bass Lines Using Chord Tones

In these exercises I will concentrate on building smooth bass lines over a series of cycle of 5ths progressions. My goal here is to find the smoothest and most interesting way to play a walking bass line with the restriction of only using chord tones. For Example:

In this commonly used IIm⁷–V⁷–Imaj⁷ progression I tried to find the chromatic approaches to link the bass line between the chord changes. On the 4th beat in the first bar I used the note C (7th of Dm^7) and on the 1st beat in the second bar I used the note B which (3rd of G^7).

Also, notice the 4th beat of the second bar I again used the note B which is the third degree of G^7. In the 1st beat of the 3rd bar I used the note C which is the root of C^{maj7}. These chromatic links help the flow of the bass line. It is important to learn these chromatic links between chord changes.

Example 1

Example 2

ESSENTIAL
BASS LIBRARY

MIROSLAV VITOUS

*I Sing The
Body Electric*
(Weather Report)
Columbia, 1972

Example 3

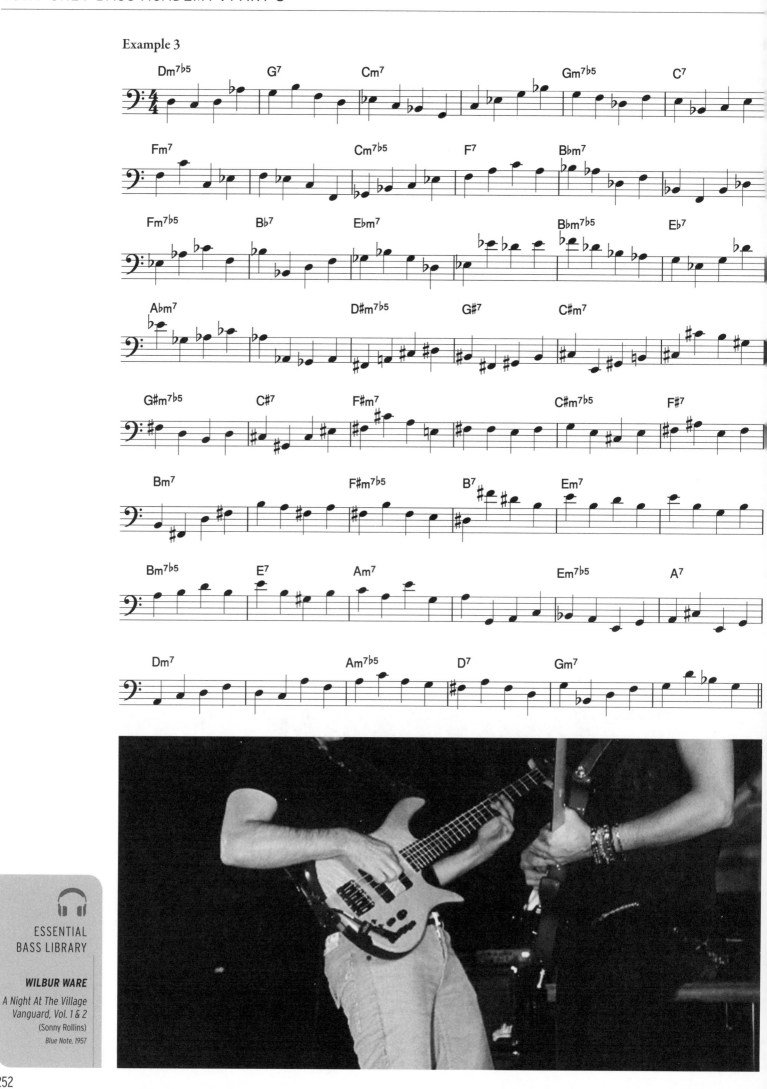

Example 4

Example 5

The use of chord tones over a Blues form.

Example 6

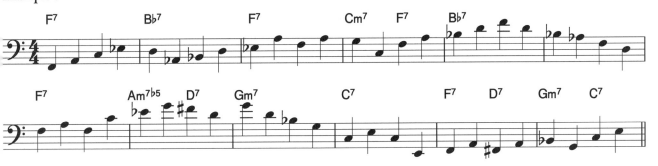

Exercise 2: Walking Bass Lines Using Chord And Scale Tones

My goal here is to create smooth walking bass lines over a series of cycle of 5ths chord progressions. In these following examples I restricted myself to using chord tones and scale tones from the appropriate chord scale. Please try to make sure your lines have a strong connection between the chord changes. The direction of your lines is very important to the flow of the music and will aid and inspire the soloist to be free.

In these following examples I used different chord types. They are: major 7, minor 7, dominant 7 and minor 7♭5. These four chord types are derived from major harmony. My walking bass lines are based on these four chord types.

C^{maj7} (Ionian)

For the minor 7 chords I am thinking of two different scale types.

In a IIm⁷–V⁷–I^{maj7} situation I will tend to think of the IIm⁷ as a Dorian sound. However, in a IIm^{7♭5}–V⁷–Im⁷ my ears can pull me to an Aeolian sound. Dorian is also acceptable in this situation, as will be shown later.

Remember to be mindful of the other musicians that you play with. Use your ears and trust your instincts to adapt to the sound and situation.

Cm⁷ (Dorian)

Cm⁷ (Aeolian)

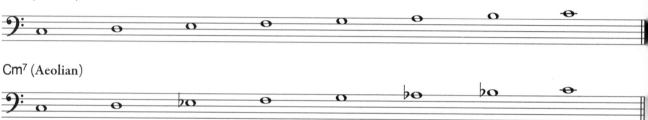

We should also consider the different ways of interpreting dominant 7 chords. Although there are many possibilities, we will look specifically at two of them:

- In the m⁷–V⁷–I^{maj7} progression we use the Mixolydian scale.
- In the IIm^{7♭5}–V⁷–Im⁷ progression my ears sometimes lean towards the Mixolydian ♭13 scale.

The Mixolydian ♭13 scale comes from the melodic minor modes.

C⁷ (Mixolydian)

C⁷ (Mixolydian ♭13)

With the minor 7♭5 I am thinking of the Locrian scale.

Cm^{7♭5} (Locrian)

Example 1

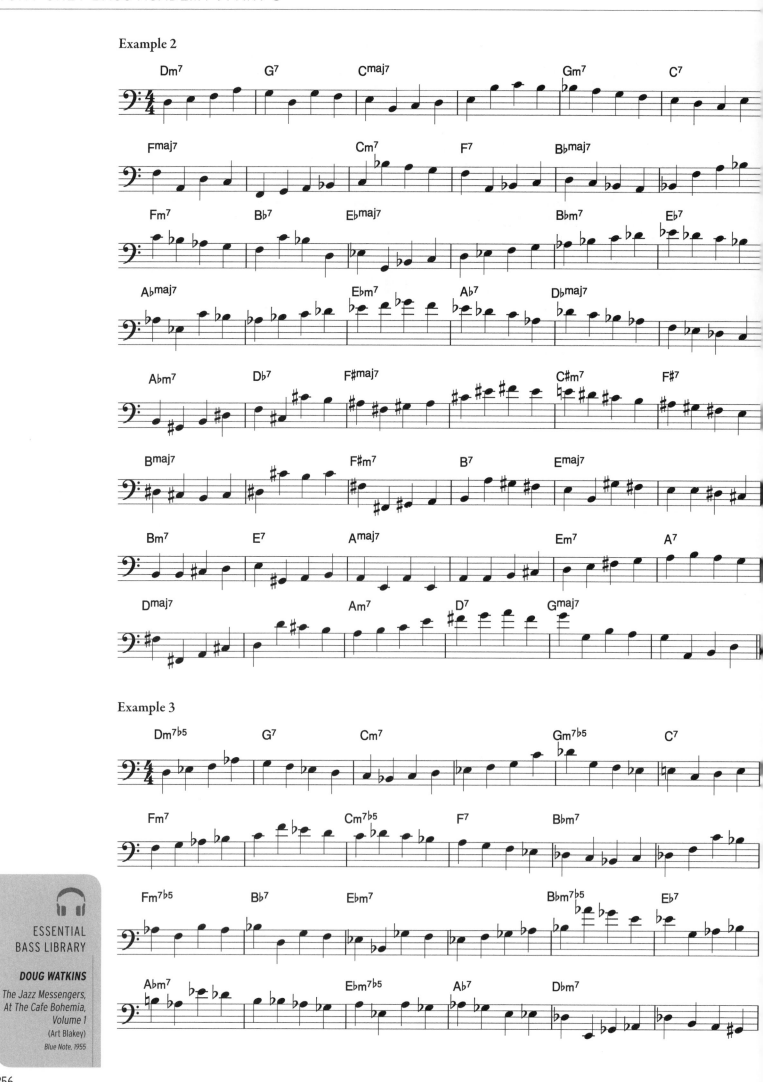

Example 4

Example 5

The use of chord tones and scale tones over a Blues form.

Example 6

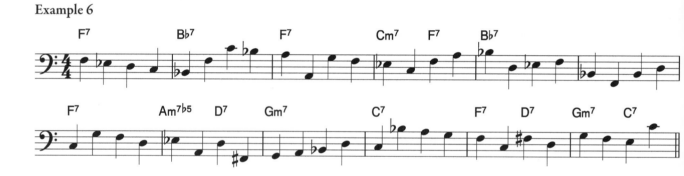

Exercise 3: Walking Bass Lines Using A Chromatic Approach To Chord Tones

The goal in this section is to create a smooth walking bass line over a series of cycle of 5ths chord progressions. In these following examples we will restrict ourselves to only using a chromatic approach to a chord tone.

The harmonic rhythm of music, in general, tends to have a strong beat/weak beat concept. The bass player's role, especially in a jazz walking bass line function, is very important as far as the harmonic pulse goes. Therefore the strong/weak concept is very important to feel and understand.

In a 4/4 piece, the chord changes occur on the first and/or third beats of the bar, and this is usually where you find the chord tones, even when the chord remains unchanged. Here is a short example to explain:

(in the key of C major)

Now it may appear contradictory that the chord tones are played on the strong beats but the weak beats are accented, however this is one of the defining characteristics of walking bass lines. When you practise walking bass lines you should play with this concept.

In these following cycle of 5ths chord progressions I try to use chord tones on the strong beats to indicate the harmony and chromatic leading tones on the weaker beats.

If the harmonic foundations are placed on the weak beats then it does not sound as good.

Example 1

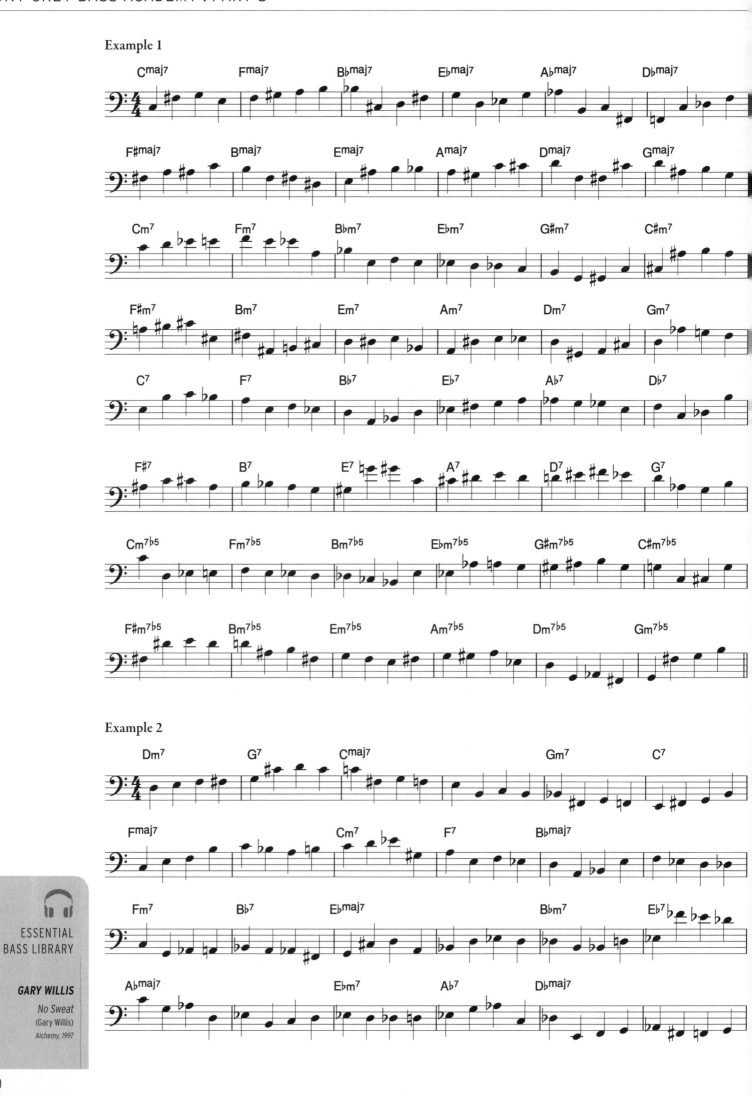

Example 2

Example 3

Example 4

Example 5

Chromatic Approaches Using The Strong Beat, Weak Beat Concept Within A Blues Form

Example 6

ESSENTIAL
BASS LIBRARY

VICTOR WOOTEN

Left Of Cool
(Béla Fleck &
The Flecktones)
Warner Brothers, 1988

Exercise 4: Walking Bass Lines Using All Techniques

My goal for these exercises is to create a series of walking bass lines using everything discussed so far.

Remember the direction of the bass line is the most important factor. There are restrictions created for these exercises purely for practice discipline, ear training and understanding.

With this exercise the rules are forgotten. If you practise the previous exercises with patience and diligence you should be able to forget the rules and create bass lines more freely and instinctively and, therefore, more importantly, musically.

Example 1

ESSENTIAL
BASS LIBRARY

VICTOR WOOTEN

A Show of Hands
(Victor Wooten)
Compass, 2011

Example 2

Example 3

Example 4

Example 5

Walking bass line over a Blues form using all the techniques given in this section

Walking Bass Lines Over One Minor 7 Chord

In the popular standards 'So What' (Miles Davis) and 'Impressions' (John Coltrane) the chord progression is Dm⁷ for 16 bars followed by E♭m⁷ for 8 bars, and finally Dm⁷ for 8 bars.

These pieces employ the Dorian mode throughout. Modal walking bass lines work in almost exactly the same way as diatonic major or minor walking bass lines, however these examples employ very few chord changes. This gives us much more freedom to construct our lines, but as always this freedom needs to be used with care to avoid compromising the structure and flow with too many ideas.

The following exercises show some different ways of keeping the lines more interesting.

EXERCISE 1

For Exercise 1 we have a 32-bar chorus using Dm⁷ and E♭m⁷ over the 32-bar progression discussed earlier. We will be using the 8-note scales and patterns based on the Dorian Scale.

The ultimate goal playing through these or any kind of chord progressions is to be completely free, using your instincts and reacting to each moment as it comes naturally. However it's important to focus on one these following techniques first to help develop your ability to deal with the concept.

At first practise these examples at a slow tempo trying to play chord tones on strong beats. Be mindful of the overall line you are going for rather than getting through one note at a time. Once you are comfortable at a tempo, raise the increments by 5-10bpm and then repeat the process. Continue until you can play through the chord progression at a challenging tempo, remembering to use all the techniques that have been learned so far.

ESSENTIAL
BASS LIBRARY

REGGIE WORKMAN

Night Dreamer
(Wayne Shorter)
Blue Note, 1964

EXERCISE 2

This exercise is similar to the previous one, based on the same 32-bar progression. This time we will superimpose some other chord progressions over the minor 7 chord(s) to make the harmony more interesting. We can exploit the strength of V–I progressions (and all similar-sounding progressions, such as II–V) to apply some movement to the relatively motionless harmonic structure.

Here are a few popular variations on the minor key chord progressions:

$$V^{7\flat9}-Im^7$$

In the key of D minor we would use $A^{7\flat9}$ (from the fifth mode of D harmonic minor) to Dm^7.

$$IIm^{7\flat5}-V^{7\flat9}-Im^7$$

In the key of D minor this would be $Em^{7\flat5}-A^{7\flat9}-Dm^7$.

The II chord comes from the second mode of D harmonic minor or the sixth mode of G melodic minor.

$$VIm^{7\flat5}-IIm^{7\flat5}-V^{7\flat9}-Im^7$$

This would be $Bm^{7\flat5}-Em^{7\flat5}-A^{7\flat9}-Dm^7$.

The VI chord is actually based on the #6, and so it is quite similar to the seventh mode of C major (B Locrian, which uses the same notes as the D Dorian scale). Superimposing these progressions over a continual Dm^7 chord works really well. Also try using these progressions as turnarounds after a sequence of bars.

Here are some superimposed progressions you could use for a Dm^7 vamp.

The term 'vamp' is commonly used in practical music playing, usually referring to an undetermined length of a single chord or short sequence of chords. In this case, we actually know the precise lengths for the Dm^7 and Em^7.

Example 1

Example 2

Example 3

ESSENTIAL
BASS LIBRARY

***REGGIE WORKMAN/
ART DAVIS***

Africa Brass
(John Coltrane)
Impulse!, 1961

Here is an example of the 32-bar chorus using Dm⁷ and E♭m⁷ over the 32-bar progression discussed earlier. I will be using examples from both Exercises 1 and 2.

Practising walking bass lines is great way to improve your knowledge of harmony. As well as practising these exercises, I strongly recommend that you transcribe as much as you can. There are countless classic recordings available, many of which can be heard on the albums suggested for your Essential Bass Library.

A FINAL WORD

Here are a few quotes which have helped me grow over the years. You can interpret them anyway you want.

"

Take care of music and it will take care of you.

— **John McLaughlin**

"

Learn as many styles of music as you can. You never know how your opportunity will come.

— **Gregg Philinganes**

"

Be careful how you practise because that is how you will sound.

— **Abe Laboriel**

"

Music is an expression of life. If you don't live, what do you have to talk about?

— **My Mother**

Acknowledgements

I would like to thank the following people for the completion of this book. Without their help and love this would not have been possible.

Firstly, to my family—June, Jack, Mam and Dad, Tim, Louise and the Kims. Also, thank you to Caroline Baxter, Sam Lung, Tom Farncombe, Leon Hughes, Frank Singer, John McLaughlin and Mike Stern.

Thank you to my endorsements from Fodera, Yamaha, Aguilar amps, DR strings, Mono cases, Zoom audio, TC electronics, Guitar-Cable.com, Source audio, and Peterson tuners.

The book is dedicated to the love and spirit of Harriet Gedge. Thank you Harriet—this book was only an idea until you made it into a reality.

PRACTICE DIARY

EXERCISES:

	KEY:	KEY:	KEY:	KEY:
DAY 1	.... mins .... bpm	.... mins .... bpm	.... mins .... bpm	.... mins .... bpm
DAY 2	KEY: .... mins .... bpm	KEY: .... mins .... bpm	KEY: .... mins .... bpm	KEY: .... mins .... bpm
DAY 3	KEY: .... mins .... bpm	KEY: .... mins .... bpm	KEY: .... mins .... bpm	KEY: .... mins .... bpm
DAY 4	KEY: .... mins .... bpm	KEY: .... mins .... bpm	KEY: .... mins .... bpm	KEY: .... mins .... bpm
DAY 5	KEY: .... mins .... bpm	KEY: .... mins .... bpm	KEY: .... mins .... bpm	KEY: .... mins .... bpm
DAY 6	KEY: .... mins .... bpm	KEY: .... mins .... bpm	KEY: .... mins .... bpm	KEY: .... mins .... bpm
DAY 7	KEY: .... mins .... bpm	KEY: .... mins .... bpm	KEY: .... mins .... bpm	KEY: .... mins .... bpm